Practicing with Paul

Practicing with Paul

*Reflections on Paul and the Practices of Ministry
in Honor of Susan G. Eastman*

EDITED BY

Presian R. Burroughs

FOREWORD BY

Richard B. Hays

CASCADE *Books* · Eugene, Oregon

PRACTICING WITH PAUL
Reflections on Paul and the Practices of Ministry in Honor of Susan G. Eastman

Cascade Books
An Imprint of Wipf and Stock Publishers
199 W. 8th Ave., Suite 3
Eugene, OR 97401

www.wipfandstock.com

PAPERBACK ISBN: 978-1-5326-0104-0
HARDCOVER ISBN: 978-1-5326-0106-4
EBOOK ISBN: 978-1-5326-0105-7

Cataloguing-in-Publication data:

Names: Burroughs, Presian R., editor. | Hays, Richard B., foreword

Title: Practicing with Paul : Reflections on Paul and the Practices of Ministry in Honor of Susan G. Eastman / Edited by Presian R. Burroughs.

Description: Eugene, OR: Cascade Books, 2018 | Includes bibliographical references.

Identifiers: ISBN 978-1-5326-0104-0 (paperback) | ISBN 978-1-5326-0106-4 (hardcover) | ISBN 978-1-5326-0105-7 (ebook)

Subjects: LCSH: Paul, the Apostle, Saint. | Bible. Epistles of Paul—Criticism, interpretation, etc. | Pastoral theology—Biblical teaching.

Classification: BS2655.P3 P7 2018 (print) | BS2655.P3 (ebook)

Manufactured in the U.S.A.   03/30/18

For The Rev. Dr. Susan Grove Eastman,
in celebration of her sixty-fifth birthday.

Contents

Foreword

As the essays in this volume attest, Susan Eastman has earned the deep respect of friends and colleagues in the field of Pauline studies. Her nuanced critical work has helped to shape the questions that many others—not only her students but also her dialogue partners within the field—now bring to the study of Paul's letters, as well as the New Testament more generally.

Susan's influence flows not from the quantity of her published work, but from the quality of its careful probing into what German scholars call *die Sache*: the actual *subject-matter* at the heart of Paul's writings. Many questions can be asked about Paul's letters: scholars can rightly explore their chronology, their background cultural/intellectual sources, their use of early pre-Pauline traditions, their social setting, their rhetorical form, or their influence on the subsequent formation of Christian theology. All such inquiries provide important perspectives on these documents, which have been so massively significant in the subsequent history of Christianity. (In this year celebrating the 500th anniversary of Martin Luther's Pauline-inspired launching of the Reformation, we are inevitably reminded again of the impact of Paul's thought not only on theology but also on world history.) But while taking all these factors fully into account, Susan has patiently and persistently focused her primary attention on the matter about which Paul wrote so passionately: the action of God in Christ and the way in which it transforms human life.

From the time Susan first arrived at Duke as a doctoral student, she brought her extensive pastoral experience to the table as a hermeneutical instrument. I do not mean that she asked simply what helpful tips Paul might offer for pastoral practice. Rather, she was asking deeper questions: how does our complex lived experience (of sin, suffering, longing, and love) intersect with Paul's radical gospel of grace? And within the serious constraints of Paul's eschatological "not yet," how can we speak with integrity of the transforming power of that gospel, its actual shaping of human experience?

These questions were framed for her in part by her studies at Yale and her reading of J. Louis Martyn's provocative work on Pauline apocalyptic thought. But her inquiry was deepened by her extensive experience as an Episcopal priest in Alaska before she returned to graduate study. As one charged with the cure of souls, she had wrestled year in and year out with the pressing issue of how Paul's message could or could not become real in the lives of the people in the congregations she was serving, as well as in her own life.

That, I submit, has been the driving concern at the heart of all of Susan's scholarly work. It is the concern that has prompted her recent turn to the study of contemporary brain science, and the creative way in which she has brought Pauline anthropology into conversation with scientific efforts to study human cognition. And it is also the concern that has made her work highly valuable for reflection on pastoral practice and the formation of Christian communities that seek to reclaim the "mother tongue" of Paul's gospel.

That brings us to the aim of the present volume. The contributors to this *Festschrift* explore from various angles how Paul's letters illuminate the practices involved in the ministries of the church. Although "ministers" often lead the church in its practices, Paul clearly expects the work of ministry to be the work of the whole body of Christ: "There are varieties of gifts, but the same Spirit; and there are varieties of services, but the same Lord; and there are varieties of activities, but it is the same God who activates all of them in everyone" (1 Cor 12:4–6, NRSV). So to speak of "ministerial formation" in a Pauline context is to speak of the shaping and upbuilding (*oikodomē*—a favorite Pauline word) of the whole community of faith for the practice of ministry. The diversity of the essays offered here mirrors Paul's passion for unity in diversity; in their distinct ways they bear witness to the truth that Paul's message can be good news for lived human experience in the flesh, in this time between the times. And, equally, all of them bear witness to the humane and salutary influence of Susan Eastman's work.

It is my honor to add to this cloud of witnesses my own word of congratulation to Susan on the occasion of her sixty-fifth birthday. It has been my privilege to know her as a student, as a colleague, and best of all to know Susan and her husband Ed as friends and companions in Christ. We are grateful, Susan, that you have led us all to a deeper grasp of grace.

Richard B. Hays

Durham, North Carolina

June 14, 2017

Acknowledgments

P AUL'S MINISTRY DEPENDED ON the faithful contributions of his coworkers, or what we might call teammates. This volume, which honors Paul
by distilling his thoughts about ministry, has depended on teamwork as
well. This *Festschrift* celebrating Susan G. Eastman's sixty-fifth birthday
would not have been possible without the generous contributions of her
friends, colleagues, and former students. Their dedicated and timely efforts,
receptivity to editorial suggestions, and willingness to participate in this
project in the first place allowed this volume to come together in record
time and with surprising delight. I deeply appreciate the opportunity I have
had to learn from their work in new ways, and I look forward to future
conversations and collaborations with these new friends.

Even before the team of writers came together, I benefitted from the
kindness and support of Richard Hays, who was then dean of Duke Divinity School and, years before that, Susan's doctoral advisor. He knew—better
than I did—how challenging and work-intensive this process would be. I
am thankful for his encouraging realism and his kindness in writing the
foreword for this volume.

Practicing with Paul would not have seen the light of day if Beverly
Gaventa had not partnered with me in finding a publisher, answering my
many questions, and allaying my concerns. I thank her for being my constant encourager and coach. I doubt I would have had the courage to venture forth without her on our team.

I also could not have completed this project without the careful editing and formatting assistance of Chad Clark. As a graduate student with
tremendous amounts of experience editing and formatting for other professors at United Theological Seminary, Chad was an invaluable member
of our team with a can-do attitude. I appreciate his hours of work and,
thanks to Dean David Watson, the opportunity to co-labor with him.

I thank the acquisitions and editorial teams of Cascade Books at Wipf
and Stock Publishers for their interest in this project and their constant

patience in fielding my many questions. It has been a joy to work with Brian
Palmer, Matthew Wimer, Chris Spinks, Shannon Carter, and Chelsea Lobey,
in particular.

I give deepest thanks to my husband, Bradley Burroughs, who—
though not a scholar of Paul but of Christian Ethics—was my biggest
support and teammate throughout this process. As one who is also in the
business of training people for ministry, he saw a need for this volume and
constantly cheered me on. I thank Brad for closely reading, editing, and offering helpful insights on my chapter. My gratitude overflows for the loving
care that Brad, family members, and friends poured out on our children,
Justus and Makaria, throughout this project and especially for Brad's patient endurance and assistance during the final weeks of the project when
our seven-month-old daughter was teething and our five-year-old son was
eager to play. I am deeply indebted to Brad and our children for making life
happen—and making it fun—as I worked on this project.

Presian Renee Burroughs

Dayton, Ohio
July 1, 2017

Abbreviations

1QH^a	*Thanksgiving Hymns*^a
AB	Anchor Bible
ABD	*The Anchor Bible Dictionary*
AH	*Against Heresies*
Alex.	*Life of Alexander*
Ant.	*Antiquitates Judaicae* (The Antiquities of the Jews)
b. Ber.	*Berakhot*
BDAG	W. Bauer, F. W. Danker, W. F. Arndt, and F. W. Gingrich, *Greek-English Lexicon of the New Testament and Other Early Christian Literature*
Bell. Jug.	*Bellum Jugurthinum* (The War with Jugurtha)
BGU	*Aegyptische Urkunden aus den Königlichen* (later Staatlichen) *Museen zu Berlin*, Griechische Urkunden. Berlin.
BJ	Bellum Judaicum (The Jewish War)
BTB	*Biblical Theology Bulletin*
BZ	*Biblische Zeitschrift*
BZNW	Beihefte zur Zeitschrift für die neutestamentliche Wissenschaft
CSCO	Corpus scriptorum christianorum orientalium
Ep.	*Epistulae*, Pliny the Younger
FRLANT	Forschungen zur Religion und Literatur des Alten und Neuen Testaments

Hell.	*Hellenica*
Hist.	*Histories*
ICC	International Critical Commentary
IKZ	*Internationale kirchliche Zeitschrift*
Int	*Interpretation*
JAAR	*Journal of the American Academy of Religion*
JBL	*Journal of Biblical Literature*
JSNT	*Journal for the Study of the New Testament*
JSP	*Journal for the Study of the Pseudepigrapha*
KEK	Kritisch-exegetischer Kommentar über das Neue Testament (Meyer-Kommentar)
LNTS	The Library of New Testament Studies
LS	*Louvain Studies*
LSJ	Liddell, H. G., R. Scott, H. S. Jones, *A Greek-English Lexicon*
LXX	Septuagint
NICNT	New International Commentary on the New Testament
NIGTC	New International Greek Testament Commentary
NovT	*Novum Testamentum*
NovTSup	Supplements to Novum Testamentum
NTS	*New Testament Studies*
OTP	*Old Testament Pseudepigrapha*, ed. J. H. Charlesworth
P. Cair. Zen.	*Zenon Papyri, Catalogue général des antiquités égyptiennes du Musée du Caire*, ed. C.C. Edgar. Cairo.
P. Giss.	*Griechische Papyri im Museum des oberhessischen Geschichtsvereins zu Giessen*, ed. O. Eger, E. Kornemann, and P. M. Meyer. Leipzig-Berlin.
Phys.	*Pyrrhoniae hypotyposes*
P. Lond.	*Greek Papyri in the British Museum*. London

P. Mich.	*Michigan Papyri*
P. Oslo	*Papyri Osloenses.* Oslo.
P. Oxy.	*The Oxyrhynchus Papyri.* Egypt Exploration Society in Graeco-Roman Memoirs. London.
P. Tebt.	*The Tebtunis Papyri.* London.
RTR	*Reformed Theological Review*
SBLDS	Society of Biblical Literature Dissertation Series
SBLECL	Society of Biblical Literature Early Christianity and its Literature Series
SBLEJL	Society of Biblical Literature Early Judaism and Its Literature
SJT	*Scottish Journal of Theology*
UMH	United Methodist Hymnal
WBC	Word Biblical Commentary
WUNT	Wissenschaftliche Untersuchungen zum Neuen Testament
ZNW	*Zeitschrift für die neutestamentliche Wissenschaft und die Kunde der älteren Kirche*

Introduction

PRESIAN R. BURROUGHS

TOO FREQUENTLY A CHASM divides biblical studies from the practices of ministry. This volume attempts to bridge that chasm. In doing so, it takes its inspiration from Susan Grove Eastman, who has provided an exemplary model of how to do so as an Episcopal priest and a professor of New Testament at Duke Divinity School. The questions she asks and invites students to ask not only plunge us into the depths of biblical studies but also into the complexities of lived Christian experience, practice, and ministry. Susan's teaching and writing merge exegetical rigor, historical awareness, theological depth, and interdisciplinary inquiry, resulting in rich practical insights. The contributors to this volume thank Susan for her courageous leadership in marking out new ways for all of us to venture across this chasm.

Because the scholarly study of the Bible requires such great attention to detail and—let's be honest—at least at times tedious investigation into the language, history, and contexts of biblical texts, biblical scholars rarely have the opportunity to elaborate the practical import of their research. Even when they see the implications, space and scholarly convention often prevent them from articulating such insights. From the other side of the divide, theologians and scholars of the practices of ministry have thousands of years of ancient and contemporary philosophical, cultural, theological, historical, and sociological issues to consider as they address the complexities of embodied, practiced life today. Although they may draw upon biblical passages, they may feel discouraged to elaborate the passages' complexities and nuances since this work appears to fall under the purview of biblical scholars. It seems to me that the Apostle Paul would have been dismayed at this situation. His attention to the details of the Bible (for him, of course, the Scriptures of Israel, what Christians now call the Old Testament) always served a practical purpose: the salvation, edification, and correction of those to whom he wrote and ministered. Meanwhile, the practical problems, questions, and activities Paul constantly faced in his ministry led him straight back to the complexities of Scripture for inspiration and guidance.

This volume offers Susan's colleagues and former students an opportunity to practice *with* Paul by illustrating the ways in which Paul's letters and theology—and the practices to which they point—breathe new life into God's people. It is an opportunity for students *of* Paul to speak into the life of the church *with* Paul by presenting their scholarly work in ways that inspire and edify followers and ministers of Jesus Christ. Each contribution delves into the details and historical contexts of Paul's letters, including the interpretation of these texts throughout the church's history. Meanwhile, each author interprets those details in relation to Christian practice and suggests implications for Christian ministry that flow out of this rich interpretive process. By modeling forms of interpretation that are practically oriented, this book provides inspiration for those who are preparing for Christian ministry and already practicing ministry as they attempt to incarnate the ways of Christ along with Paul. The chapters, then, follow Susan—who travels alongside Paul—as they demonstrate a variety of ways in which rigorous biblical study can speak to Christian living today.

In the first chapter, Michael Gorman illustrates that practicing with Paul necessarily presses ministers (and all Christians for that matter) into a life of participation with Christ's humiliation, suffering, and death. Such participation is the mark of Christian integrity, requiring leaders and laypeople alike to rely upon God's abundant grace.

Drawing together the interrelated Pauline concepts of grace and gift in chapter 2, John Barclay illustrates the reciprocal nature of giving and receiving that shapes the body of Christ and the larger community. In conversation with asset-based community development, he conveys a Pauline vision of Christian ministry *with* the economically poor since the poor and the rich both give and receive.

Seeking to grasp the implications of a Pauline-inspired apocalyptic imagination for preaching, in chapter 3 Charles Campbell highlights the dangerous, disruptive, perception-transforming nature of preaching *with* Paul. He illustrates this form of preaching by the example of Oscar Romero, who boldly spoke out against the injustices inflicted upon the poor of El Salvador and was ultimately martyred for his faith.

Chapters 4 and 5 reveal two areas in which Paul's letters have been used in oppressive ways that seem fundamentally to go *against* practicing *with* Paul. In chapter 4, Beverly Gaventa illustrates how several Pauline passages have been employed to curtail women's leadership in church communities despite Paul's own practice of co-laboring with women in ministry.

By thinking with Paul about the body of Christ, Gaventa shows how this image points toward the fundamental inclusivity of the church in its ministries and gifts. In her first of two contributions, Lisa Bowens examines how African Americans have counteracted slavery and racism by reinterpreting Paul—the same author used by whites to support slavery. Bowens demonstrates how African Americans have walked *with* Paul—finding in his letters words of liberation—in the struggle for justice and liberty.

Recognizing that the destructive effects of sin and death are experienced now as suffering, Ann Jervis in chapter 6 reflects on Paul's understanding that God has interrupted and transformed death-constrained time through the resurrection of Jesus Christ. Paul's message that God's people now live in Christ's salutary, liberative time serves as a timely reminder to those who suffer and those who minister to the suffering.

Examining the implications of Paul's prayer life and his requests for prayer, Robert Moses demonstrates in chapter 7 how Paul's theology and practice of prayer levels social, economic, and gender hierarchies. Despite the uncertainties and struggles of life, prayer leads God's people into the mysterious, peaceful presence of God and must remain an ecclesial practice that is open to all.

In chapter 8, Lisa Bowens illuminates the way in which Paul's ministry and the ministries of all those who practice in his stead bring them into spiritual battle. This spiritually attuned warfare attempts to rescue the minds and hearts of people who are oppressed by deceptive and destructive forces, not through rhetorical prowess but by the strength of God.

Colin Miller argues in chapter 9 that the human person reflects the image of God and so makes faith in the risen Christ realizable. Because persons in poverty make the poor Christ real to us, directing us to true faith in Christ, Miller maintains that all churches ought to include the financially poor in their midst and recognize the immeasurable contributions such persons make to the well-being of the ecclesial community.

In addition to those with scant economic resources, the church and its weekly worship services ought to incorporate people of all ages, as Emily Peck-McClain argues in chapter 10. Reflecting on the image of the body of Christ, Peck-McClain suggests that age-segregated ministry cripples the body. Paul's metaphor of the body instead encourages us to strengthen Christ's body by validating and incorporating the gifts and contributions of people of all ages and abilities.

Considering the negative effects of sin on the nonhuman creation, Presian Burroughs demonstrates in chapter 11 that Paul's theology of creation teaches God's people to attend to creation and stand in solidarity with its suffering and liberation. In so doing, they exercise Christlike, loving self-restraint, transforming their destructive activities (especially destructive forms of growing and eating food) into those that support the well-being of all creation.

In chapter 12, Mary Schmitt and Bishop Samuel Enosa Peni of South Sudan reflect on the complexities of Paul's injunction in Rom 12:18 to "pursue peace." They argue that peacemaking—even in war-torn places such as South Sudan—depends upon the power of the reconciling and peacemaking God, who calls us to pursue peace no matter the responses of others.

Examining the Christian's relationship to power, specifically ruling powers, in chapter 13 Douglas Harink argues that God's promises of justice depend not on the zeal and activity of Christians but on the Messiah's own work of justice. With Paul, Harink invites Christians to trust in the resurrecting and creating power of God for peace and justice rather than the characteristically violent and ultimately failed attempts of political regimes.

Tracing Paul's extraordinary and courageous efforts to establish peace with other Christian leaders, Douglas Campbell in chapter 14 argues that a primary way in which we practice *with* Paul is by becoming peacemakers in hostile homes, churches, and communities. Such peacemaking requires Christian leaders to bear the fruit of the Spirit and be formed in the practices of restorative justice, gentle and self-controlled speech, and extravagant patience.

Philip Ziegler fittingly finishes this volume by examining Christ's overcoming of death through death, as explained in Hebrews, a book that was long considered to be a homily written by Paul. Reflecting on the radical nature of God's grace in saving people through Jesus' death, as exposited by Paul and carried forth in Hebrews, Ziegler highlights ways in which Christians attending those who are dying might help them face death with comforting faith.

It is with great joy that we present these offerings to Susan and to the body of Christ, which she loves so dearly. May they illuminate the complexities of Paul's life, ministry, and writings for the edification of God's people as they practice *with* Paul by following the crucified and resurrected Christ.

1 ——————————————————————————————

Participation and Ministerial Integrity in the Letters of Paul

Michael J. Gorman

For we cannot do anything against the truth, but only for the truth.

—2 Corinthians 13:8

I T IS A DISTINCT pleasure to contribute to this volume honoring my friend and colleague Susan Eastman. Susan's appointment at Duke to teach in the ministerial division as well as the biblical division has always appealed to me, as I have also tried to bridge that divide in my own teaching and writing. Of great significance to each of us has been the theme of "participation" in Paul, and I wish to take up that theme in this essay. What does it mean for a minister of the gospel to live "in Christ" with integrity?

The Need for Ministerial Integrity

Offering such a heading for this initial section may sound something like proposing an article for a medical journal with the title, "The Need for Physician Competence": it is an exercise in stating the obvious. But the obvious is not always so obvious—or practiced. As I was preparing this essay, I received word of reported widespread domestic abuse among clergy in Australia. Closer to home, I have taught (as a Protestant) in a Roman Catholic seminary for more than a quarter-century, which means I—and my colleagues and students, not to mention their families, friends, peers, and bishops—have lived through intense periods of hurt, scandal, repentance, change, and so on.

The issue of integrity—consistency between professed belief and actual practice—is not new to the Christian community. In fact, it is a major concern in the Pauline letters, and it cuts both ways. On the one hand, some of Paul's critics say, "His letters are weighty and strong, but his bodily presence is weak, and his speech contemptible" (2 Cor 10:10).[1] Paul is also disparaged for not accepting the Corinthians' financial support but, instead, supporting himself with manual labor (2 Cor 11:7–11) while perhaps stealing from the collection for Jerusalem (2 Cor 12:14–18). Therefore, as we will see, Paul often feels the need to defend the integrity of his ministry.

On the other hand, Paul was not one to mince words when it came to the question of others' integrity, of their not living and ministering in ways that are "worthy of the gospel of Christ" (Phil 1:27; see also Gal 2:14):

1. In Gal 2:4 Paul speaks of what happened during a meeting with Jerusalem leaders, when "false believers [were] secretly brought in, who slipped in to spy on the freedom we have in Christ Jesus, so that they might enslave us [meaning at least Paul and the uncircumcised gentile Titus]."

2. Only a few verses later, in Gal 2:11–14, Paul tells the Galatians how he excoriated Cephas (Peter) and Barnabas for their hypocrisy, for "not acting consistently with the truth of the gospel" (2:14), after they had withdrawn from table fellowship with gentiles. Paul says he "opposed him [Cephas] to his face, because he [Cephas] stood self-condemned" (2:11).

3. In 1 Corinthians, Paul finds serious fault with a whole range of people, at least some of whom are "ministers" or leaders: those responsible for fracturing the community (1:10—4:21); those exercising alleged personal rights to the detriment of fellow Christians and to themselves (6:1–11; 8:1—11:1); those engaging in inappropriate sexual relationships (5:1–11; 6:12–20); those turning the Lord's supper into a pagan banquet for the elite (11:17–34); and those with esteemed spiritual gifts feeling superior and making others feel inferior (chapters 12–14).

4. In 2 Corinthians, Paul has sharp words for those he sarcastically calls "super-apostles" (11:5; 12:11) for arrogantly offering what he considers to be a false Jesus, Spirit, and gospel (11:4). He calls them "boasters [who] are false apostles, deceitful workers, disguising themselves as apostles of Christ," just as "Satan disguises himself as an angel of light" (11:13–14).

1. All scriptural quotations are from the NRSV, unless otherwise indicated.

What is it that these various behaviors represent for Paul? They are failures of integrity. While there are certainly various dimensions of the problem, the fundamental issue is that the behaviors are inconsistent with the gospel narrative, the story of Christ. And for Paul, that story is narrated clearly, with wide-ranging implications for all who claim to believe it, in Philippians.

The Starting Point: Christ's Participation with Us

As Susan Eastman has frequently pointed out, our participation in Christ, in his story, is dependent on and derives from Christ's initial participation with us, in our human story.[2] Here is how Paul narrates Christ's participation with us in the second chapter of his letter to the Philippians (the translation is mine):

> Let this same mind-set—this way of thinking, feeling, and act-ing—be operative in your community, which is indeed a fellow-ship in Christ Jesus, who,
>
> although [x] he was in the form of God,
>
> did not [y] consider this equality with God as something to be exploited for his own advantage,
>
> but rather [z_1] emptied himself
>
>   by taking the form of a slave;
>
>   that is,
>
>   by being born in the likeness of human beings.
>
> And being found in human form,
>
> he [z_2] humbled himself
>
>   by becoming obedient to death—
>
>   even death on a Roman cross. (Phil 2:5–8)

We should note four things about this text.

First, it is clearly a story of Christ's participation with us, a drama with two main events: his incarnation and his death on the cross. The incarnation (indicated by [z_1] above) is presented as Christ's self-emptying (kenosis) and self-enslavement, or total self-giving. Christ's death (indicated by [z_2]

---

2. See, e.g., Eastman, *Paul and the Person*, esp. chapter 5, and various articles refer-enced there.

above) is similarly presented as his complete self-humbling and obedience (to the Father), even to the point of accepting the cruelest form of death known in antiquity: crucifixion, reserved for slaves and other despicables. This, then, is not a résumé of advancement but of downward mobility: the counterintuitive, countercultural narrative of a strange way of becoming and being human.

Second, these two acts of incarnation and death ($[z_1]$ and $[z_2]$) are actually part of a larger story. The movement of this story is indicated by the position of these two acts within a sequence that includes the other parts of the narrative labeled above as [x] and [y]. This narrative pattern may be summarized as "although [x], not [y] but [z]," meaning:

> although [x] status,
>
> not [y] selfish exploitation of that status
>
> but [z] self-renunciation and self-giving.[3]

That is, although [x] Christ possessed the highest imaginable status, equality with God, he did not [y] use that status for his own selfish gain but [z] voluntarily chose to become human and die for the good of others. (I use $[z_1]$ and $[z_2]$ above because the third part of the pattern occurs as two events.) Although Paul does not explicitly spell out the loving, others-oriented character of this death (that is, he died for us and for our sins), this aspect of Christ's death is implied by the context (2:1–4) and made explicit elsewhere in Paul's letters.[4] As we will see below, this narrative pattern is essential to Paul's understanding of ministry and ministerial integrity.

Third, there is a possible significant twist to this story of Christ if one word in the translation is altered. The phrase that begins verse 6, "although he was in the form of God," appears in nearly every translation with similar wording, starting with the initial word "although" (or "though"). A more literal translation from the Greek would be simply "being in the form of God," which could mean something like "*while* he was," or "*although* he was" (the standard interpretation), or even "*because* he was."

A number of scholars have proposed this last option as the best translation: "because he was in the form of God, he did not consider this

---

3. See, e.g., Gorman, *Cruciformity*, 89–91, 164–69, and elsewhere. Even this larger narrative is not the full story, which ends not with death but with exaltation (Phil 2:9–11). This aspect of the story does not, however, directly impact our understanding of integrity.

4. For Paul, Christ's death for us and our sins has multiple meanings, but it is most importantly the manifestation of both Christ's love and the Father's love, which are ultimately the same love (Rom 5:5–8; 8:35–39; 2 Cor 5:14; 13:13; Gal 2:20).

equality with God as something to be exploited for his own advantage, but rather emptied himself . . . and humbled himself." That is, Christ did what he did not *in spite of* his being divine but *because of* his being divine. If this option is correct, then the story tells us not only something remarkable about Christ, but also something profound about God: that God is inherently self-giving and even self-humbling, self-lowering. To put it differently: *Christ's acts of self-emptying incarnation and self-giving death were acts of divine integrity*—of God doing what God claims to be and in fact is. God is downwardly mobile.[5]

This is a strange way of being God, too. Humans generally expect God, or the gods, to be *upwardly* mobile, to seek the glory that is rightfully theirs, or at least to express the divine nature in terms of manifesting power and glory. For this reason we might translate verse 6 as "although and because he was in the form of God," meaning "although we do not expect God to act this way, but because Christ is the true form of the true God, he emptied and humbled himself because it is the nature of God to do precisely that." Christ's participation in our human story was the unexpected (to us) but natural ultimate manifestation of God's character: self-giving love.

The fourth and last point about Phil 2:6–8 is another translation issue, namely verse 5, which connects the story of Christ back to the exhortations to humility and love in 2:1–4. The translation offered here, "Let this same mind-set—this way of thinking, feeling, and acting—be operative in your community, which is indeed a fellowship in Christ Jesus," draws attention to two important aspects of the Christ-story and its relevance to the Philippians, to Paul, and to us. In the first place, the word "mind" or "mind-set" includes thinking but also feeling and acting.[6] Secondly, this translation makes it clear that the Philippians (and all believers) are to consider the needs of others, in humility and love, precisely because they are now a fellowship that lives together *in* Christ, the one whose story is a story of self-emptying, self-giving love for others.

For a Christian community or individual, to live with integrity is to live in Christ, to participate in him by living according to the story of Christ told in Philippians 2:6–8. It is to live in the narrative shape of "although (and perhaps also because) [x], not [y] but [z]," the Christ-pattern.

We turn now to see how that pattern of participation played out for Paul as a minister of the gospel who sought to live with integrity—to practice what he preached.

---

5. See Eastman, "Philippians 2:6–11," 1–22; Gorman, *Inhabiting*, 9–39.

6. See Fowl, *Philippians*, 28–29, 36–37, 89–90.

Participation and Ministerial Integrity in Philippians

We begin with Paul's letter to the Philippians, since that is where the Christ-pattern is found. There are three principal examples of ministerial integrity as participation in Christ within this letter.

First, we have Paul himself. Paul writes to the Philippians from prison, and the Roman chains have had quite an impact on the apostle. Amazingly, in spite of his circumstances, Paul writes with joy in the midst of suffering and—no less amazingly—affirms that his imprisonment has actually contributed to the spread of the gospel (1:12–14).[7] At the same time, Paul's experience has led him to contemplate his possible fate and its positive consequences:

> For to me, living is Christ and dying is gain. If I am to live in the flesh, that means fruitful labor for me; and I do not know which I prefer [or possibly "choose"]. I am hard pressed between the two: my desire is to depart and be with Christ, for that is far better. (Phil 1:21–23)

But Paul's understandable "selfish" desire to die and be with Christ, which would be a personal gain for him, is checked by his Christlike concern and love for others, especially the Philippians, and by his commitment to the further expansion of the gospel's impact. This Christlike mind-set literally envelops (in 1:19–20 and 1:24–26) the expression of feeling hard pressed between life and death:

> For I know that through your prayers and the help of the Spirit of Jesus Christ this will turn out for my deliverance. It is my eager expectation and hope that I will not be put to shame in any way, but that by my speaking with all boldness, Christ will be exalted now as always in my body, whether by life or by death. . . . But to remain in the flesh is more necessary for you. Since I am convinced of this, I know that I will remain and continue with all of you for your progress and joy in faith, so that I may share abundantly in your boasting in Christ Jesus when I come to you again. (Phil 1:19–20, 24–26)

In other words, although [x] Paul felt dying would be gain and perhaps even willed his own death, he did not [y] allow that self-centered sentiment and desire to define him but rather [z] thought and acted in consideration of others. The Christ-pattern is powerfully present in these words.

7. For Paul's joy, see 1:4, 18; 2:2, 17–18; 4:1, 10.

In addition to Paul, we also have the examples of Timothy and Epaphroditus. About Timothy, Paul writes the following:

> I hope in the Lord Jesus to send Timothy to you soon, so that I may be cheered by news of you. I have no one like him who will be genuinely concerned for your welfare. All of them are seeking their own interests, not those of Jesus Christ. But Timothy's worth you know, how like a son with a father he has served with me in the work of the gospel. I hope therefore to send him as soon as I see how things go with me; and I trust in the Lord that I will also come soon. (Phil 2:19–24)

In this passage, Paul criticizes some people, apparently gospel ministers and even his colleagues, for "seeking their own interests" (*ta heautōn*, 2:21) which is precisely what Paul in 2:3–4 told the Philippians not to seek (*ta heautōn*, 2:4). Why? Because Christ did not seek his own interests. That is, these are ministers lacking integrity.

Timothy, on the other hand, has "worth," or integrity, as a minister. His service (*edouleusen*) has been son-like (2:22), meaning Paul-like, which ultimately means Christlike, for Christ took the form of a servant/slave (*doulou*, 2:7). The Christ-pattern here is once again evident, even in the words chosen to describe Timothy. It could be said of him that although (and perhaps because) [x] other ministers seek their own interests, he [y] did not imitate them but rather [z] imitated his father in ministry (Paul), and Christ himself, by seeking the good of others in self-giving service to them.[8]

Immediately after his words about Timothy, Paul writes the following about Epaphroditus as he urges the Philippians to welcome him back:

> Still, I think it necessary to send to you Epaphroditus—my brother and co-worker and fellow soldier, your messenger and minister to my need; for he has been longing for all of you, and has been distressed because you heard that he was ill. He was indeed so ill that he nearly died. But God had mercy on him. . . . Welcome him then in the Lord with all joy, and honor such people, because he came close to death for the work of Christ, risking his life to make up for those services that you could not give me. (Phil 2:25–27a, 29–30)

Above all else, Epaphroditus is someone who puts the needs of others—both those of Paul and those of the Philippians—above his own, acting as

---

8. Paul's calls to imitate him (e.g., Phil 3:17; 4:9) are ultimately exhortations to imitate Christ (1 Cor 11:1).

a messenger or representative (Gk. *apostolos*, 2:25) of the Philippians to Paul, but ultimately as a messenger of Christ. This is made clear in 2:30, not only in the phrase "the work of Christ," but also in the phrase "he came close to death." In Greek, the words "close to death" (*mechri thanatou*) are the same words used to describe Christ's obedience "to the point of death" (*mechri thanatou*, 2:8).[9] That is, because [x] Epaphroditus was the *apostolos* of the Philippians and of Christ, he did not [y] concern himself with the risk involved but [z] demonstrated Christlike sacrificial love for the Philippians and for Paul.

Philippians, then, bears testimony to the fundamental meaning of integrity in Paul as participation in the story of Christ by adhering to the Christ-pattern of "although/because [x] not [y] but [z]." We turn now to see this pattern of participation as integrity on display in three other letters.

Participation and Ministerial Integrity in 1 Thessalonians

Many scholars believe that 1 Thessalonians was the first letter from Paul that has been preserved, though some think Galatians is earlier. In either case, 1 Thessalonians is certainly earlier than Philippians, and yet echoes of the Christ-pattern we find in Phil 2:6–8 appear as a narrative of Paul's ministry in this earlier letter.[10]

It is clear from 1 Thessalonians that Paul has a good relationship with the believers there. His initial ministry in Thessaloniki (see 1:1—2:2; 2:13–16) had borne fruit, in spite of opposition to the apostle and persecution of the new believers. The Thessalonians had grown in holiness (faithfulness, love, hope) in spite of ongoing persecution—something about which Paul had been concerned, but good news received via Timothy had relieved him (2:17—3:13). The exhortations in the letter have the upbeat tone of "keep on keeping on" (e.g., 4:1, "do so more and more").

Nonetheless, Paul feels it necessary to defend his and his colleagues' own ministerial integrity. Much of the letter's second chapter is devoted to just that: a denial of their insincerity and a description of their Christlike

---

9. This phrase can mean "to the actual point of death" (Christ) or "nearly to the point of death" (Epaphroditus).

10. This suggests either that Paul incorporated an existing (pre-Pauline) poem or hymn into Philippians (a common theory) or that the text he wrote to the Philippians embodies his own essential Christology that predates its specific inclusion in Philippians. I lean toward the latter explanation.

ministry among the Thessalonians.[11] The chapter begins with a reminder that the Pauline mission in both Philippi and Thessaloniki has been troubled by opposition, and yet that mistreatment has not stopped Paul and friends (2:1–2; cf. 2:14–17). This is because they have not behaved like some orators and teachers in antiquity, who were self-seeking deceivers, peddling their wares or otherwise improperly enticing their hearers and seeking human approval (2:3–6).

Paul's defense of his (i.e., their) integrity is full of the language of participating in Christ, embodying the Christ-pattern, even as he employs rich imagery to express it. Intriguingly, Paul identifies his team's ministry as both maternal (2:7b) and paternal (2:11–12) in nature.[12] The Christ-pattern emerges in the words that precede and follow the maternal image:

> Nor did we seek praise from mortals, whether from you or from others, though we might have made demands [or, better, "thrown our weight around"[13]] as apostles of Christ. But we were gentle among you, like a nurse tenderly caring for her own children. So deeply do we care for you that we are [or "were"] determined to share with you not only the gospel of God but also our own selves, because you have become very dear [*agapētoi*, "beloved"] to us. You remember our labor and toil, brothers and sisters; we worked night and day, so that we might not burden any of you while we proclaimed to you the gospel of God. (1 Thess 2:6–9)

The echo of the basic structure of Phil 2:6–8 is clear even in the English translation—"though . . . not . . . but." The idea is this:

> Although [x] we have a certain authority as apostles, we did not [y] seek human glory or throw our weight around and coerce you in any way, but rather we [z] treated you lovingly like parents, sharing with you not only our words but our lives, our very selves.

It is also possible that the opening thought here, once again, should be translated "because"—*because* we are apostles." That is, apostolic authority in Christ is inherently maternal and paternal, self-giving and guiding, but non-coercive. With either translation, the point for Paul is essentially the same: he and his team acted with integrity, for the Thessalonians and God

---

11. See Johnson, *1 & 2 Thessalonians*, 57–85.

12. There is scholarly debate about the original text of 2:7b and about its correct translation, but the debate does not really affect the main point of the maternal image and thus need not detain us.

13. See CEB; similarly, NAB, NET, NJB.

are witnesses to "how pure, upright, and blameless our conduct was" (2:10). The solid proof of this integrity is the fact that Paul and colleagues worked night and day to support themselves (2:9; cf. 2 Thess 3:6–12).

But there is more. Somewhat hidden within this pastoral imagery is another specific allusion to the Christ-pattern: the determination "to share with you not only the gospel of God but also our own selves" (2:8b). This phrase likely refers to the apostolic parental care and hard work. Yet "our own selves" also encompasses the very heart and soul of the apostles; the Greek phrase is, in fact, "share . . . our own souls" (*metadounai tas heautōn psychas*). And the idiom of giving one's soul/life probably derives from similar early Christian language referring to Jesus' own self-offering in death. For instance, in Mark 10:45 (= Matt 20:28), Jesus says, "For the Son of Man came not to be served but to serve, and to give his life (*dounai tēn psychēn autou*) a ransom for many."[14]

Finally, it is worth noting the phrase "night and day," used of the apostles' practice of working in self-support (2:9). The same phrase reappears in 3:10—"Night and day we pray most earnestly that we may see you face to face and restore whatever is lacking in your faith." Christlike apostolic self-giving can take many forms, from hard work to teaching to prayer.[15]

Participation and Ministerial Integrity in 1 Corinthians

Many of Paul's important claims about integrity that we have seen in Philippians and 1 Thessalonians appear also in the Corinthian correspondence. In these two letters Paul is explaining in some detail what a Christ-shaped, cross-shaped community looks like and what a Christ-shaped, cross-shaped minister of the gospel looks like. Although 1 Corinthians emphasizes the former and 2 Corinthians the latter, each letter has something to say about both subjects—which are, of course, closely interrelated.

In 1 Cor 9 Paul offers himself as an example of the "although/because [x] not [y] but [z] pattern." He writes autobiographically to urge certain Corinthians primarily to stop eating meat in the precincts of pagan temples so as not to cause other Christians to fall back into idolatry. The meat-eaters have either explicitly or implicitly claimed to possess the right ("liberty" in some translations) to do so (chapter 8, esp. 8:9), so Paul challenges that

---

14. See also John 10:11, 15b, 17. In addition, John 15:13 and 1 John 3:16 use similar language for disciples' participation in such self-giving love.

15. In chapter 7, Robert Moses highlights the ways in which Paul was a man of prayer and expected his Christian siblings to pray with and for him.

right by letting them know that he and Barnabas have given up legitimate apostolic rights (to be supported financially and to take their spouses with them; 9:3–14) for the benefit and salvation of others.[16] He writes,

> Nevertheless, we have not made use of this right, but we endure anything rather than put an obstacle in the way of the gospel of Christ. . . . But I have made no use of any of these rights, nor am I writing this so that they may be applied in my case. Indeed, I would rather die than that—no one will deprive me of my ground for boasting! If I proclaim the gospel, this gives me no ground for boasting, for an obligation is laid on me, and woe to me if I do not proclaim the gospel! For if I do this of my own will, I have a reward; but if not of my own will, I am entrusted with a commission. What then is my reward? Just this: that in my proclamation I may make the gospel free of charge, so as not to make full use of my rights in the gospel. For though I am free with respect to all, I have made myself a slave to all, so that I might win more of them. (1 Cor 9:12b, 15–19)

This text has obvious similarities to 1 Thess 2. The Christ-pattern is once again crystal clear: "although [x] we had certain apostolic rights, we did not [y] exercise them but rather [z] supported ourselves." The echo of Phil 2 is especially strong in verse 19: "I have made myself a slave [literally "enslaved myself," *emauton edoulōsa*] to all" is reminiscent of Christ's "taking the form of a slave" (*doulou*, Phil 2:7).

It is also clear that while Paul became a slave (metaphorically speaking) voluntarily, as did Christ, there is a certain compulsion or obedience involved because not to do what he did would be to lack integrity (1 Cor 9:15–18).[17] In other words, it is also true that "*because* [x] we are apostles of Christ who happen to have certain rights, we [y] did not exercise those rights, which would be for our own advantage, but rather [z] acted for the benefit of others, just as Christ did."

Paul offers himself to the Corinthians as a model of Christ, both here and in a similar passage a little later in the letter, where he says, "Be[come] imitators of me, as I am of Christ" (11:1).[18] It is therefore evident that the

16. The Greek word *exousia* is best translated "right," not "liberty," in this context (8:9; 9:4–6, 12, 18). For further reflection on how Paul encourages those in Christ to restrain their own dietary rights for the benefit of others, see Presian Burroughs's chapter 11.

17. For a discussion of how *involuntary* slaves employed Paul's epistles to protest and resist slavery, see Lisa Bowens's chapter 5.

18. The words of 11:1 are preceded by these: "Do not seek your own advantage, but that of the other. . . . Just as I try to please everyone in everything I do, not seeking my

Christ-pattern is for all believers. All ministers of the gospel are first of all Christians, and all Christians are also ministers; Christ is the pattern for each and all. Integrity is necessary for all who are in Christ, and Christlikeness is the standard for integrity.[19]

Participation and Ministerial Integrity in 2 Corinthians

Second Corinthians is in large measure a focused defense of Paul's ministry. As in 1 Thess 2, there are two main components to the defense: (1) his ministry is not one of deceit or peddling, and (2) his ministry is cruciform, or cross-shaped, and therefore Christlike. (In fact, Paul often uses "we" language, meaning that the defense is, again, of both him and his colleagues.)

One of the first things Paul says about himself and his team actually combines both main claims:

> But thanks be to God, who in Christ always leads us in triumphal procession, and through us spreads in every place the fragrance that comes from knowing him. For we are the aroma of Christ to God among those who are being saved and among those who are perishing; to the one a fragrance from death to death, to the other a fragrance from life to life. Who is sufficient for these things? For we are not peddlers of God's word like so many; but in Christ we speak as persons of sincerity, as persons sent from God and standing in his presence. (2 Cor 2:14–17)

Paul here shockingly compares ministers to those who have been conquered by a Roman general or emperor and dragged through the streets of Rome in a "triumph," surrounded by burning incense, after which they would normally be slain. Ministers of the gospel, then, are like those on a procession to death. This is, for Paul, the obvious proof that they are clearly not engaging in their ministry for personal gain as peddlers. The claim that Paul and his team are not cunning peddlers also appears in 4:1–2 and, implicitly, in 6:6–7 ("purity . . . truthful speech"); the latter passage also combines the claim of a death-like existence (6:4–10) with the corollary claim of obvious integrity: "We are putting no obstacle in anyone's way, so that no fault may be found with our ministry" (6:3).

---

own advantage, but that of many, so that they may be saved" (10:24, 33). All of these texts are part of a long essay on a single but complex topic (8:1—11:1). "Not seeking one's own advantage" is a central dimension of love (13:5).

19. Paul also speaks about his ministerial integrity/Christlikeness in 1 Cor 3–4, but space does not permit consideration of those texts.

At the same time—and this is the fundamental paradox of ministry in Paul's eyes—such a life of "death" is ultimately life-giving, both for ministers (6:9) and for those to whom they minister:

> We are afflicted in every way, but not crushed; perplexed, but not driven to despair; persecuted, but not forsaken; struck down, but not destroyed; always carrying in the body the death of Jesus, so that the life of Jesus may also be made visible in our bodies. For while we live, we are always being given up to death for Jesus' sake, so that the life of Jesus may be made visible in our mortal flesh. So death is at work in us, but life in you. . . . So we do not lose heart. Even though our outer nature is wasting away, our inner nature is being renewed day by day. (2 Cor 4:8–12, 16)

This is what Paul means when he speaks of "being transformed into the same image [of Christ, 4:4] from one degree of glory to another" (3:18); it is also what he means when he says ministers like him are simultaneously out of their mind for God and "in their right mind" for others (5:13). Much of 2 Cor 10–13 is Paul's "fool's speech" in which, among other things, he foolishly "boasts" in his Christlike weakness, suffering, and love. He thereby shows himself, in an important sense, to be a fool—but a fool with integrity.[20]

Throughout 2 Corinthians, Paul commends himself—that is, his integrity—but only by commending his participation in the love and sufferings of Christ for others (e.g., 2:4; 6:4–12; 11:11; 12:6–10). This is how Paul knows that his ministry is grounded not in himself but in the grace of God (1:12; 12:9) and the power-in-weakness of the indwelling Christ (12:9). Therefore, he says, "I will most gladly spend and be spent for you" (12:15a), for "everything we do, beloved, is for the sake of building you up" (12:19b; see also 13:10) and "we rejoice when we are weak and you are strong" (13:9a).

Reflections for Today

In the spirit of Susan Eastman, we do not want to leave this study of Paul's integrity in the past. Instead, we may reflect briefly on five dimensions of this integrity that speak across the centuries.

First is the need for sincerity, of freedom from duplicity. Ministry can definitely tempt us to seek power, prestige, and even money—and it can happen, increasingly over time, either without our noticing it or with our *approving* of it as God's reward for our faithfulness.

---

20. For Paul's talk of being a "fool," see 11:1, 16–21; 12:6, 11. See also Charles Campbell's reflections on Paul as the foolish preacher in chapter 3.

Second is the need for self-giving, for seeing ministry as the offering of ourselves, not just our words. The Pauline team gave themselves in concrete ways to the communities they formed, leaving us not merely a model but a mandate. Why? Because their self-giving derived from their own life in Christ, their own participation in his participation in our humanity. Why? Because they were recipients of God's own self-giving love.

Third, this participation, if it is truly participation in the resurrected crucified Christ, will naturally take on a downwardly mobile trajectory that is—paradoxically—life-giving. What this means will vary from minister to minister, from time to time, and from place to place; it will require commitment and discernment.

Fourth, such participation will require collegiality: support from others in ministry, from family members, and even from those who are the principal recipients of one's ministry.

Finally, integrity cannot be sustained without prayer and without dependence on God's grace. If we believe, with Paul, that by the Spirit Christ lives in us to empower us in our weakness, then knowing the reality of this indwelling love through an ongoing life of prayer will be the key to ministry that is worthy of the gospel of Christ.

Bibliography

Eastman, Susan Grove. *Paul and the Person: Reframing Paul's Anthropology*. Grand Rapids: Eerdmans, 2017.

———. "Philippians 2:6–11: Incarnation as Mimic Participation." *Journal for the Study of Paul and His Letters* (2010) 1–22.

Fowl, Stephen E. *Philippians*. Grand Rapids: Eerdmans, 2005.

Gorman, Michael J. *Cruciformity: Paul's Narrative Spirituality of the Cross*. Grand Rapids: Eerdmans, 2001.

———. *Inhabiting the Cruciform God: Kenosis, Justification, and Theosis in Paul's Narrative Soteriology*. Grand Rapids: Eerdmans, 2009.

Johnson, Andy. *1 & 2 Thessalonians*. Grand Rapids: Eerdmans, 2016.

2 _____

Paul, Reciprocity, and Giving with the Poor

John M. G. Barclay

A FRIEND RECENTLY POSED ME a teasing question: what is the opposite of giving? My instinctive answer was: receiving. Is it not obvious that giving and receiving are opposite actions? But a little more reflection made me reconsider. Are giving and receiving really opposites, or are they complementary aspects of a single phenomenon of gift? If we position gift and receipt in an antithetical relationship, we might reinforce an opinion common in the modern West, and at first sight well supported by a Christian ethic, that the highest form of gift, indeed the perfect gift, is a gift which expects no return, a gift "with no strings attached," a gift "free" of reciprocal exchange and *quid pro quo*. There are, indeed, circumstances when the one-way gift is the best form of gift, and there are conditions in which no other form of gift is proper or even possible. But is that always and necessarily the case, or is the reciprocity of gift-receipt-return another perfect form of gift, with equally strong Christian support? I have learned much from Susan Eastman in many rich conversations on this topic over recent years, and I wish here to explore some of the Pauline resources for an ethic of giving that is centrally about reciprocity, exchange, and mutual benefit. According to this ethic, the opposite of giving is not *receiving*, but *keeping* (declining to give), because receiving and giving are conjoined in the proper exchange and circulation of gift, a system of reciprocity that in the right circumstances is a form of gift as good as, and sometimes better than, a one-way, no-return gift. After outlining core characteristics of Paul's theology of gift (or grace), and of the reciprocal dynamics of gift-exchange, I wish to add Paul's voice to the current debates about community development and the sometimes toxic results of what we like to consider "charity" and "service."

Participation in the Gift-Dynamic of Christ

As Susan Eastman has rightly insisted, when Paul speaks of believers' participation in Christ (incorporation "into Christ," and life "with Christ" and "in Christ"), he presupposes the prior participation of Christ in the human condition, the coming of the Son of God who "was found in human form" and was "obedient unto death" (Phil 2:6–8; see also Gal 4:4–7; Rom 8:3).[1] Christ's participation in the human condition not only enables our participation in Christ, it also grounds, through the Spirit, the "newness of life" (Rom 6:4) that is the energizing source of all Christian behavior. Thus, Paul's ethic of human gift-giving is part of, and integral to, his theology of grace. That is immediately obvious not just in the linguistic link between divine grace (*charis*) and the gifts of the Spirit (*charismata*, e.g., 1 Cor 1:4–7), but also in the theological connections Paul draws between the grace (*charis*) of Christ and the gift (*charis*) that Macedonia and (he hopes) Achaia are making toward the church in Jerusalem (2 Cor 8:1, 4, 6, 7, 9). The nodal point of connection between grace and gift is articulated in 2 Cor 8:9. This sentence is normally translated, "for you know the grace of our Lord Jesus Christ, that though he was rich, yet for your sakes he became poor, so that through his poverty you might become rich."[2] This is a perfectly possible translation: it figures Christ's richness (understood in non-material terms) as a form of possession that he renounced in becoming poor (a movement generally taken to refer to the incarnation), through which believers themselves become rich (in non-material terms). But it is not very clear how this fits the context, where the Corinthians are being asked to make a material donation but are not required to make themselves poor (8:13): if the Corinthians are expected to imitate or participate in the Christ-event, it is not very clear what aspect is meant to shape their lives. Moreover, in the context, the language of wealth or riches seems to designate not quantity of possession but scale of generosity: for instance, in the immediately preceding context, Paul had noted the "wealth" of the Macedonians, which consisted not of their possessions but of their generosity (8:2; 9:11). Thus an equally possible, and arguably better, translation of 2 Cor 8:9 would run like this (with explanation in parentheses): "For you know the grace of our Lord Jesus Christ, that *because* he was rich (rich in generosity) he became

---

1. See Eastman, *Paul and the Person*, chapter 5. All scriptural quotations are from the NRSV, unless otherwise indicated.

2. I have discussed the translation options in more detail in Barclay, "Because He was Rich," 331–44. Colin Miller also reflects on the poverty of Christ and its implications for understanding people experiencing poverty as those who bear the image of the Lord in chapter 9 of this volume.

poor (in the incarnation), so that by his poverty (his saving adoption of the human condition) you may become rich (rich in Christlike and Christ energized generosity)." The participial clause (*plousios ōn*) can be translated as easily "because he was rich" as "although he was rich," and there is a good case for taking the parallel phrase in Phil 2:6 this way ("because he was in the form of God, he emptied himself").[3] If Christ was rich, it was because he was full of the self-giving love of God; and if we are enriched, it is not so we might *have* much (material or spiritual) but so we might *give* much (or have much by giving). We do not become rich materially (this is not a version of the prosperity gospel), nor do we become rich simply in the sense of enjoying spiritual blessings. We become rich precisely as he was and is rich; that is, in the self-diffusing love that is the core of the life of God.

On this reading, the ultimate connection between divine grace and human generosity is mutual participation: Christ's participation in the human condition enables, indeed creates, our participation in Christ and in the gift-momentum of his grace. Grace, we may say, gives us not *something* but *someone*—that is, Godself—and in an important sense gives us ourselves, the new life that we live in and from the resurrection of Christ (Gal 2:19–20). We are not our old selves, loaded with extra divine benefits (and responsibilities); we are new selves, drawn by the Spirit into the very life of God. And this means that God is not just the source or the initiator of the movement of grace—not just the fountain from which grace flows or the generator that creates its current. God is the flow, the momentum, the energy itself, the One we enter into and commit ourselves to as we enter God's (still transcendent) agency of grace.

Reciprocity in Gift

When Paul figures this grace at work in the Christian community, even across a geographical distance, he figures it not as a one-way momentum, but as a gift that flows in both (or all) directions, with givers of grace also its receivers, and receivers also its givers. Consider the Jerusalem collection,

---

3. See Gorman, *Inhabiting the Cruciform God*, 28 (following Charles Moule, Stephen Fowl, and others) and Gorman, pp. 3–5 of the present volume. For theological exposition of the reading "because he was rich" in 2 Cor 8:9, see Tanner, *Economy of Grace*, 79: "by becoming one with us in Christ, the Word, while remaining rich, acquires our poverty and neediness, for the purpose of giving us what we as mere creatures do not have or own by nature—the very riches of God's own life, its holiness and incorruptibility." To this I would add: "and its wealth of generosity." Cf. Tanner, *Economy of Grace*, 84: "Jesus entered into our poverty for the sake of the poor, but he did so as someone rich with the Father's own love."

for which he labored so hard over so many years. In Rom 15 he describes this collection not as an initial gift but as a return gift: if the gentiles have enjoyed a partnership with Jerusalem in relation to spiritual blessings, they are pleased to—in fact they are obliged to—make this service to the poor among the saints in material terms (15:25–29). "They are obliged" (Rom 15:27): Paul does not shy away from the language of obligation, as if proper gifts should be free of such things; he simply states the obvious implication of a gift in ancient terms, that it puts its recipients under obligation.[4] In any case, this gift and counter-gift (which is both voluntary and obliged) tie together communities of different ethnicity across hundreds of miles, and if there are "strings" attached to the original gift, they are the strings of fellowship in grace and common dependency on grace, not just the human ties of gift-exchange. In 2 Cor 8–9 Paul approaches this collection from a different angle and now speaks of the *charis* that Macedonia is willing—and Corinth should be willing—to contribute to the saints in Jerusalem. This gift will represent the overflow of God's grace to and through the Macedonian and Corinthian believers, since "God is able to provide you with every gift in abundance, so that by always having enough of everything, you may abound in every good work" (2 Cor 9:8). When Jerusalem receives this gift, says Paul, "they will long for you and pray for you, because of the surpassing grace of God given to you" (9:14). Indeed, this gift will overflow in many thanksgivings to God (9:12), who is the source of the gift that flows between them: "thanks be to God for his indescribable Gift" (9:15).

But here again Paul does not figure this as a one-way relationship. Apart from the longing and prayer on the part of the believers in Jerusalem, Paul imagines a further reciprocity between Jerusalem and Corinth that initially takes us by surprise: "I do not mean that there should be relief for others and pressure on you, but it is a question of a fair balance between your abundance and their need, so that *their abundance may be for your need*, in order that there might be a fair balance" (8:13–14).[5] Paul does not clarify how Jerusalem will be in surplus and in what sense they will be able to meet the needs of the Corinthians, and one might imagine that the Corinthians, who were all too conscious of excelling in everything (see 2 Cor 8:7), might not have been pleased to be thought of as standing in any sort of need.[6] But it is clear that what Paul envisages here is a system of reciprocity, a movement of benefits not only in one direction but also in the other, with

4. See Barclay, *Paul and the Gift*, chapter 1.
5. On the notion of "fair balance" or "equality" here, see Welborn, "That There Might Be Equality," 73–90.
6. For further reflection on 2 Cor 8:13–15, and its Exodus citation, see Barclay, "Manna," 409–26.

the two communities tied together both by generosity and by need. The Macedonians' gift is noted in 8:1–4 for its extraordinary generosity (actually the product of divine grace, 8:1), but superabundant generosity does not necessarily imply another perfection of gift, non-circularity.[7] Even extreme generosity is compatible with reciprocity: a generous gift is not necessarily, or in principle, one-way. The Macedonians gave out of their poverty, with a remarkable degree of self-sacrifice. But the goal of this generosity is to establish or cement a relationship that is in principle—and at best—*two-way*, not one-way; a relationship that will somehow benefit the Macedonians as well as the believers in Jerusalem.

When we look elsewhere at Paul's ethical instructions, the norm that comes into view time and again is not one-way gift giving but reciprocity, the circulation of gifts in systems of mutual benefit. To be sure, there are a number of places where Paul encourages generosity by urging believers not to seek their own interests. In Rom 15:1–3 the strong are told to bear the weaknesses of those without power and not to please themselves: "Each of us must please our neighbor for the good purpose of upbuilding. For Christ did not please himself, but as it is written, 'The insults of those who insult you have fallen on me'" (15:2–3). Serving the neighbor will mean forgoing some rights and freedoms, and entering deeply into their social and psychological condition.[8] But Paul is careful to ensure that this is not a one-way, condescending relationship in which one side welcomes the other, tolerating their foibles from a position of superior self-sufficiency. Far from it: the two sides are told to "welcome one another" (15:7), and it is expected that the building up will go in both directions: "Let us pursue what makes for peace, and for the building up *of one another*" (14:9).[9] In other words, the self-giving of the strong is intended to create or sustain relationships where both sides have something to contribute to the other. The power of the host (to welcome the other) is distributed evenly and mutually, because each is expressing and passing forward the welcome that they have received from Christ ("welcome one another as Christ has welcomed you," 15:7). In order to create this reciprocal flow of gifts, Paul has to warn against the natural instincts of selfishness and overcome the all-too-human inclination to keep rather than to give. But the relationships he intends to

7. On different perfections of gift see Barclay, *Paul and the Gift*, chapter 2.

8. Forgoing some rights is a theme Gorman traces in chapter 1. In chapter 11, Presian Burroughs suggests another dimension of this neighborly service involves self-restraint on behalf of the nonhuman creation.

9. In the present volume, Mary Schmitt and Samuel Enosa Peni (chapter 12) and Douglas Campbell (chapter 14) consider the timely Pauline themes of peace and peacemaking.

promote are mutually enriching because the divine gifts are circulated so that no one is self-sufficient or enjoys the permanent superiority of the omni-competent giver.

Hence, love does not seek its own interests (*ta heautēs*, 1 Cor 13:5). Paul instructs, "Do not seek your own advantage (*to heautou*), but the advantage of others" (10:24), just as "I try to please everyone in everything I do, not seeking my own advantage (*to emautou sympheron*), but the advantage of others" (10:33). Christ himself is the supreme example (although also much more than that): his self-emptying, in becoming human and becoming a slave (Phil 2:6–8), is related (in one function of the Philippian hymn) to the preceding instruction that each should "look not to your own interests (*ta heautōn*) but to the interests of others" (2:4). Even here some (perhaps better) texts read, "look not to your own interests but *also* (*kai*) to the interests of others" (2:4), which suggests that the two sets of interests are not mutually exclusive.[10] But however we read that phrase, the wider context indicates that, where *each* person is to look to the interests of others, the framework and primary goal is social solidarity and thus the collective interests of *everyone*.[11] What Paul seeks to inculcate here is not self-sufficient individuals who do nothing but give to others, but a community of shared sympathy and mutual support in co-dependence on the Spirit (*koinōnia pneumatos*, 2:1). Where compassion and sympathy are shared, it would be unthinkable that one member would be allowed merely to suffer for the benefit of others, since each person would have everyone else looking out for their interests.

Paul frequently talks about doing things to or for one another (*allēlois* or *eis allēlous*) and such phrases occur no less than thirty-two times in the undisputed letters. Believers are to greet *one another* (with a holy kiss, Rom 16:16; 1 Cor 16:20); they are expected to encourage *one another* (1 Thess 4:18; 5:11) and warn or instruct *one another* (Rom 15:14). Above all, they are to love *one another* (Gal 5:13; Rom 12:10; 13:8), as the love of God flows within the community in all directions. The notion of "bearing *one another's* burdens" (Gal 6:2) implies that there are no self-sufficient individuals able to carry their own load together with others': all need the help of other people in carrying their own burden, and they are bound together in need and therefore in mutual support. Even Paul exemplifies this phenomenon. When he looks forward to strengthening the believers in Rome with some spiritual gift, he immediately corrects himself to indicate that they will be "*mutually* encouraged by the faith that is in one another,

---

10. A wide range of early manuscripts (including P46, and the codices Sinaiticus and Alexandrinus) include *kai*, and it should probably be judged the superior reading.

11. For the significance of community in Paul's ethics, see Horrell, *Solidarity and Difference*.

both yours and mine" (Rom 1:11–12). That correction indicates that Paul is fully aware that the one-way gift can appear patronizing, as an implicit claim to superior power. Here and elsewhere Paul backs off from making himself the patron of his churches and anticipates instead a kind of mutual patronage, where each will have something to contribute to the other.[12] But since the gifts they share are ultimately not their own, but merely what they have received from God, this would be better figured not as mutual patronage, but as mutual brokerage—each being a broker of divine generosity to the other.[13] Thus, when Paul reflects on his relationship to the church in Philippi, he recognizes their gift to him as part of their relationship of "give and take" (Phil 4:15), though the source and energy of this mutual benefit is their common sharing in the grace of God (1:6). Indeed, their mutuality, in which each is enabled to give to the other, is precisely how the generosity of God binds them together.

The fullest demonstration of this principle of reciprocity—and of its social ramifications—is the Pauline metaphor of the body (1 Cor 12:12–26; Rom 12:3–8), as Beverly Gaventa and Emily Peck-McClain also illustrate in chapters 4 and 10, respectively. In this metaphor, the members of the body are explicitly described as united in mutual contribution. The gifts of the Spirit (*charismata*) are distributed around the body, to individual members, so that no part can say that it is self-sufficient, and none can be dispensed with or disparaged as superfluous. "The eye cannot say to the hand, 'I have no need of you,' nor can the head say to the feet, 'I have no need of you'" (1 Cor 12:21). "Need" is a strong word: it betokens vulnerability, exposure, the necessity to receive. Thus, all the parts of the body are bound together both in gift and in need. The gift-and-return here may not be bilateral: there are more than two parts to the body, so gifts will circulate around the body in both direct and indirect forms of reciprocity, a system that an anthropologist might dub "generalized reciprocity."[14] Thus, what I give may not be matched by a return gift from the recipient but by a return from elsewhere in the community: as gifts circulate among us, everyone is constantly in the process of both giving and receiving. In the Corinthian situation this is clearly directed against the development of internal hierarchy and division

12. Another way in which all people—whether rich or poor—may contribute to the well-being of others is through prayer, as Robert Moses explains in chapter 7.

13. See Briones, *Paul's Financial Policy*.

14. Marshall Sahlins used this phrase to refer to the indefinite reciprocity (generalized in kind) operative in intimate relationships (e.g., family) (Sahlins, *Stone Age Economics*, 194–95). But it is also commonly used for multilateral, indirect forms of reciprocity (generalized in scope), where the benefits of cooperation are diffused and not limited to bilateral relations.

(1 Cor 12:22–25). That the parts of the body care for one another, to the same degree and in the same way, is what prevents the community from flying apart into mutual indifference.

Crucially, this reciprocity is fueled and maintained by the fact that all parties are recipients of the Spirit's gifts—what they pass on to others is what they themselves have received. Thus, the reciprocity between givers and receivers—in which each party is both (at one time or in one respect) a giver *and* a receiver—is not just a pragmatic arrangement or a political device. It is a means of entering into the generosity and self-giving love of God. Note that we enter this not only when we give (flowing in the momentum of gift that is at the heart of God) but also when we receive, because what we receive is that same momentum as it comes to us through others. Paul's image of the body suggests that we are designed both to give and to receive, and the same is true for everyone else with whom we are in relationship. They too are designed to enjoy the dignity and privilege of being givers, and if we decline their gift or refuse their return, we are denying them the opportunity of entering into the momentum of grace as fully as we are claiming for ourselves. In other words, the one-way gift can be bad for the recipients of such gifts not only because they may be psychologically humiliated or socially demeaned, but because they end up spiritually crippled. If we refuse to accept a return we are denying others the means by which they become rich *in giving to us*!

To put the matter this way might suggest that the promotion of reciprocity has become a convenient mask for self-interest. To be sure, there are significant dangers in certain forms of gift-reciprocity, and not every kind of reciprocity is good. The dangers particularly concern the problems of power and the potential for manipulation. Every gift involves some shift in the balance of power: at the moment of giving—and in that respect—the giver is superior to the recipient, and a differential of power, small or great, is created between them. If this is badly handled, the recipient can be humiliated by the gift and can be put under an unwelcome, even harmful, obligation. Gifts that expect a return can be overwhelming, oppressive, and manipulative. If the power-superiority of the giver is employed to leverage a particular return or to alter the allegiances of the recipient, the gift becomes a bribe. This was a problem already well recognized in antiquity, where the Hebrew Scriptures forbid the receipt of gifts by those who adjudicate lawsuits (e.g., Exod 23:6–8) and where Greek city-states struggled to counteract the obligations that their aristocrats had acquired through gift-relations with fellow aristocrats in competing cities.[15] Today this problem is familiar to us as

15. See Herman, *Ritualised Friendship*.

"bribery and corruption"—the power of the gift to oblige the recipient to make partial decisions and to act against the interests of their employer or their state. It is natural in such circumstances to cut the strings and either to ban the gift altogether or to insist that the gift should be one way only, with no strings attached.

Banning the gift may indeed be the only solution in certain circumstances, and there are also conditions where a one-way gift is both necessary and ideal. But there are also ways of limiting or equalizing the power relations in gift giving, by ensuring that the asymmetry in one direction is balanced by an equally powerful (though not necessarily identical) asymmetry in the other. In conditions of generalized reciprocity, where giving and receiving is diffused within a community, the power of gifts is equally diffused and less easily a means of manipulation. Different circumstances will allow different solutions, but the material we have surveyed strongly suggests that a one-way gift is not the only form of good gift and not necessarily the best: reciprocal giving can be an equal, though different, good. It is important here to avoid three common errors, which have crept into our conceptuality of gift giving, especially in the modern West.

1. It is a mistake to think that a benefit to others is necessarily in competition with a benefit to oneself, or vice versa. According to the common zero-sum configuration of gifts, if I gain benefit in a relationship or through an action, my gain must be deducted from yours: the more for me, the less for you; the benefit of an action is divided between us. But there is no good reason to adopt this model of mutual exclusion: what I give may be 100 percent for your benefit but may *also* benefit me, not least in the development of a relationship (of friendship or mutuality) that enriches us both at the same time.

2. It is a mistake to figure social relationships on a spectrum between selfishness (or self-interest), at one end, and selflessness (or self-sacrifice), at the other, if mutual benefit is figured as a compromise or mid-way point between these poles. This is a very common mental picture that reinforces the mistake of the zero-sum: it suggests that a relationship of reciprocity and co-interest must be tainted by some element of self-interest and that only a relationship utterly free of benefit to me can be regarded as truly loving or other-directed.

3. It is a mistake to define *altruism* as giving-without-return. Altruism can have a range of senses and at its most basic simply means action for the sake of the other. But recent centuries have seen a philosophical (and sometimes theological) pull toward defining altruism as

giving-without-return, on the understanding, famously articulated by Jacques Derrida, that "for there to be a gift, there must be no reciprocity, return, exchange, countergift, or debt."[16]

These three mistakes are mutually reinforcing, but they are all unnecessary and should be resisted. It is undoubtedly the case that some forms of gift-reciprocity do not bring real benefit to the recipient and are disguised—or self-deceiving—forms of selfishness. But this is by no means always or necessarily the case. Relationships of mutual benefit or co-interest, such as a well-functioning friendship or a well-balanced marriage, are characterized by the constant interplay of gift and receipt: they reflect the vulnerability of the human condition and give both parties the dignity and privilege of being the giver. According to Paul, this is not an accident or an unfortunate compromise of an ideal, unilateral gift. It is precisely how we are designed to flourish as we participate in the flow of divine generosity in Christ. And there is good reason to think that this is the most helpful model for gift-relationships in general, including those that operate with and among the poor.

Beyond Charity

Giving without allowing and enabling a return sounds heroic and self-sacrificial, but it easily turns toxic. A large range of empirical evidence relating to both international aid and local charitable interventions has demonstrated this toxicity on a number of levels.[17] As we have seen, the giver is always, in some respect, in a position of superior power, and if this relationship becomes permanently one-sided, that asymmetry is exacerbated and continually reinforced. From that inequality comes the humiliation or demeaning of the recipient, all the more damaging since it exacerbates what is often already a psychology of shame or despair among those in long-term material need. The fatalism and negativity, even nihilism, that can take hold of whole communities in a prolonged economic downturn is well documented, especially where such communities feel "left behind" by more affluent groups. In these conditions, well-meaning charity can quickly become condescending and patronizing, since it disregards the local resources that are waiting to be developed and further disempowers the weak. Doing *for* others, rather than doing *with*, can create debilitating dependencies, which discourage

16. Derrida, *Given Time*, 12. For exposition of this modern trajectory, see Barclay, *Paul and the Gift*, 51–63.

17. For some recent discussions of this issue, see Corbett and Fikkert, *When Helping Hurts*; Lupton, *Toxic Charity*.

and limit the agency of the poor themselves. Much as Christians love to adopt a "service" ethos, and prefer to give than to receive, the effects of their charity can be disastrous: short-term "missions" to the developing world, the one-way donations of rich churches to those in poorer parts of town, even soup kitchens and similar homelessness projects that fail to encourage the agency of the homeless can become toxic and counterproductive. What might be appropriate in an emergency can create, over time, a debilitating dependency, which may reinforce the donors' sense of moral, financial, and social superiority and can end up doing more harm than good.

Language is revealing. When communities are described as "deprived," they are figured as having no resources of their own—nothing to give. On this deficit model, outsiders arrive to solve "problems" and meet "needs," but the surplus-to-need momentum is entirely one way. Donors give to recipients and service providers supply the needs of beneficiaries: agency is only expected of the donor in relation to a grateful, but essentially passive, recipient. Ironically, this can create not less but greater distance between the two parties: there is no solidarity here, only self-sufficiency on one side and dependency on the other. In reaction to this, it is not uncommon to hear calls for the poor to become self-reliant and independent; but that is to fall back into another version of modern individualism (or limited-horizon social isolation). If our vision is not independence but *interdependence* in relationships of mutual enhancement, the goal is not to have everyone capable of "standing on their own two feet," but to have all able and willing to bear one another's burdens (Gal 6:2). Here no one is self-sufficient, but all are mutually linked both in giving and in receiving support.

Although Paul speaks of this reciprocity explicitly only in connection to relationships among believers, he does extend the giving of benefits beyond the boundaries of the church (e.g., Gal 6:10: "let us work for the good of all, and especially for those of the household of faith"). Moreover, the range of what he considers God-given gifts can include what is gifted in the created world (e.g., 2 Cor 9:10: "he who supplies seed for the sower and bread for food"). There is some warrant, then, for taking an important hermeneutical step: what Paul says about gifts and their circulation in the body of Christ is structurally parallel to what may be said about all the gifts of humanity, natural as well as spiritual, within the world as well as the church. The gifts of "common grace" may not be recognized as divinely sourced by the majority of those who receive and use them—it is the task of mission to make people aware of their source—but they are gifts nonetheless, given by God to be developed, deployed, and circulated. Thus, there is a deep resonance between a Christian theology of reciprocal gift giving and the principles of community engagement that have come to be known as "Asset-Based Community Development" (ABCD).[18] The philosophical and pragmatic roots of this perspective on community development lie in sources as diverse as Paulo Freire's liberation insights[19] and Saul Alinsky's rules of community organizing,[20] but its primary principles include:

1. The expectation that the community itself will already contain multiple gifts—skills, resources, and capabilities. The aim is to discover and develop these resources, including local experience, wisdom, ingenuity, resilience, and social connectivity, so as to develop confidence and creativity and build local capacity, leadership, and initiative.

2. The determination to bring in outside resources, financial or personal, *only* in such a way as to develop and enhance the gifts already present and being developed within the community and not to supplant or diminish them.

3. The desire to create partnerships, cooperation, and solidarity, both within local communities and, where appropriate, with other agencies; but these latter are expected to become engaged as mutual beneficiaries in the development of the community and not to remain "outside" agencies, which operate from a benevolent but lofty distance.

The model in ABCD is not the soup kitchen, where lines of "needy" people are given aid by self-sufficient donors, but the potluck supper, where everybody brings something to the table, of whatever sort, however small or big.[21] Of course, there will be crisis conditions where the soup kitchen or famine relief is not only appropriate but urgently necessary. But it is easy to get stuck in that model—not least because it fits so well with our desire to be givers and assuages our guilt at being in surplus—and never move beyond it to the harder and more demanding vocation of working not *for* but *with* the poor. In my limited experience (in a former mining village in the northeast

18. See Asset-Based Community Development Institute at http://www.abcdinstitute.org. The institute describes itself as "at the center of a large and growing movement that considers local assets as the primary building blocks of sustainable community development. Building on the skills of local residents, the power of local associations, and the supportive functions of local institutions, asset-based community development draws upon existing community strengths to build stronger, more sustainable communities for the future." Its principles are now key to the Church of Scotland's "Priority Areas" initiative and are being adopted by churches, as well as secular organizations, all over the world.

19. Freire, *Pedagogy of the Oppressed.*

20. Alinsky, *Rules for Radicals.*

21. For this image I am indebted to Michael Rhodes, from whose experience I have learned much.

of England), such presence, involvement, and mutuality is always complex and often messy, but it is also hugely enriching and far more productive than the "pure" one-way altruism that refuses relational exchange.

In his recent book, *A Nazareth Manifesto*, Sam Wells has made a powerful theological case for looking beyond doing (or being) *for* others, so as to bring into focus the end goal of being *with*.[22] Drawing on a theology of the Trinity and the incarnation, and looking to an eschatology figured as the endlessly rich enjoyment of *presence with* (with God, with one another, and with a restored creation), Wells offers a theological argument that starts from a different place from that outlined above, but reaches the same conclusions. As he rightly insists, participation, mutuality, and solidarity are ends in themselves, not a means to some other end; they are the destination and not the route. If the focus is on the process (not the projects) and on people (not outcomes), we can follow God's purpose to bring us out of alienation and isolation into participation and reconciliation. On this view, there is no "for"—even Christ's gift *for us*—that is not also intended to result in "with"—Christ *with* us so that we might be *with* each other. There is no receipt of the gift that is not designed to enable participation in the energy and reciprocity of the gift-dynamic. As Wells writes, altruism is not the goal if by altruism we consider "that the only noble way is to seek nothing for oneself and to seek only the benefit of others."[23] That, as he says, is neither sustainable nor the true image of our eschatological goal.

Readers might have thought there must be some mistake in the wording of my title. Surely it should read, "giving *to* the poor" not "giving *with* the poor." If people are poor, do they not, by definition, have nothing to give? Paul would not have agreed (see 2 Cor 8:1–4) for at least two reasons. First, he expects that everyone is gifted enough *in some respect* to be able to give to others, even if not in material terms. And second, he expects any giving in one direction to be matched by giving in the other, creating an equalizing partnership based on mutuality and *co-interest*, so that everyone is in a position of both giver and receiver. As Wells insists, "the Christian relationship to poverty is thus not fundamentally working on behalf of the poor but developing reciprocal relationships and expecting to receive from the poor."[24] Where churches have gone beyond figuring themselves as the ever-giving (but, in fact, eventually exhausted) donors, they have been able to establish partnerships in poor communities with others whose talents are

---

22. Wells, *Nazareth Manifesto*.

23. Ibid., 116. See above on one modern definition of altruism as "giving-without-return."

24. Ibid., 65.

already rich and ripe for development. And in this coalition of friends there can develop honest, fruitful, and genuinely transformative relationships that enrich all parties, including the local church.[25] And then, in fact, "the poor" no longer become a generalized category, different from "us," but such labels give way to people, with personal names and rich and complex histories, just like everyone else. In the pooling of talents, we all learn both to give and to receive, and in so doing we are all drawn deeper into relationship with one another and with God, whose grace is what passes between us.

Bibliography

Alinsky, Saul. *Rules for Radicals: A Pragmatic Primer for Realistic Radicals.* New York: Vintage, 1989.

Barclay, John M. G. "'Because He Was Rich He Became Poor': Translation, Exegesis, and Hermeneutics in the Reading of 2 Cor 8.9." In *Theologizing in the Corinthian Conflict: Studies in the Exegesis and Theology of 2 Corinthians,* edited by Reimund Bieringer, Ma. Marilou S. Ibita, Dominika A. Kurek-Chomycz, and Thomas A. Vollmer, 331–44. Biblical Tools and Studies. Paris: Peeters, 2013.

———. "Manna and the Circulation of Grace: A Study of 2 Corinthians 8:1–15." In *The Word Leaps the Gap: Essays on Scripture and Theology in Honor of Richard B. Hays,* edited by J. Ross Wagner, C. Kavin Rowe, and A. Katherine Grieb, 409–26. Grand Rapids: Eerdmans, 2008.

———. *Paul and the Gift.* Grand Rapids: Eerdmans, 2015.

Briones, David. *Paul's Financial Policy: A Socio-Theological Approach.* London: T. & T. Clark, 2013.

Corbett, Steve, and Brian Fikkert. *When Helping Hurts.* Chicago: Moody, 2009.

Derrida, Jacques. *Given Time: 1, Counterfeit Money.* Translated by Peggy Kamuf. Chicago: University of Chicago Press, 1992.

Eastman, Susan. *Paul and the Person: Reframing Paul's Anthropology.* Grand Rapids: Eerdmans, 2017.

Freire, Paulo. *Pedagogy of the Oppressed.* Harmondsworth, UK: Penguin, 1972.

Gorman, Michael J. *Inhabiting the Cruciform God: Kenosis, Justification, and Theosis in Paul's Narrative Soteriology.* Grand Rapids: Eerdmans, 2009.

Herman, Gabriel. *Ritualised Friendship and the Greek City.* Cambridge: Cambridge University Press, 1987.

25. I speak from my own experience and from the experience of many others with whom I have spoken. In a recent discussion paper for the Church of Scotland, written by Derek Pope, upbeat reports are given of situations where churches have applied the perspectives of ABCD and a number of principles are enunciated, including: "Priority Areas are not problematic communities, but good places to live, abundant communities, full of gifted people. God is at work in these communities and is seen in the faithful daily lives of those who live in them. We should decide that we will no longer support or develop programmes or projects based on 'meeting the needs' of these communities, but instead commit to 'working with,' building friendships, sharing our strengths and resources. We should declare that we are no longer going to relate to people as passive recipients of our services, but only as gifted companions on the way."

Horrell, David G. *Solidarity and Difference: A Contemporary Reading of Paul's Ethics.* London: T. & T. Clark, 2005.

Lupton, Robert D. *Toxic Charity: How Churches and Charities Hurt Those They Help (And How to Reverse It).* New York: Harper Collins, 2011.

Sahlins, Marshall. *Stone Age Economics.* 2nd ed. London: Routledge, 2004.

Tanner, Katherine. *Economy of Grace.* Minneapolis: Fortress, 2005.

Welborn, Laurence L. "'That There Might Be Equality': The Contexts and Consequences of a Pauline Ideal." *NTS* 59 (2013) 73–90.

Wells, Sam. *A Nazareth Manifesto: Being with God.* Chichester: Wiley Blackwell, 2015.

3

The Disruptive Sermon:
Preaching and Apocalyptic Imagination

CHARLES CAMPBELL

A FTER GRACIOUSLY READING A book I co-authored, *Preaching Fools*, Susan Eastman commented to me, "You know, Chuck, this is really a book about apocalyptic imagination." No, Susan, actually I didn't know that. But her comment got me thinking. And ever since then, I've been trying to sort out what she meant. I've been pondering preaching and apocalyptic imagination, trying to glean the primary characteristics of this form of imagination and to explore its significance for preaching. This chapter is thus a response to Susan's comment about *Preaching Fools*. When she reads it, she may remark, "No, Chuck, this is not what I meant at all." But at least our conversation will continue.[1]

Apocalyptic Imagination

Previously when I thought of "apocalyptic," I had in mind a literary genre—a book like the Apocalypse of John. I thought of literature with wild, spectacular imagery and trips to heaven guided by angels and visions of the future. There are misogynistic images that demean women. There is violent warfare imagery as the battle rages between the forces of God and the forces of evil. There are swords and horses and plagues and blood—slaughter everywhere. There are good reasons many Christians avoid apocalyptic, though it does

---

1. This chapter is a distillation of lectures given at Saint Meinrad Seminary and School of Theology, Lancaster Theological Seminary, Hazelip School of Theology at Lipscomb University, and Leipzig University in Germany. I am grateful for the comments I received from participants at those lectures. This article also develops some material from Campbell and Cilliers, *Preaching Fools*, which is further developed in my commentary on 1 Corinthians in Westminster John Knox's Belief Series.

feel at times as if these traditional apocalyptic images give voice to the world in which we are living.

Recently, however, scholars have moved beyond considering apocalyptic simply as a particular genre with distinctive literary and metaphorical characteristics. Rather, apocalyptic is understood more as a theological orientation, a perception that crosses many genres in Scripture. Apocalyptic is a form of imagination. At the heart of apocalyptic imagination is a *theology of interruption*, to borrow a phrase from the Belgian theologian Lieven Boeve.[2] Apocalyptic imagination, that is, lives in the space where the new age invades and interrupts the old. It lives in that threshold space in which the new age *has* broken in but in which the old age continues aggressively to challenge the new. That is the character, as Boeve notes, of interruptions. There is a twofold dynamic at work—both continuity and discontinuity. What is interrupted—in this case, the old age—does not cease to exist. At the same time, however, what is interrupted does not continue as if nothing had happened. And in the case of Christ, something decisive has happened. There *is*, thus, a conflictual dynamic to apocalyptic because of the ongoing tensive relationship between the old age and the new creation.[3] And apocalyptic imagination lives and moves in that space of interruption in which the new has decisively interrupted the old but has not fully or finally overcome it.

Paul's proclamation of the cross in 1 Corinthians, as many New Testament scholars now argue, is precisely this kind of apocalyptic interruption. The cross interrupts or invades the old age—the old myths and conventions and rationalities of the world.[4] The cross unmasks the powers of this age (1 Cor 2:6–8) for what they are: not the divine regents of life, but the agents of domination, violence, and death. The cross inaugurates the new age or new creation in the midst of the old. And through this interruption of the old age by the new, the cross creates a space where believers may be liberated from the powers of this age both to resist their deadly ways and to begin living in the new creation.[5]

2. See Boeve, *God Interrupts History*.

3. For an extended reflection on time and the concept of already/not yet, see chapter 6 by Ann Jervis.

4. See Martyn, "Epistemology," 89–110, and "From Paul," 279–97; and Brown, *Cross and Human Transformation*.

5. For a more thorough discussion of the principalities and powers, which is not possible here, see Campbell, *Word*. Also, Wink, *Powers*. The phrase, "the powers of death," used as an all-encompassing summary of the character of the "principalities and powers" of the old age is taken from Stringfellow, *Ethic for Christians*.

As a result of this apocalyptic interruption, Christians stand at the "juncture of the ages" or the "turn of the ages."[6] Believers stand "in-between," in a kind of liminal or threshold space where the two ages overlap, where the old is passing away while the new has not yet fully come. This space, like all liminal spaces, is an unsettling space in which the old-age frameworks and certainties and assumptions no longer hold, even as they continue seeking to take people captive.[7] This liminal space is a dynamic space of movement from one place to another, in this case movement from the old age to the new—a movement that is never complete until the final coming of the new creation.

Paul signals the character of this space when, in 1 Corinthians, he emphasizes that believers are "being saved" (sōzesthe, 1:18, 15:2).[8] This phrase depicts the tensive, dynamic character of the Christian life and the Christian community at the juncture of the ages. The Christian life is neither settled nor complete until the powers of this age are fully overcome and God is all in all (15:24–28). In the apocalyptic space inaugurated by Christ's crucifixion and resurrection, the Christian life is a pilgrimage from the old age that has been interrupted to the new that has not yet fully come.

In this space apocalyptic imagination is born. And this imagination has a specific characteristic. It functions, to draw an image from New Testament scholar J. Louis Martyn, as a kind of bifocal vision—or bifocal discernment.[9] Such discernment simultaneously perceives both the old-age powers of death continuing their work in the world and the life of the new creation, which has disrupted the world but often remains hidden to those who lack the perception to recognize it. William Stringfellow, an Episcopal lay theologian and radical Christian, has put it this way: Such discernment enables one "to see portents of death where others find progress or success but, simultaneously, to behold tokens of the reality of the Resurrection where others are consigned to confusion or despair"; it involves "perceiving the saga of salvation within the era of the Fall."[10]

---

6. Martyn, "Epistemology," 89, 92; Brown, Cross and Human Transformation, 124.

7. For a discussion of how Paul confronted these challenges as a form of spiritual battle, see Lisa Bowens's chapter 8 in this volume.

8. Sōzesthe is connected with both crucifixion (1:18) and resurrection (15:2) at the beginning and end of Paul's letter. The term highlights the "futuristic nuance of the present tense;" "salvation is now, but it is also in process, to be completed at the Day of the Lord." See Fee, First Epistle, 720, n. 32.

9. I will use the terms "perception" and "discernment" because "bifocal vision" does not refer to physical sight.

10. Stringfellow, Ethic for Christians, 138–9.

Indeed, *perception* is at the heart of the word "apocalyptic." In Scripture the Greek term for "reveal" is *apocalyptō*, from which comes apocalypse/revelation. *Apocalyptō* involves an unveiling, an uncovering, an unmasking of the invasion of God that has taken place. It is a new kind of perception, a new kind of imagination. In John's Apocalypse, for example, that is what the "seer" of Patmos offers us in the midst of his grotesque, shocking imagery; he offers a new kind of perception. The almighty empire, which claims to be the divine giver of life, is perceived to be a death-dealing beast. The martyrs killed by the Roman Empire are actually triumphantly singing praises to God. The slaughtered Lamb—the one crucified by the empire—is actually the one who reigns. The future belongs not to caesar, but to the lamb that sits on the throne. John is engaged in a battle, to be sure, but a battle for perception, a battle for the imagination.

And in 1 Corinthians Paul preaches with this same kind of apocalyptic imagination. He's unveiling God's hidden interruption of the old age in the crucifixion of Jesus Christ. Throughout the opening of 1 Corinthians, Paul engages in one interruption after another. But the pivotal moment comes in 1:18, when he turns to the proclamation of the cross: "For the message about the cross is foolishness to those who are perishing, but to us who are being saved it is the power of God."[11] Here Paul, with a strong "but," proclaims the cross as an interruption—an interruption of the old-age understandings of power and wisdom. In the midst of the powerful, dominating, militaristic Roman Empire, Paul proclaims the power of the cross.[12] Paul's preaching is disruptive folly. Theologically, it was unimaginable that the Messiah—the Christ—would be crucified. Philosophically, it was unthinkable that the divine could hang in the flesh on a cross. Politically, it was inconceivable that the Messiah would liberate Israel through crucifixion. And culturally, it was impossible that one shamed on the cross could be honored as the Christ.[13] Crucified Messiah. Powerful cross. These were incommensurable realities. Neither the theological nor philosophical nor political nor cultural imagination could entertain such an idea. They were shocking, even blasphemous paradoxes.[14] Foolishness.

Paul too wages a battle for perception. He seeks to interrupt the perception of the Corinthians so they might discern God's wisdom and power in the foolishness and weakness of the cross. He seeks to "perceptually

---

11. All scriptural quotations are from the NRSV, unless otherwise indicated.

12. In chapter 13, Douglas Harink reflects at length on the Christian's relationship with governing authorities.

13. For a concise description of these issues, see Hengel, *Crucifixion*, 6–7.

14. Welborn, *Paul, the Fool of Christ*, 23.

unbalance" the Corinthians so they might discern the God who is simultaneously revealed and hidden in the cross of Jesus Christ.[15] Paul, that is, calls the Corinthians—and us—to perceive with bifocal discernment, with apocalyptic imagination.

The Fool as an Agent of Apocalyptic Imagination

At the point at which Paul interrupts the powers of this age and invites us to perceive God simultaneously revealed and hidden on the cross, the apostle speaks of the gospel as foolishness, and he adopts the role of the fool (1 Cor 1:18–25; 4:10). He holds up folly and the fool as agents of apocalyptic imagination. A brief look at these odd figures suggests the appropriateness of Paul's claim, for fools engage in two primary activities: 1) they interrupt, and 2) they are agents of perception.

Fools interrupt. They interrupt the taken-for-granted myths, rationalities, and presuppositions of the world, which so often hold us captive and keep us from new life. At the deepest level fools do not simply seek to entertain or be funny, though often they do work through these means. Rather, they seek to interrupt business as usual. As Enid Welsford has written, fools "melt the solidity of the world."[16] They interrupt the truths and assumptions that are supposedly "written in stone."

So Paul intentionally and specifically *adopts* and *enacts* the role of the fool. It is the appropriate role for him at the juncture of the ages. For Paul too is melting the solidity of the world. "We have become a spectacle to the world, to angels and to mortals," Paul writes of himself and the other apostles (4:9). "We are fools for the sake of Christ" (4:10). The Greek word translated "spectacle," placed parallel to "fools," is *theatron*, which means a theater-act.[17] Paul thus declares that in preaching the cross he plays a role similar to the spectacle enacted by the fool in the Roman theater. As is the case in later theatrical forms through the centuries, in the Roman theater the fool is a lower-class buffoon, who is identified with the poor and engages in transgressive, disruptive behavior. He mocks the words and deeds of the serious and honorable characters; he resists privilege and authority and gives voice to what no one else dares to say.[18] As a result of this disruptive behavior, the fool often suffers both verbal and physical abuse.

15. Brown, *Cross and Human Transformation*, 158.

16. Welsford, *Fool*, 223.

17. Welborn, *Paul, the Fool of Christ*, 50–51. See also "*theatron*," in Kittel and Bromiley, *Theological Dictionary*, 42–43.

18. Welborn, *Paul, the Fool of Christ*, 32, 36–37, 149.

It is precisely this role that Paul assumes. He should be imagined as a theatrical fool, dashing unexpectedly onto the stage and disrupting the entire play with his shocking words and antics. Like the theatrical fool, Paul identifies with the "low and despised" (1:28) and engages in transgressive behavior. Through the proclamation of the cross, he disrupts the world's understandings of power and wisdom. He interrupts all the serious and honorable characters on the world's stage. He says things that no one else dares to say. He proclaims his foolish gospel: the crucified Christ is the wisdom and power of God. Indeed, by depicting God on the cross, Paul engages in the most extreme folly imaginable. He proclaims a paradoxical, even blasphemous word in mind-bogglingly transgressive speech: a "gallows-bird" embodies the divine.[19] Fools interrupt. And Paul, through his preaching, plays this disruptive role.

Fools, however, interrupt with a purpose. At the deepest level, they interrupt in order to change perspective and create a space where the new might break in, where new ways of perceiving and living might happen. They interrupt in order to reframe reality and open up the possibility for a different kind of wisdom and another way of life.

Jesters, for example, are often paired with persons in power, whether kings or emperors or archbishops or professors. And they interrupt the myopic and oppressive assumptions of those in power, usually on behalf of the common people. In so doing, they challenge these powerful people to perceive the world differently and exercise their power differently. Indeed, one scholar has suggested that court jesters were often physically different from others for precisely this reason. A jester might be a short person or a hunchbacked person not simply for the purpose of entertainment or ridicule and not simply because such people were no threat to the ruler. Rather, such jesters physically embodied a different perspective on the world. A short person saw the world differently from a person of more common stature. Similarly, a hunchbacked person literally had a different perspective on the world from those who stood up straight. Such people embodied in a physical way the central purpose of the fool: to interrupt in order to challenge and reframe perspective.[20]

In playing the fool, Paul likewise seeks to change our perception of the world. In taking on the role of the theatrical fool and making a "spectacle" of himself (4:9), Paul invites people to a new kind of perception. *Theatron*, the word translated "spectacle," is a cognate of the word *theaomai*, which

---

19. Ibid., 180, 146–47.
20. Otto, *Fools Are Everywhere*, 27, 31.

means "to see, to look at, to behold."[21] *Theatron* involves a kind of attentive looking or beholding, as the English word "spectacle" actually suggests. As the foolish theater act, Paul invites an attentive looking, just as the audience in the theater must attend to the spectacle of the play. He invites people to perceive in the folly of his words and his life the inbreaking of the new age. As a spectacle, that is, Paul the fool interrupts in order to facilitate a new and different perception.

Paul seeks what New Testament scholar Alexandra Brown calls a "perceptual transformation" among his hearers. He seeks to move them from the perspective of the old age, in which the cross is a "symbol of suffering, weakness, folly, and death," to the perspective of the new creation, in which the cross is "the transforming symbol of power and life."[22] Through his disruptive, foolish preaching Paul intentionally leaves his hearers "perceptually unbalanced."[23] He places believers in the liminal, "being-saved" space on the threshold between the old age and the new, where we might move, even if at times uncertainly, from one perspective to the other. That is the work of apocalyptic imagination—and the fool. So Paul takes up the role of the fool in interrupting the world and seeking to change perception.

Indeed, Paul's *rhetoric* is often the rhetoric of the fool. He employs a wide range of rhetorical forms, from irony to sarcasm to hyperbole to parody.[24] His language is transgressive and disruptive. His rhetoric is shaped by shocking, unsettling paradoxes: Crucified Messiah. Powerful cross. Foolish wisdom. Weak power. Resurrected body. Within the context of the old age, Paul's rhetoric is crazy; it is nonsensical and disorienting. He takes common assumptions and subverts them by repeatedly holding together "unconventional and destabilizing pairings of opposites."[25] It is as if one is left standing in the middle of a carnival house of mirrors, disoriented and off balance, having to discern what is truth and what is illusion.

Paul thus interrupts and seeks to change perception by using the rhetoric of the fool. He invites believers to discern with apocalyptic imagination the God who is both revealed and hidden in Jesus Christ.

21. "*Theaomai*," in Arndt and Gingrich, *Greek English Lexicon*, 353. See also "*theaomai*" in Kittel and Bromiley, *Theological Dictionary*, 317–18.

22. Brown, *Cross and Human Transformation*, xii, 14.

23. Ibid., 158.

24. See, e.g., 1 Cor 4:8–13 for an extraordinary combination of sarcasm, irony, hyperbole, and parody. Such language runs through 1 Corinthians.

25. Brown, *Cross and Human Transformation*, 30.

Preaching and Apocalyptic Imagination

Preaching with apocalyptic imagination thus involves four general characteristics. First, apocalyptic preaching *interrupts*. It employs transgressive rhetoric that disrupts the myths and conventions and rationalities of the old age, which lead to death. Such preaching engages in creative resistance to the powers of this age that hold people captive and often prevent them from even imagining alternatives to the conventions and assumptions of the world. Second, through these interruptions, such preaching creates an unsettled, *liminal space* in which people may move—and always keep moving—from the old age to the new. Apocalyptic imagination does not shut down or tie up or close off, but rather instigates and sustains liminality, that in-between space where the movement of the Spirit occurs. Such preaching seeks to set and keep believers on pilgrimage. It seeks to build up, not a secure and settled church, but a people who are "being saved" (1 Cor 1:18, 15:2). Third, such preaching is concerned with *perception* and *discernment*. The preacher is a fool, proclaiming a foolish gospel. Preachers seek to unmask the deadly ways of the old age and help people discern the inbreaking, though often hidden, new creation. God has already invaded and changed the world through the cross and resurrection of Jesus Christ. Apocalyptic imagination seeks to create the space where new perception becomes possible. Finally, such preaching, like fools of all ages, *does not take itself too seriously*. For discernment is the gift of the Spirit. No eloquent words or human wisdom can give the mind of Christ, but only the power of the cross and resurrection through the movement of the Spirit (2:1–5). So such preaching is content to play the fool and proclaim the disruptive promise of our odd God: "God's foolishness is wiser than human wisdom, and God's weakness is stronger than human strength" (1:25).

The Example of Oscar Romero

Oscar Romero, Archbishop of San Salvador from 1977–80, was one of the most remarkable preachers of the twentieth century, though he has been virtually ignored in the homiletical literature in North America. Few people outside of El Salvador probably think of Romero primarily as a preacher, even though he once said about himself, "I make no other claim than that of being a simple preacher of the word of God."[26] I have been teaching preaching for almost thirty years, and it has just been in the past few years, following two trips to El Salvador, that I myself have discovered Oscar Romero

---

26. Cited in Reid, "Romero the Preacher," 20.

the preacher. His sermons are quite remarkable. They are at odds with the creative homiletical thought that was emerging in the United States during the 1970s and '80s. His sermons are not narrative, they are not inductive, they often have three points, and they rarely develop a single focus. They are long and sometimes complicated—his final Sunday sermon, the day before he was martyred, lasted one hour and forty-five minutes. They don't fit the reigning "mainline" homiletical paradigms in North America, so they have been ignored. But they *do* embody aspects of apocalyptic imagination.

Romero, like the apocalyptic fool, identified with the poor, interrupted and unmasked the powers of death, and sought to change perceptions in the face of the horrific activity of brutal governmental and economic powers. He lived and proclaimed the foolish way of the cross. And he was, himself, finally, "crucified." On Monday, March 24, 1980, during Lent, Romero was shot and killed in the chapel of the hospital where he lived. He was saying a mass on the anniversary of the death of a friend's mother. Unlike in the movie, Romero was not killed as he held up the chalice while celebrating the Eucharist. Rather, he was shot as he concluded his sermon. He was martyred while he was preaching.

Romero's apocalyptic preaching from 1977–80 was the result of an interruption in his own life. He had been a rather traditional, scholarly priest and bishop—a seemingly safe pick for archbishop, the people in power assumed. Then in March of 1977 his friend and fellow priest, Rutilio Grande, was murdered. That crucifixion changed Romero's preaching; he decided that as archbishop he had to "take a stand."[27] Grande's death graphically unmasked for him the powers of death at work in El Salvador. And that crucifixion led Romero, through his preaching, to interrupt those powers on behalf of the poor and oppressed people in his country, among whom he had lived and served. It led him boldly to proclaim his understanding of where Christ is to be discerned. As the liberation theologian Jon Sobrino wrote of Romero:

> He found in the poor that which is scandalous in the mystery of God understood in a Christian sense: in those whom history crucifies is made present the crucified God. . . . The kenotic dimension of God—God's emptying himself, in other words—goes on being foolishness, a scandal. . . . It is made manifest in the poor, in the oppressed and the repressed of God's people. In their faces Romero saw the disfigured countenance of God.[28]

---

27. Quoted in Rocca, *Oscar Romero*, 80. Thanks to Duke doctoral student, Alma Ruiz, who provided invaluable suggestions about my treatment of Romero.

28. Sobrino, "Theologian's View," 27.

As Romero himself said in one of his sermons, "The guarantee of one's prayer is not saying a lot of words. The guarantee of one's petition is very easy to know: how do I treat the poor? Because that is where God is. . . . What you do to [the poor], you do to God. The way you *look* at them is the way you *look* at God."[29]

Romero's foolish, apocalyptic preaching grew out of his attention to God, whom he discerned in the lives of El Salvador's poor. In his sermons Romero repeatedly and boldly *interrupted* and *unmasked* the old-age powers of death that were oppressing and slaughtering these people. In many of his sermons Romero would spend significant amounts of time naming those individuals who had been murdered or had disappeared during the preceding week, sometimes working his way methodically through each day of the week. Warning his congregation to beware of the manipulation of the news, Romero also interrupted the lies and propaganda of the media with true accounts of the atrocities. Following the murder of the priest Octavio Ortiz Luna and several other young men, he proclaims emphatically, "The official statement that the media published is filled with lies from beginning to end."[30] Then, right in the middle of the sermon, he reconstructs the events surrounding the murders based on eyewitness accounts. Not surprisingly, the radio station that aired his sermons was bombed on several occasions. As both Jesus and Paul discovered, the apocalyptic imagination creates conflict; the powers of this age do not take kindly to interruptions.

Romero knew the risks, but he also knew his calling to preach the disruptive, apocalyptic Word: "If it is really God's word," he proclaimed, "it can explode, and not many are willing to carry it. If it were defused, no one would be afraid to [carry it]."[31] It was risky foolishness to preach the way he did. Interestingly, Mary, who saw her own son tortured and killed, becomes a model of this kind of disruptive preaching for Romero. Mary raises her voice in "holy rebelliousness," Romero proclaims in one sermon, and she says to God, "Disperse the arrogant of mind and heart; throw down the rulers from their thrones and lift up the lowly" (quoting Luke 1:51–52).[32]

Through his sermons Romero, like Paul, was not just interrupting. He was also inviting a new and different perception of the world and of God. Time and again, he repeats this homiletical aim; in his preaching he seeks to

29. Romero, *Violence of Love*, 34–35. Italics mine. Similarly, Colin Miller in chapter 9 of this volume explains that the poor reveal the poor Christ to God's people by their presence in the ecclesial community, pointing toward our constant need to be face to face with the poor.

30. Romero, "Assassination."

31. Cited in Reid, "Romero the Preacher," 25.

32. Romero, "Birth of the Lord," 3.

"illuminate" the realities in El Salvador through the light of the gospel.[33] Like the Apostle Paul before him, he repeatedly invites people to learn to look, to discern with bifocal perception the hidden revelation of Christ. Romero's sermonic interruptions created a space in which people might perceive the world differently and live in it differently. In his final Christmas Eve sermon he invites believers to this kind of bifocal discernment:

> Tonight we do not look for God among the opulence of the world, or among the idolatries of wealth or among those eager for power or among the intrigues of the powerful. God is not there. Let us look for God with the sign announced by the angels: resting in a manger and wrapped in swaddling clothes made by the humble peasant woman of Nazareth—poor swaddling clothes and a little hay on which this God-made-man rested, on which this King of the ages becomes accessible to humankind as a poor child.
>
> Today is the time to look for this child Jesus, but do not look for him in the beautiful images of nativity sets but look for him among the children lacking proper nutrition who have gone to sleep this evening with nothing to eat. Let us look for him among the poor newspaper boys who sleep in the doorways wrapped in today's paper. Let us look for him in the shoeshine boy who perhaps has earned enough to buy a small gift for his mother. Let us look for him in the newspaper boy who, because he did not sell enough papers, is severely reprimanded by his stepfather or stepmother. How sad is the history of these children. Yet Jesus takes on all of this tonight.[34]

Throughout his preaching Romero was also envisioning a new age, a new creation. He proclaimed an order characterized not by the domination and violence of the powers of this age, but by mutuality and love. He sought to redeem, to liberate, both oppressor and oppressed so that all might live in peace and justice. Sometimes he would invite people to discern the new creation breaking into the world even now. "Christ has begun a new era here on earth," he proclaimed, "and blessed are those who discover the secret of the resurrection because for them, despite criminal actions and evil, life in the world becomes the power and the framework for salvation."[35] And he called the church to embody that perception amidst the stark realities of El Salvador. Indeed, even the countless crucifixions he witnessed spoke to him

---

33. See, for example, his final Sunday homily, Romero, "Church in the Service," 2–3.
34. Romero, "Birth of the Lord," 2–3.
35. Romero, "Assassination," 6.

of the resurrection power of God that transcends death even in the midst of it. The title of one of his most famous sermons employs destabilizing pairs of opposites to invite bifocal discernment: "An Assassination that Speaks of Resurrection."

At other times, Romero envisioned the fulfillment of God's reign as a hope for the future. We are a pilgrim people, he regularly repeated, journeying toward the reign of God. The Eucharist itself, which Romero proclaimed as a foretaste of the heavenly liturgy, enacted the liminal reality of the church as it lives and often struggles in the space between Christ's interruption of the old age and the fulfillment of God's new creation.[36] At the funeral mass for Octavio Ortiz Luna, Romero proclaims this tensive hope: "We question ourselves as we gather in the presence of these bodies that are not dead but are journeying to true life so that we, the community that is still on pilgrimage, might become more secure in the hope that is so alive in the hearts of all of you."[37]

In his final homily Romero bears witness to this vision of God's fulfillment, while never losing sight of the ongoing struggle of the Christian life. One of the readings for this final mass was 1 Cor 15:20–28, which contains the vision of Christ's overcoming all the principalities and powers: "Then comes the end," Paul writes, "when Christ hands over the kingdom to God the Father, after he has overcome every principality and every power and every force. For he must reign until he has put all his enemies under his feet. The last enemy to be destroyed is death" (15:24–26).[38] Romero's homily that day, though not based on this text, alludes to Paul's words and conveys the spirit of Paul's hope.[39] Quoting, as he often did, a document from Vatican II, Romero both names the powers of death that continue to deform human life and also shares his vision of "the end":

> We do not know the time for the consummation of the earth and of humanity, nor do we know how all things will be transformed.

36. Romero, "Assassination," 2.

37. Ibid., 2.

38. Romero, "Last Homily." I have translated *archēn*, *exousian*, and *dynamis* as "principality, power, and force," which is more appropriate than the NRSV's translation, "ruler, authority, and power."

39. The text for the homily itself was John 12:23–26, which also proclaims a compelling vision requiring bifocal discernment: "Jesus answered them, 'The hour has come for the Son of Man to be glorified. Very truly, I tell you, unless a grain of wheat falls into the earth and dies, it remains just a single grain; but if it dies, it bears much fruit. Those who love their life lose it, and those who hate their life in this world will keep it for eternal life. Whoever serves me must follow me, and where I am, there will my servant be also. Whoever serves me, the Father will honor.'"

As deformed by sin, the shape of this world will pass away; but we are taught that God is preparing a new dwelling place and a new earth where justice will abide, and whose blessedness will answer and surpass all the longings for peace which spring up in the human heart. . . . On this earth that Kingdom is already present in mystery. When the Lord returns it will be brought into full flower. (*Gaudium et Spes*, #39)[40]

Following this affirmation, Romero echoes Paul's words in 1 Cor 15, again revealing the tensive character of the Christian life: "I think we do not aspire in vain in these times of hope and struggle."[41]

Moments after he preached these words, the powers of this age crucified Oscar Romero, just as they had crucified Jesus (2:6–8). He was martyred because he would not be quiet. Even when nothing seemed to be changing, he would not be silent; he would not stop preaching. And he would not resort to any other weapon than the Word. Even when the Word seemed so weak and foolish before the powers of this age. Even when it resulted in his death.

Interruption. Unmasking. Perception. Discernment. Envisioning. These are the homiletical tools of apocalyptic imagination. As the witness of the Apostle Paul and Archbishop Romero reveals, however, such preaching is risky. Fools who rely on words to apocalypse the God who is revealed and hidden on the cross can never control the outcome of their preaching. There are no guarantees. For such preachers, faithfulness is more important than effectiveness or success. One interrupts the powers of death and seeks to create the possibility for new life in the conflictual, liminal space between the ages. But the future and the fulfillment belong to God.

Bibliography

Arndt, William F., and F. Wilbur Gingrich. *A Greek English Lexicon of the New Testament and Other Early Christian Literature*. Chicago: University of Chicago Press, 1957.

Boeve, Lieven. *God Interrupts History: Theology in a Time of Upheaval*. New York: Continuum, 2007.

Brown, Alexandra. *The Cross and Human Transformation: Paul's Apocalyptic Word in 1 Corinthians*. Minneapolis: Fortress, 1995.

Campbell, Charles L. *1 Corinthians*. Belief: A Theological Commentary on the Bible. Louisville: Westminster John Knox, 2018.

———. *The Word Before the Powers: An Ethic of Preaching*. Louisville: Westminster John Knox, 2002.

40. Romero, "Last Homily," 1.

41. Ibid., 2. See 1 Cor 15:2, 14, 58.

Campbell, Charles L., and Johan H. Cilliers. *Preaching Fools: The Gospel as a Rhetoric of Folly*. Waco: Baylor University Press, 2012.

Fee, Gordon D. *The First Epistle to the Corinthians*. NICNT. Grand Rapids: Eerdmans, 1987.

Hengel, Martin. *Crucifixion: In the Ancient World and the Folly of the Message of the Cross*. Translated by John Bowden. Philadelphia: Fortress, 1977.

Kittel, Gerhard, ed., and Geoffrey W. Bromiley, trans. *Theological Dictionary of the New Testament*. Vol. 3. Grand Rapids: Eerdmans, 1965.

Martyn, J. Louis. "Epistemology at the Turn of the Ages." In *Theological Issues in the Letters of Paul*, 89–110. Nashville: Abingdon, 1997.

———. "From Paul to Flannery O'Connor with the Power of Grace." In *Theological Issues in the Letters of Paul*, 279–97. Nashville: Abingdon, 1997.

Otto, Beatrice K. *Fools Are Everywhere: The Court Jester Around the World*. Chicago: University of Chicago Press, 2001.

Reid, Barbara E. "Romero the Preacher." In *Archbishop Romero: Martyr and Prophet for the New Millennium*, edited by Robert Pelton, 17–32. Scranton, PA: University of Scranton Press, 2006.

Rocca, Roberto Morozzo de la. *Oscar Romero: Prophet of Hope*. Translated by Michael J. Miller. London: Darton, Longman and Todd, 2015.

Romero, Oscar. "An Assassination that Speaks of Resurrection." January 21, 1979. http://www.romerotrust.org.uk/sites/default/files/homilies/an_assassination_that_speaks_of_resurrection.pdf.

———. "The Birth of the Lord." December 24, 1979. http://www.romerotrust.org.uk/sites/default/files/homilies/birth_of_the_lord.pdf.

———. "The Church in the Service of Personal, Community, and Transcendent Liberation." March 23, 1980. http://www.romerotrust.org.uk/sites/default/files/homilies/in_service_of_transcendent_liberation.pdf.

———. "Last Homily of Archbishop Romero." March 24, 1980. http://www.romerotrust.org.uk/homilies-and-writings/homilies/final-homily-archbishop-romero.

———. *The Violence of Love*. Translated by James R. Brockman. Maryknoll, NY: Orbis, 1988.

Sobrino, Jon. "A Theologian's View of Oscar Romero." In *Voice of the Voiceless: The Four Pastoral Letters and Other Statements*, by Archbishop Oscar Romero, 22–51. Translated by Michael J. Walsh. Maryknoll, NY: Orbis, 2003.

Stringfellow, William. *An Ethic for Christians and Other Aliens in a Strange Land*. Reprint, Eugene, OR: Wipf and Stock, 2004.

Welborn, L. L. *Paul, the Fool of Christ: A Study of 1 Corinthians 1–4 in the Comic-Philosophic Tradition*. Early Christianity in Context. London: T. & T. Clark, 2005.

Welch, Sharon D. *A Feminist Ethic of Risk*. Minneapolis: Fortress, 1990.

Welsford, Enid. *The Fool: His Social and Literary History*. Gloucester, MA: Peter Smith, 1966.

Wink, Walter. *The Powers that Be: Theology for a New Millennium*. New York: Doubleday, 1998.

4

Gendered Bodies and the Body of Christ

BEVERLY ROBERTS GAVENTA

Despite the immense role Paul's letters played in the formation of western Christian theology, ecclesial discussions of Paul in the United States have tended to gravitate around specific issues of the day. Paul's letters provided fodder for both sides of the nineteenth century debate about slavery.[1] The status of women, particularly the status of women in the church, stimulated discussion of Paul's letters during much of the twentieth century. More recently, comments taken from Paul's letters have played a significant role in intense ecclesial debates about homosexuality.[2]

On the status of women, there are some obvious landmarks in the scholarly discussion regarding Paul. Krister Stendahl produced his slender volume, *The Bible and the Role of Women*, in the course of a protracted debate in the Church of Sweden regarding women's ordination.[3] The title might well have been *Some Pauline Texts and the Role of Women*, since Stendahl passed over the Gospels in three quick pages before rounding up the usual exegetical suspects: 1 Cor 11:11–12; 14:34–35; Eph 5:22–23; 1 Tim 2:11–15; and of course Gal 3:28. In the early 1970s Robin Scroggs identified Paul as the "one clear voice in the New Testament asserting the freedom and equality of woman in the eschatological community."[4] Scroggs's argument for separating the "establishment Paul" from the "historical" Paul depended on setting aside passages from Ephesians, Colossians, and the Pastorals, as

1. For some introduction to the texts and their treatment, see Noll, *Civil War*, 33–35, 38, 50, 60, 100, 115–16, 120, 147; and Perkinson, "Enslaved by the Text," 121–41.

2. The literature on this question is voluminous. A good overview of the issues and the bibliography regarding Rom 1:26–27 in particular appears in Hultgren, *Paul's Letter*, 616–22.

3. Stendahl, *Bible and the Role of Women*.

4. Scroggs, "Paul and the Eschatological Woman," 283–303; see also his subsequent Scroggs, "Paul and the Eschatological Woman: Revisited," 532–37.

44

well as 1 Cor 14:33b–36, and bringing forward 1 Cor 11:2–16 and Gal 3:28. Scroggs also took into account the greetings of women in Phil 4:2–3 and in Rom 16:1–16. In a thoughtful response, Elaine Pagels suggested that Paul may have proclaimed freedom in the early stages of his ministry, but he later found the radical results of that freedom abhorrent.[5]

Best known of these landmarks is Elisabeth Schüssler Fiorenza's 1983 volume, *In Memory of Her: A Feminist Theological Reconstruction of Christian Origins*.[6] As the subtitle suggests, Fiorenza undertook to produce a history of early Christianity that would show how an original "discipleship of equals" was undermined by patriarchalization. Her assessment of Paul is similar to that of Pagels, in that she finds the early vision of equality in Gal 3:28 modified in subsequent developments in 1 Corinthians. She treats Colossians and Ephesians separately, regarding them as post-Pauline.

These landmarks are by no means the only features of the interpretive territory, but they serve to make my point: discussion of Paul and gender has largely gravitated around a slender handful of texts.

Although scholars were largely unaware of the fact at the time, challenges to standard interpretations of these texts were not new in the church's life.[7] To take a few examples: in 1539 French reformer Marie Dentière invoked John 4 and Mark 16 as counter-witnesses to the silencing of women in 1 Cor 14:34, since the Samaritan woman announces the news of Jesus and Mary Magdalene is commissioned to do so following the resurrection.[8] A century later, Quaker preacher Hester Biddle called on Phoebe in Rom 16:1 and the female coworkers of Phil 4:3 as evidence in her defense when she was arrested for preaching in public.[9] Decades later, Anglican Mary Astell engaged in a close reading of 1 Cor 11, concluding that Paul allows women to pray and prophesy in worship, but he wants them to do so in conformity to the customs of decency that prevailed in his era.[10] By the middle of the nineteenth century, British activist Josephine Butler identified the Pauline texts subjecting women to male authority as historical accidents that should not detract from the larger biblical message of hope for women.[11] One of the salutary developments in the biblical scholarship of recent decades is

5. Pagels, "Paul and Women," 538–49.

6. Fiorenza, *In Memory*.

7. Although, see Fiorenza's brief discussion regarding *The Woman's Bible* in Fiorenza, *In Memory*, 11–13.

8. Here I rely on the fine collection edited by Marion Taylor with the assistance of Agnes Choi (Taylor, *Handbook of Women Biblical Interpreters*, 157).

9. Ibid., 73.

10. Ibid., 46.

11. Ibid., 104.

the recovery of these previously overlooked contributions that anticipate arguments developed at greater length in the twentieth century.

Despite this history and the remarkable proliferation of books and articles concerning Paul and women in the decades since the important contributions of Stendahl, Scroggs, Pagels, and Fiorenza, the same questions about the same texts appear regularly, especially in the ecclesial arena. Robin Scroggs's initial article on the subject breathes with confidence that reasonable people will come to see Paul as he does, and I shared that expectation in my early years of teaching. It was easy to anticipate the day when the study of Paul's letters would have moved beyond the assumption that Paul is personally responsible for the limited roles of women in faith communities.

Although that shift has taken place in some corners of the church's life, in others—and certainly outside the church—the assumption that Paul is, in George Bernard Shaw's memorable phrase, "the eternal enemy of Woman"[12] (sic) has proven to have lasting power.[13] Complicating things further, other issues have come to the foreground even as that earlier debate persists. Disputes over the place of gay and lesbian Christians in the church have dominated in many parts of church life in recent decades, and those disputes also prominently feature exegetical arguments over Pauline texts. It will not be surprising if questions about what gender is and what gender identity does also find Paul's letters to be contested territory.

An abiding difficulty in this long history remains the constricted character of the questions we raise. By "constricted" I mean both the range of texts introduced into discussion and the character of the questions put to those texts. People continue to debate the interpretation of individual texts, pitting Gal 3:28 against 1 Cor 11:2–16 and Rom 16:1–16 against 1 Cor 14:33b–35 (and Eph 5:22–24 and 1 Tim 2:8–15). People also continue to confine their questions about gender to issues of church leadership, asking who can be authorized to become leaders, without taking into account the range of issues that constitute leadership, how it functions, and especially what leadership should mean in the life of the church. Further, discussion focuses on gender roles without reflecting on larger questions about what it means to be human in relationship to God. In other words, there is something doggedly one-dimensional in our reflection on Paul and gender.

---

12. Shaw, "Preface on the Prospects of Christianity," 550.

13. In chapter 5, Lisa Bowens demonstrates how Pauline texts have also been used as enemies of black slaves in the United States. The potential negative effects of Pauline texts are compounded when race and gender intersect in the bodies of black female ministers, as she illustrates on pp. 69–71 of the present volume.

It is possible to expand the discussion, however, both by expanding the texts brought to the foreground and by expanding the questions asked. In earlier work, I explored the various instances when Paul applies to himself an apostolic labor imagery that is unmistakably maternal (as in 1 Thess 2:5–8; Gal 4:19; 1 Cor 3:1–2; 15:8; see also Rom 8:22–23), asking what light that imagery might shed on his understanding of leadership and its implications for the church.[14] In this essay, I want to step further back to ask how Paul's use of the "body of Christ" might be suggestive for thinking theologically about gender.[15] My proposal is that the diversity Paul finds to be non-negotiable within the body of Christ provides us with a way of thinking constructively about the diversity of human lives—gendered human bodies—within the body of Christ. This way of approaching things seems to be especially fitting for our honoree, since in her teaching and writing Susan Groves Eastman exemplifies the engaged thinking along *with* Paul I wish to undertake here.[16]

As is well known, the connection between the church and Christ's body appears twice in the undisputed Pauline letters, 1 Cor 12 and Rom 12, although there are brief references in 1 Cor 6:15, 10:16, and 11:29 that may anticipate Paul's usage later.[17] Scholars generally agree that the phrase adapts a widely used metaphor about the nature of society as a body. For example, Plutarch asks, "Do we not in this world of ours often have a single body composed of separate bodies, as, for example, an assembly of people or an army or a band of dancers, each one of whom has the contingent faculty of living, thinking, and learning" (*Moralia* 426A; LCL). And Cicero similarly employs the body as an analogy for the state:

> So kings, commanders, magistrates, senators, and popular assemblies govern citizens as the mind governs the body; but the master's restraint of his slaves is like the restraint exercised by the best part of the mind, the reason, over its own evil and weak elements, such as the lustful desires, anger, and the other disquieting emotions. . . .[T]he parts of the body are ruled like sons on account of their ready obedience, but the evil parts of the mind

14. Gaventa, *Our Mother*. Major contributions to the study of that imagery have emerged, including Eastman, *Recovering Paul's Mother Tongue*; Gerber, *Paulus und Seine "Kinder"*; and McNeel, *Paul as Infant*.

15. See also chapter 10, where Emily Peck-McClain considers body of Christ imagery in relation to intergenerational ministry.

16. It is a pleasure to offer this essay in honor of a wise and gifted colleague, from whom I have learned immensely.

17. Ephesians 4–5 takes Paul's usage further, but the disputed authorship of that letter places it outside the scope of this essay.

are restrained with a stricter curb, like slaves. . . . (*De Republica* 3.25.37)

Both the comparison and the use of body imagery to encourage unity are common fare in ancient political discourse.[18] Just as we adapt Hamilton lyrics for political slogans or take up the rock standards of the 1960s in television commercials, Paul adapts a widely used image for his own context.

The Body of Christ in 1 Corinthians 12

Communication with believers in Corinth has become problematic, making it altogether understandable that Paul might resort to a familiar image such as the "body" when writing to Corinth. An earlier letter from Paul to the Corinthians has apparently produced less than desirable results (see 1 Cor 5:9), an experience with which most teachers and preachers will be familiar. Paul needs all the help he can muster in his effort to address these conflicting factions.

Chapters 11–14 take up a number of issues related to worship, including the self-presentation of women who are praying and prophesying, the celebration of the Lord's Supper, and the character of spiritual gifts and how they should be valued and employed. These issues do not arise out of thin air or from Paul's leisurely reflection on topics that might be of interest. In every case he has learned of some specific problem, whether from the Corinthians themselves or from others.

At least from Paul's perspective, there are some among the Corinthians who have experienced certain dramatic spiritual gifts and who are happy to exalt themselves before others. In the outset of the letter, Paul acknowledges that the Corinthians have been blessed with spiritual gifts (1:5); he also signals early on that they (or some of them) are "puffed up" and regard themselves as "already" in possession of spiritual benefits (4:6–13).[19] Now he takes up what appears to be competition over the particularly dramatic gifts of prophecy and speaking in tongues, which he addresses at length in chapter 14.

Contemporary Christians may find these conflicts over spiritual gifts foreign to their experience, but we have ample conflicts of our own. Discussions about whether Don's tenor voice is more valuable to the church's mission than Coretta's direction of the stewardship campaign might come

---

18. For evidence in support of this assertion, see Mitchell, *Paul and the Rhetoric of Reconciliation*, 157–64.

19. All scriptural quotations are from the NRSV, unless otherwise indicated.

as a surprise to us. But consider whose voice carries the greater weight in decision-making: is it that of the third-generation Moore family who owns a chain of grocery stores or that of the recently arrived Gonzalez family who struggles with the mortgage payments? Status indicators may have shifted, but questions about status and relative contributions to the body of Christ are no less relevant now than they were in first century Corinth.

In the Corinthian context of competition regarding spiritual gifts, Paul claims that believers are members of the body of Christ. He begins by reminding the Corinthians that the declaration "Jesus is Lord" can be made only by means of the Holy Spirit's intervention, framing the entire discussion in light of divine action (12:1–3). If the most fundamental confession of the Christian faith comes by way of the Spirit, it should not be surprising to learn that spiritual gifts also are just that—gifts.[20] That very point comes to expression in 12:4–11: the *charismata*, whatever they are, all come about through the very same Spirit. Moreover, the Spirit distributes these gifts to each individual just as it wishes (12:11). What Paul implies but does not state here is that the gifts that follow from the initial gift of faith are not possessions or achievements; therefore, any gloating or competition about them is absurd. To this point, however, he has left room for the gifts to be ranked according to status or preference.

To address that gap, Paul next turns to the common analogy of the body: just as a body is a single entity but has many parts, "we" all were baptized into a single body, namely, the body of Christ (12:12–13). The foot cannot secede from the body because it is not an eye; neither is the whole body made of the eye. The various parts of the body cannot exist independently of one another (12:14–26). In fact, they have need of one another to such an extent that when one part suffers an injury, the whole body suffers. The congregation is not made up simply of the one who stands in the pulpit or the one who warms the furnace in January. It is at a loss if Don's voice is silenced or when Coretta's organizational skills are lost.

In the context of Corinth, it appears that the problem is with those who bask in their own special gifts of speaking in tongues and prophesying, since Paul will soon elaborate the importance but also the dangers associated with these particular gifts (see 14:1–40). The argument is also reversible: it would work equally well in settings where the problem is envy on the part of those who long for the recognition and achievement of those whose gifts are more dramatic or generous.[21]

20. On Paul's understanding of gift and its importance for ministry, see John M. G. Barclay's chapter in this volume as well as Barclay, *Paul and the Gift*.

21. Peter Schaeffer's brilliant play *Amadeus* offers an extended case study of such envy. The modestly talented court composer Antonio Salieri finds himself in the

The Body of Christ in Romans 12

Paul employs "body of Christ" language again and more briefly in Rom 12. The chapter opens with a call for presenting to God the whole person ("your bodies") as a fitting response to God's mercies and a plea for transformed minds that are able to discern God's will. Dividing up Paul's letters into "theological" and "ethical" sections is misleading, given that Paul's ethics are theocentric and his theology constantly has lived experience in view; nonetheless, Rom 12:1–2 marks an important transition as Paul moves from his lengthy discussion of God's faithfulness to Israel into a sustained discussion of Christian life.

Immediately following this transitional statement, Paul's first admonition concerns hubris. Robert Jewett's translation brings out Paul's play on words at work in 12:3: "For I say through the grace given to me to everyone who is among you, do not be superminded above what one ought to be minded, but set your mind on being sober-minded."[22] The caution about being "superminded" has everything to do with avoiding hubris. A few lines below, Paul returns to the topic with another warning against thinking too highly of one's own views (12:16). By contrast with 1 Cor 12–14, with its discussion of speaking in tongues and prophecy, here Paul writes in fairly general terms, which makes it difficult to know whether he has any particular instances of hubris in mind.[23] Other parts of the letter suggest at least two possibilities. Romans 11:13 and 18 warn gentiles in no uncertain terms ("I am talking to you gentiles!")[24] against boasting over the Jewish "remainder" who do not recognize Jesus as God's intended Messiah; and Rom 14 urges that those who have differing understandings of Jewish food laws not "judge" one another but engage in "upbuilding."[25] In other words, at several

---

presence of Wolfgang Amadeus Mozart, whose brilliance both overwhelms and enrages Salieri. Recognizing his own mediocrity and the divine inspiration of Mozart's music, Salieri plots to destroy the young upstart by way of striking back at God for this injustice: "You are the Enemy! I name thee now—*Nemica Eterno!* . . . To my last breath I shall *block* You on earth, as far as I am able!" (Schaeffer, *Amadeus*, 47). Regrettably, the filmed version of this play effaces this element.

22. Jewett, *Romans*, 736.

23. This is one of the several problems bound together in what scholars refer to as the "Romans debate," which is the debate over the occasion and purpose of the letter. The scholarly literature on this set of questions is extensive; for a general introduction, see Gaventa, "Paul and the Roman Believers," 93–107.

24. Author's translation.

25. For further discussion of Rom 14 in relation to Christlike eating, see chapter 11 by Presian Burroughs.

junctures in this letter we see Paul's concern that believers not inflate their own opinions or status over those of others.

In this context, Paul writes that just as a body is singular but has many parts and the parts do not all have the same function, so in the one body that is Christ, the members belong to a single body but have different gifts. Gift language overflows in 12:6a: "we" have "gifts (*charisma*) that differ according to the gift (*charis*) given (*didōmi*) to us." The differences within the body result from the abundance of divine giving, to which Paul draws ample attention here. That reference to the varied gifts within the body becomes the springboard for a series of comments about the gifts and their use (12:6–8). English translations struggle to do justice to the Greek here, but these lines appear to encourage extravagance in the employment of one's gifts. The one who is gifted in "giving," is described as "generous," implicitly urging such generosity.

Nowhere does Paul warn against the danger of undervaluing one's own gifts. A life of teaching in a wide variety of settings inclines me to wish Paul had added a few lines here about undervaluing of gifts. Although I have seen a good deal of hubris, I have as often seen those who undermine their own gifts, who do not trust them, who are afraid of the consequences of employing them. Romans 12:3–8 comes close, with its insistence that God gives the gifts, and its implication that the gifts are there to be used rather than neglected.

Unity versus Uniformity in the Body of Christ

Paul's use of body of Christ imagery affirms both that Christ's body is single and that its numerous and diverse members have a single purpose. That singular character comes to expression starkly in the well-trodden lines of Gal 3:28: "There is no longer Jew or Greek, there is no longer slave or free, there is no longer male and female; for all of you are one in Christ Jesus." Earlier interpreters found this vision to be liberating (as in the work of Fiorenza, Scroggs, and Stendahl noted above), but more recent discussions point out the stultifying possibilities of sameness. Taken together with Paul's admonitions about upbuilding (Rom 14:19; 1 Cor 8:1; 10:23; 14:12, 16) and sharing a way of thinking (Rom 12:16; 14:5; 1 Cor 1:10; 2 Cor 13:11; Phil 2:2; 4:2), Paul's notion of the single body sets off alarms, raising as it does the fear of conformity. Yung Suk Kim, for example, contends that body of Christ language can mark out "an exclusive boundary that silences the voice of marginality."[26] "Belonging" to the body suggests to Kim a closed notion of community, isolated from the larger world.

Calls for unity can indeed be experienced and can function as oppressive, since unity can be reduced to uniformity of thought and action. And border guards can emerge (self-appointed or otherwise) who patrol the perimeter for infractions, whether from the inside or the outside. This is especially a danger where a single group—in this case, white males—have patrolled the interpretive border and have implicitly or otherwise claimed for themselves—or functionally retained—the keys to the interpretive cupboard.[27]

The question for me, however, is whether Paul's letters themselves understand the singular body of Christ to be a uniform community, a congregation of sameness. Such a conclusion is hard to sustain: oneness in the body of Christ is not sameness. That is quite obvious with respect to spiritual gifts. The argument in 1 Corinthians against boasting on the basis of one's gifts presupposes that there are and will continue to be a range of gifts, each of which contributes to the whole. Similarly, Rom 12 specifies that God has distributed an array of gifts, each of which is to be used extravagantly.

A similar logic underlies Paul's complex treatment of Jew and gentile in relation to one another. In Galatians, where some of Paul's fellow Jews have preached that only those gentiles who become Jews through circumcision and law observance are eligible for membership in Christ's body (by means of their membership in Abraham), Paul claims that there is "no longer Jew or Greek." That is, there is no place in the body of Christ for such human-made distinctions. But in Romans, where it appears that gentile arrogance is a threat, Paul patiently insists on the priority of God's dealings with Israel (see, e.g., 1:16; 9:1–5; 15:27), while also contending for God's graciousness toward gentiles. In fact, his argument about God's bringing about salvation

26. Kim, *Christ's Body*, 1.

27. Here I have in mind not simply the fact that historically the vast majority of biblical scholars have been white males but also the current infatuation with "complementarian" interpretations that reinscribe male authority and privilege. In their 2016 pamphlet on male-female relationships, Wayne Grudem and John Piper explicitly maintain that women may only teach Scripture to children and to groups of women, not to groups of men or to women and men together. To be fair, they do concede that it is acceptable for individuals to read books written by women, which opens the door slightly for women as interpreters of Scripture; yet the entire tenor of the pamphlet suggests that all such decisions are to be made by men based on their own (male) searching of Scripture. Women are nowhere imagined as sharers in the enterprise of discerning Scripture's meaning for the life of the church, which means, in effect, that men retain the keys to the interpretive cupboard (Grudem and Piper, *50 Crucial Questions*).

for Jew and gentile appears to depend on their continued difference, as in 11:11–32.

Difference persists in the body of Christ; it may even be said to flourish. To be sure, there are places where Paul draws lines around the community, most notably in 1 Cor 5, where he castigates the Corinthians for their tolerance of a man who is sleeping with his stepmother. Yet those instances do not negate the considerable diversity that persists, not as a tolerated weakness or evil but as a necessity. Spiritual gifts differ and all are needed, just as the parts of the body are needed. Jew and gentile differ, they continue to differ, but they share a single place in the body of Christ.

Well in advance of the contemporary discussions of diversity, Ernst Käsemann anticipated the polyform nature of the church in Paul's thought:

> Paul finds it important for the church to remain polyform. Only in this way can it pervade the world, since the world's everyday reality is not to be conformistic. It is impossible to cope with the everyday life of the world if one is out for uniformity. Uniformity is petrified solidarity. People who are the same have nothing to say to one another and cannot help one another. They remain introverts and cannot do justice to the constantly differing situations of life, a changing environment or people in their varying individualities. The necessity and blessing of Christian liberty as a state of being in the presence of Christ is not to give everyone the same thing but to give and allow everyone what is his.[28]

Gendered Bodies and the Body of Christ

This notion of the singular yet polyform body of Christ could also help us to think in a more generous, more capacious way about gendered human bodies. In all our differences, our bodies matter. Following on the observations above from Käsemann, it is not just that there is room for diversity or that diversity is to be respected, but that diversity matters, even that the diversity of human bodies matters.

It is not a denial of the particularity of Christ (i.e., that he was a Jewish male) to say that the body of Christ is polyform, that it must be. Just as the body contains ethnic and racial differences, it contains male and female differences as well as those whose bodies are differently gendered.

Further, that body of Christ has no place for a hierarchy among the different bodies contained within it. This is manifestly clear when Paul asks

28. Käsemann, "Theological Problem," 119.

what would happen to the body if all of its parts were an eye or all were an ear (1 Cor 12:17–21). Neither males nor females are capable of being the body on their own. To the extent that there is a hierarchy, it is entirely one in which Christ himself is ruler. The place of "boss" is filled, and nothing is said here that suggests men have any more claims to the priority than do women.

To be specific: calling to service is not restricted along gender lines so that arguments about complementarity find no grounding here. In addition, the greetings of Rom 16 have their place in the discussion; Paul introduces Phoebe the deacon, Junia the apostle, and various other women without any indication that their work is restricted by gender. Even the confusions of 1 Cor 11:2–16 have their place, since for all its twists and turns, the argument works to preserve the role of women who pray and prophesy in the gathered community, as Robert Moses also argues on pp. 99–102 of the present volume.

We can take this reflection on the irreducibly polyform character of Christ's body further: what if we imagine that the *charismata* identified by Paul actually include our sexual identities? That notion of gender as gift appears to come closer to a contemporary understanding of gender than the notion of hierarchy at work in Rom 1:18–32, where cultural understandings of masculinity and femininity are very much in play. If our identities as women, as men, or as persons beyond gender binaries are given to us rather than achieved by our own behavior, then we have the basis for maintaining both singular identity in Christ and received bodies of varying identities.

I am not for a moment suggesting that this was Paul's own view. He participates in the understanding of gender regnant in his own period, as do we all. What I am suggesting, instead, is that his notion of the body of Christ may have implications for our thinking and rethinking about gender in our own time.

In the context of ministry, what do these conclusions mean? What does all this reflection about the body of Christ mean in lived experience? At the very least, it means welcoming individuals and their talents, quite apart from their gender. That in turn means acknowledging that God's creation of the human body takes many forms and that none of those forms can claim privilege over the others, any more than the eye can "say to the hand, 'I have no need of you'" (1 Cor 12:20). Given the deep conflicts of our time and our widespread unwillingness to listen to one another, that is an excellent place to begin.[29]

The charge comes very often that, when the church welcomes the vocations of women or when it includes LGBTQ folks fully, it does so because

---

29. On this point, see Brian Bantum's powerful essay, "Who Decides," 26–29.

it listens more carefully to the culture than to the gospel, because it cares more about maintaining memberships and social acceptability than about the gospel. Of course, the gospel is always deeply connected with culture, as it has been at least since Jesus taught with parables drawn from agricultural life and Paul with strategies drawn from Greco-Roman rhetoric.[30] Instead of capitulation to the culture, recognizing the radical character of diversity within Christ's body may arise from the truly radical nature of God's grace. It is not that we have capitulated to culture—which is now the mantra—but because the deep impulses of the gospel compel us to gratitude and wonder in the face of our own inclusion, a gratitude and wonder that spills over into a welcome for all God's "others."

Many conversations around these issues disabuse me of any rosy conviction that the argument I have sketched here will persuade those for whom gender hierarchy is part and parcel of the gospel. Quite apart from whether that happens, I hope that this essay serves to encourage a way of thinking along *with* Paul. I would like us to move away from the entrenched practice of parsing the lines of Paul's letters for theological propositions and ethical guidelines that must be replicated narrowly. And I long for us to move toward a thinking along *with* Paul as we discover for our time the singular claim of the body of Christ.

Bibliography

Bantum, Brian. "Who Decides What My Body Means?" *Christian Century* 134 (2017) 26–29.

Barclay, John M. G. *Paul and the Gift*. Grand Rapids: Eerdmans, 2015.

Eastman, Susan. *Recovering Paul's Mother Tongue: Language and Theology in Galatians*. Grand Rapids: Eerdmans, 2007.

Fiorenza, Elisabeth Schüssler. *In Memory of Her: A Feminist Theological Reconstruction of Christian Origins*. New York: Crossroad, 1983.

Gaventa, Beverly Roberts. *Our Mother Saint Paul*. Louisville: Westminster John Knox, 2007.

———. "Paul and the Roman Believers." In *The Blackwell Companion to Paul*, edited by Stephen Westerholm, 93–107. Malden, MA: Wiley-Blackwell, 2011.

Gerber, Christine. *Paulus und Seine "Kinder": Studien zur Beziehungsmetaphorik der Paulinischen Briefe*. BZNW 136. Berlin: de Gruyter, 2005.

Grudem, Wayne, and John Piper. *50 Crucial Questions: An Overview of Central Concerns about Manhood and Womanhood*. Wheaton, IL: Crossway, 2016.

Hultgren, Arland. *Paul's Letter to the Romans: A Commentary*. Grand Rapids: Eerdmans, 2011.

30. It is tempting to wonder whether this argument goes back to Paul's own context: did some of those who resisted the full inclusion of gentile believers accuse Paul of selling out to culture in order to bulk up the numbers of his mission?

Jewett, Robert. *Romans*. Hermeneia. Minneapolis: Fortress, 2007.

Käsemann, Ernst. "The Theological Problem Presented by the Motif of the Body of Christ." In *Perspectives on Paul*, 102–21. Philadelphia: Fortress, 1971.

Kim, Yung Suk. *Christ's Body in Corinth: The Politics of a Metaphor*. Minneapolis: Fortress, 2008.

McNeel, Jennifer Houston. *Paul as Infant and Nursing Mother: Metaphor, Rhetoric, and Identity in 1 Thessalonians 2:5–8*. SBLECL 12. Atlanta: SBL, 2012.

Mitchell, Margaret. *Paul and the Rhetoric of Reconciliation: An Exegetical Investigation of the Language and Composition of 1 Corinthians*. Louisville: Westminster John Knox, 1992.

Noll, Mark A. *The Civil War as a Theological Crisis*. Chapel Hill: University of North Carolina Press, 2006.

Pagels, Elaine. "Paul and Women: A Response to Recent Discussion." *JAAR* 42 (1974) 538–49.

Perkinson, James W. "Enslaved by the Text: The Uses of Philemon." In *Onesimus Our Brother: Reading Religion, Race, and Culture in Philemon*, edited by Matthew V. Johnson, James A. Noel, and Demetrius K. Williams, 121–41. Minneapolis: Fortress, 2012.

Schaeffer, Peter. *Amadeus*. New York: Harper and Row, 1980.

Scroggs, Robin. "Paul and the Eschatological Woman." *JAAR* 40 (1972) 283–303.

———. "Paul and the Eschatological Woman: Revisited." *JAAR* 42 (1974) 532–37.

Shaw, George Bernard. "Preface on the Prospects of Christianity." In vol. 4 of *The Bodley Head Bernard Shaw: Collected Plays with Their Prefaces*, 455–579. London: Max Reinhardt, Bodley Head, 1972.

Stendahl, Krister. *The Bible and the Role of Women: A Case Study in Hermeneutics*. Translated by Emilie T. Sander. Philadelphia: Fortress, 1966.

Taylor, Marion. *Handbook of Women Biblical Interpreters: A Historical and Biographical Guide*. Grand Rapids: Baker, 2012.

5

Liberating Paul: African Americans' Use of Paul in Resistance and Protest[1]

LISA BOWENS

"SLAVES, BE OBEDIENT TO them that are your masters according to the flesh" (Eph 6:5).[2] These words of Paul and others like them have caused great harm, wreaking havoc upon the bodies and minds of African Americans for centuries. With such a caustic message, how could African Americans possibly utilize the words of the apostle in their struggles for equality and justice? By considering the reception of Paul's letters among African Americans, with specific attention to their historical use of Paul in resistance and protest, we will discover the ways in which African Americans have done just that. The ensuing exploration participates in the rise of reception history in biblical scholarship and illustrates one of the tenets of this new area: "Biblical texts not only have their own particular backgrounds and settings but have also been received and interpreted, and have exerted influence or otherwise have had impact in countless religious, theological, and aesthetic settings."[3] As this esay will demonstrate, African American Pauline hermeneutics—that is, the use and interpretation of Pauline Scripture—has impacted the lives of many African Americans in terms of religious thought and experience and has been employed by them to resist oppression and protest dehumanization.[4] The present analysis begins with a brief discussion

1. It is an honor to offer this essay to Susan Eastman, a companion in the struggle for freedom.

2. All biblical citations are from the King James Bible, the version used by the writers discussed in this essay.

3. Klauck et al., *Encyclopedia*, 1:ix.

4. This essay is part of a larger research project in which I engage in a historical, biblical, and theological analysis of African American Pauline hermeneutics from the 1700s to the present.

of the complicated historical relationship that African Americans have had with Paul's writings. It will then examine excerpts from blacks who used Paul to protest slavery as well as an excerpt from Zilpha Elaw, a nineteenth century black woman who adopted Pauline language to reject denials of her call to preach. And, finally, this essay will conclude with some implications of this exploration for Christian ministers today.

African Americans and Paul

When discussing the relationship between African Americans and Paul's letters, one often hears the account of Howard Thurman and his grandmother, Nancy Ambrose. The following excerpt from Thurman's *Jesus and the Disinherited* merits full citation:

> During much of my boyhood I was cared for by my grandmother, who was born a slave and lived until the Civil War on a plantation near Madison, Florida. My regular chore was to do all of the readings for my grandmother—she could neither read nor write. Two or three times a week I read the Bible aloud to her. I was deeply impressed by the fact that she was most particular about the choice of Scripture. For instance, I might read many of the more devotional Psalms, some of Isaiah, the Gospels again and again. But the Pauline epistles, never—except, at long intervals, the thirteenth chapter of First Corinthians. My curiosity knew no bounds, but we did not question her about anything.
>
> When I was older and was half through college, I chanced to be spending a few days at home near the end of summer vacation. With a feeling of great temerity I asked her one day why it was that she would not let me read any of the Pauline letters. What she told me I shall never forget. "During the days of slavery," she said, "the master's minister would occasionally hold services for the slaves. Old man McGhee was so mean that he would not let a Negro minister preach to his slaves. Always the white minister used as his text something from Paul. At least three or four times a year he used as a text: 'Slaves, be obedient to them that are your masters, as unto Christ.' Then he would go on to show how it was God's will that we were slaves, and how, if we were good and happy slaves, God would bless us. I promised my Maker that if I ever learned to read and if freedom ever came, I would not read that part of the Bible."[5]

5. Thurman, *Jesus*, 19–20.

This poignant selection illustrates how slave masters and white ministers often used Paul's words to justify the cruel practice of slavery. In their misappropriation, Scripture tied the existence and identity of an entire people to slavery. Thurman's grandmother repeated the words of the minister: "It was God's will that we were slaves." African Americans' existence was wholly dependent upon slave status since this was God's predetermined destiny for them.

However, not only were Paul's words used to justify slavery but a common belief was that the story of Ham in Gen 9:18–27 sanctioned slavery as well. Josiah Priest, a proslavery advocate, represents the prevalent sentiments of the time regarding this passage of Scripture in *Slavery as it Relates to the Negro or African Race*. Priest writes:

> The appointment of this [Negro] race of men to servitude and slavery was a judicial act of God, or in other words was a divine judgement. There are three evidences of this, which are as follows:
>
> First—The fact of their being created or produced in a lower order of intellectuality than either of the other races . . . is evidence of the preordination of their fate as slaves on the earth as none but God could have done or determined this thing.
>
> Second—The announcement of God by the mouth of Noah, relative to the whole race of Ham, pointing out in so many words in the clearest and most specific manner, that they were adjudged to slavery . . . that they were foreordained and appointed to the condition they hold among men by the divine mind, solely on account of the foreseen character they would sustain as a race, who, therefore were thus judicially put beneath the supervision of the other races.
>
> Third—The great and everywhere pervading fact of their degraded condition, both now and in all time . . . that the negro race as a people, are judicially given over to a state or peculiar liability of being enslaved by the other races.[6]

Priest captures the scriptural hermeneutics of his period in these passages. Because of their descent from Ham, as this interpretation goes, slavery of blacks was ordained by God. The evidence of this preordained status is their intellectual inferiority, the prophetic utterance of Noah's curse, and their degraded condition, which demonstrates that their enslavement lasts for all time. As one can see, Paul's admonition of "[s]laves, obey your masters" (Eph 6:5; Col 3:22), which was frequently preached by white slaveholders

---

6. Priest, *Slavery*, 83.

and their ministers, cohered well with this understanding of the Old Testament passage. The apostle was seen as merely endorsing what was "evident" from Genesis.

Slave owners' distorted use of Scripture and the laws they implemented, which they believed to be sanctioned by the Bible, sought to prevent or limit slaves' access to Scripture and thereby underscored "one of the greatest fears of slaveholding society: that religion, if taught honestly, was full of revolutionary possibilities."[7] Although sometimes white slave owners permitted black ministers to preach to the slaves, more often than not white ministers preached to them, and the message they proclaimed was, "Slaves, obey your masters." That slaveholders tried to derail and control African Americans' access to the Bible testifies to the liberating power of Scripture.

Remarkably, despite the repeated attempts of slaveholders to drill into the hearts and minds of their slaves, through Scripture, that God appointed slavery for them, slaves refused to believe it. Albert Raboteau writes about slaves' resolve regarding this issue: "In opposition to the slaveholder's belief, the slave believed that slavery was surely contrary to the will of God. John Hunter, a fugitive from slavery in Maryland, attested to this belief: 'I have heard poor ignorant slaves, that did not know A from B, say that they did not believe the Lord ever intended they should be slaves, and that they did not see how it should be so.'"[8]

The choice of Thurman's grandmother to disregard, to a great extent, Paul's writings is understandable in light of the circumstances. As C. Michelle Venable-Ridley eloquently writes,

> Because of Thurman's grandmother's aural contact with the Bible, she was able to reject those portions of the biblical text that insulted her sense of dignity as an African American and as a woman. She likewise was able to embrace those sections of the Bible that affirmed her sense of self-worth as an enchained woman of color.[9]

No doubt other African American slaves followed the same trajectory as Thurman's grandmother. However, it is also important to note that African Americans' relationship with Paul is a complicated one and, while the story of Nancy Ambrose offers a powerful snapshot into some aspects of that relationship, it does not tell the entire story of that relationship. Other features of that relationship exist, for "African Americans have struggled for more than two centuries to reinterpret and revise a distorted gospel received from

---

7. Pierce, *Hell Without Fires*, 41.

8. Raboteau, *Slave Religion*, 309.

9. Venable-Ridley, "Paul and the African," 213.

White Christians."[10] And part of this reinterpretation and revision involved "rescuing" Paul from the hands of white slaveholders and employing him in the liberation fight.

In her essay "Paul and the African American Community," Venable-Ridley states that one of her goals is "not to redeem but to reclaim the writings of Paul as a religious source for the African American community."[11] The present project reveals that historically many African Americans considered Paul's words to be a redemptive force and so he became a religious resource for them as well as a political resource. For these interpreters the religious and the political were intricately linked and could not be separated, and Paul's words provided spiritual nourishment and the biblical basis to protest unjust laws and to resist the dehumanization of slavery promulgated by the distorted gospel of white Christian slaveholders and preachers. The apostle's words also provided black women preachers the scriptural means by which to resist those who would deny them the pulpit because of their race and gender. These rich early interpretive trajectories of African American Pauline hermeneutics provide an important glimpse into Paul's significance in the black struggle for justice.

1774 Petition to Governor of Massachusetts

As early as 1774 slaves interpreted Paul to argue their case for freedom. Below is a petition written to the governor, council, and representatives of Massachusetts with Pauline references italicized:

> The Petition of a Grate Number of Blackes of this Province who by divine permission are held in a state of Slavery within the bowels of a free and christian Country
>
> Humbly Shewing
>
> That your Petitioners apprehind we have in common with all other men a naturel right to our freedoms without Being depriv'd of them by our fellow men as we are a freeborn Pepel and have never forfeited this Blessing by aney compact or agreement whatever. But we were unjustly dragged by the cruel hand of power from our dearest frinds and sum of us stolen from the bosoms of our tender Parents and from a Populous Pleasant and

---

10. Ibid., 214.

11. Ibid. See Abraham Smith's insightful essay on Paul and African Americans (Smith, "Paul and African American," 31–42) and the more recent important discussion on Paul by Emerson Powery and Rodney Sadler (*Genesis*, 113–44).

plentiful country and Brought hither to be made slaves for Life in a Christian land. Thus are we deprived of every thing that hath a tendency to make life even tolerable, the endearing ties of husband and wife we are strangers to for we are no longer man and wife then our masters or mestreses thinkes proper marred or onmarred. Our children are also taken from us by force and sent maney miles from us wear we seldom or ever see them again there to be made slaves of for Life which sumtimes is vere short by Reson of Being dragged from their mothers Breest. Thus our Lives are imbittered to us on these accounts By our deplorable situation we are rendered incapable of shewing our obedience to Almighty God *how can a slave perform the duties of a husband to a wife or parent to his child* How can a husband leave master and work and cleave to his wife *How can the wife submit themselves to there husbands in all things. How can the child obey thear parents in all things. There is a grat number of us sencear ... members of the Church of Christ how can the master and the slave be said to fulfil that command Live in love let Brotherly Love contuner and abound Beare yea onenothers Bordenes How can the master be said to Beare my Borden when he Beares me down whith the Have chanes of slavery and operson against my will* and how can we fulfill our parte of duty to him whilst in this condition and as we cannot searve our God as we ought whilst in this situation Nither can we reap an equal benefet from the laws of the Land which doth not justifi but condemns Slavery or if there had bin aney Law to hold us in Bondege we are Humbely of the Opinon ther never was aney to inslave our children for life when Born in a free Countrey. We therefor Bage your Excellency and Honours will give this its deu weight and consideration and that you will accordingly cause an act of the legislative to be pessed that we may obtain our Natural right our freedoms and our children be set at lebety at the yeare of Twenty one for whoues sekes more petequeley your Petitioners is in Duty ever to Pray.[12]

The disruptive nature of the gospel is evident in the slaves' powerful words in which they argue that slavery and Christianity are irreconcilable.[13] How do these slaves argue for this incompatibility? They utilize Pauline language. Echoing Paul's call in Gal 6:2 to believers to "[b]ear ye one another's burdens," they forcefully declare that slavery prevents the fulfillment of the

12. Founders' Constitution, *Slave Petition*, 3:432–33. Portions of this petition are also cited by Raboteau, *Slave Religion*, 290–91.

13. Michael Gorman in chapter 1 of this volume highlights the importance in Christian ministry of the Pauline concept of voluntary, metaphorical slavery, which differs immensely from forced, literal slavery.

apostle's words. By placing burdens upon black slaves and creating the heavy chains of slavery and oppression, white masters do the opposite of what the apostle commanded. Through their citation and interpretation of Gal 6:2, the slaves adamantly decree that slavery counteracts Christian behavior, for whites do not carry the burdens of their black brothers and sisters; instead, they create them. Additionally, while white slave owners often began and ended their scriptural exegesis with Eph 6:5–6; Col 3:22–24; or 1 Tim 6:1–2, these slaves maintained that true scriptural exegesis began in Eph 5:22 with instructions to wives and continued until 6:4 with instructions to fathers. However, the practice of slavery, which separates family members from one another, violates all of the household admonitions set forth by the apostle. Slavery, these petitioners exclaimed, impedes husbands from loving their wives, wives from submitting to their husbands, and children from obeying and being instructed by their parents. The slaves skillfully raise the question of how they can love their wives and their children if they are taken from them. Slavery prohibits them from obeying Almighty God in carrying out their Christian duties to their families. The apostle's words, these writers reason, condemn slavery and the actions of the white slave owners; they do not condone them.

Interestingly, all of this language occurs after the writers designate this country as "free and Christian." Such language frames their subsequent use of Paul. If this country is "free and Christian," then it ought to follow the apostle's words. These writers resisted the prevalent notion that it was God's will for them to be slaves and that they had to obey their masters. They protested whites' interpretation and use of Paul to justify enslaving them and interpreted the apostle's words for themselves. Their act of interpreting Paul on their own terms was an act of resistance and protest, an act that can be delineated for heuristic purposes in three ways: 1) They began their interpretation of Scripture where *they* wanted to begin (Eph 5:22) and not where their white enslavers chose to begin. This meant they were seizing "hermeneutical control" of Pauline Scripture.[14] 2) They engaged in "exegetical reversal" disputing whites' ownership of Paul to sanction slavery and instead proclaimed that Paul himself condemns slavery with his very words. 3) They appealed to familial language to undercut "slaveholding religion."[15] This familial language resonated in two spheres: both the natural family and the Christian family. The slaves insisted that their identities as members of families were primary; their identity as husbands, wives, and children negated

---

14. Braxton, *No Longer*, 12.

15. This phrase comes from Frederick Douglass, who makes a profound distinction between the Christianity of Christ and "slaveholding religion" (Douglass, "Narrative," 592).

American slave status. When Paul spoke of families he included them, and so they should not be disregarded. While whites asserted that Paul's words bestowed slavery upon blacks, these slaves challenged this idea and insisted that the apostle recognized them as human beings with families that needed nurture and love like any other. In terms of the Christian family, these petitioners cite Heb 13:1: "Let brotherly love continue."[16] How can brotherly love coexist with the wretched practice of slavery? The two, these slaves contend, are mutually exclusive. These authors maintained that the apostle supported their natural right to freedom and upheld their declaration that they should not be enslaved to anyone. To petition the governor and other governmental leaders with the apostle's words, the same apostle who had been used to justify their enslavement, was a bold move for these early writers to make. It demonstrated they recognized their agency in interpreting Scripture for themselves and their right to claim and proclaim this holy writ.

Lemuel Haynes, 1753–1833

Lemuel Haynes, who for a period of time lived as an indentured servant, critiqued the use of the Ham story in Genesis by white Christian proslavery proponents. As we noted in the earlier discussion of Josiah Priest, the story of Ham was used extensively by supporters of slavery to justify the practice. As Katie Cannon observes, this belief that enslaving blacks was a "judicial act of God" and "necessary to the veracity of God Himself" enabled whites to see blacks as non-human property.[17] With this basic belief system in place, it became easy to portray "people with Black skin as demonic, unholy, infectious progenitors of sin, full of animality and matriarchal proclivities."[18] As Cannon indicates, the Ham story provided biblical sanction for blacks' slavery, and for some whites it even provided the idea that part of the curse was a curse of blackness. Slaves' black skin proved that they were evil descendants of Ham deserving subjugation.

Writing in the eighteenth century, near the year of 1776, Lemuel Haynes was skeptical of whites' use of the Ham passage stating that "Whethear the Negros are of Canaans posterity or not, perhaps is not known by any mortal under Heaven."[19] And again he declares, "Our glorious

---

16. Smith notes that many blacks attributed Hebrews to Paul ("Paul and African American," 34).

17. Cannon, "Slave Ideology," 11–12.

18. Ibid.

19. Haynes, "Liberty," 24. See John Saillant's important discussion of Lemuel Haynes and other early black exegetes (Saillant, "Origins," 236–50).

hygh priest hath visably appear'd in the flesh, and hath Establish'd a more glorious Oeconomy. . . . It is plain Beyond all Doubt, that at the comeing of Christ, this curse that was upon Canaan, was taken off."[20] As illustrated by these quotations, part of Haynes's critique of this story's interpretation lies in recognizing the improbability of knowing the identity of Canaan's descendants.[21] Yet his resistance to this interpretation of the narrative also rests upon echoing Paul's words in Gal 3:13 where the apostle states, "Christ has redeemed us from the curse of the law, being made a curse for us: for it is written, Cursed is everyone that hangeth on a tree." Using the apostle's language, Haynes grants that even if blacks were descendants of Canaan, Christ's death removes this curse and therefore delegitimizes the use of the Ham narrative. The curse and, as a result, slavery were eradicated by Christ's advent.

Haynes's work also protested the slave trade. Some whites saw the slave trade as an action of divine providence, for through it Africans were "Christianized" and "civilized." From this perspective, the slave trade really was a blessing to the Africans because it allowed them to be freed from their savage lands and customs in order to experience "civilization." Most of all, slavery permitted them to live in a "Christian" nation. But the brutality of slavery belied such a view. A couple of citations make this clear. David Walker states:

> But Christian Americans not only hinder their fellow creatures, the Africans, but thousands of them will absolutely beat a coloured person nearly to death, if they catch him on his knees, supplicating the throne of grace. . . . Yes, I have known small collections of coloured people to have convened together for no other purpose than to worship God Almighty, in spirit and in truth, to the best of their knowledge; when tyrants, calling themselves patrols . . . would burst in upon them and drag them out and commence beating them as they would rattle-snakes— many of whom, they would beat so unmercifully, that they would hardly be able to crawl for weeks and sometimes for months.[22]

Also, Frederick Douglass relates the following:

> For between the Christianity of this land, and the Christianity of Christ, I recognize the widest possible difference—so wide, that to receive the one as good, pure, and holy, is of necessity to reject the other as bad, corrupt, and wicked. To be the friend

20. Ibid., 25.
21. Saillant, "Origins," 238.
22. Walker, "Our Wretchedness," 195.

of the one, is of necessity to be the enemy of the other. I love
the pure, peaceable, and impartial Christianity of Christ: I
therefore hate the corrupt, slaveholding, women-whipping,
cradle-plundering, partial and hypocritical Christianity of this
land. Indeed, I can see no reason, but the most deceitful one,
for calling the religion of this land Christianity. I look upon it
as the climax of all misnomers, the boldest of all frauds, and the
grossest of all libels.[23]

The unspeakable horrors captured in these passages and endured by many
slaves contradict any notion of slavery as being a blessing to Africans. Walker underscores the hypocrisy of the idea of a Christian nation when slaves
were not even permitted to pray and, if caught doing so, suffered egregiously.
Similarly, Douglass refuses to believe that the Christianity practiced in this
country corresponds at all with the Christianity of Christ. Both Walker and
Douglass deny the beneficence of slavery.

The belief that divine providence approved of the slave trade so that
slaves could find salvation was ludicrous to Haynes as well. To refute the notion of slavery's benefit, Haynes used the apostle's words in Rom 3:8 and 6:1
that declare, respectively, "And not rather, (as we be slanderously reported,
and as some affirm that we say,) Let us do evil, that good may come? Whose
damnation is just;" and "What shall we say then? Shall we continue in sin,
that grace may abound?" By drawing on these texts, Haynes demonstrates
that, just as in Paul's day when some were exclaiming "let us do evil so that
good may come," whites wanted to commit evil in promoting the slave trade
so that "good" (civilizing Africans and causing them to become Christians)
may result.[24] Haynes avers that the apostle's answer to his readers in the
first century is the same answer he gives to Haynes's audience: "God forbid."
In his use of Paul here to condemn whites' view of slavery, Haynes calls
slavery sin ("Shall we continue in sin?"), a move that many white Christians
at the time could not and would not make. Haynes asserts that instead of
slavery being a blessing to the African, it is the exact opposite. It is sin that
God through Paul forbids continuing. For those who do engage in it, their
damnation is a righteous one as evidenced by the apostle's words. Haynes's
hermeneutical effrontery was both a penetrating and an ingenious move on
his part. Reversing the whites' practice of having the apostle preach to the
slaves, in essence, Haynes depicts the apostle as preaching to the white slave
owner and minister, "Shall you continue in sin, that is, participate in slavery
and the slave trade? God forbid!"

23. Douglass, "Narrative," 1:592.

24. Haynes, "Liberty," 26.

Zilpha Elaw, 1790–1873[25]

Zilpha Elaw was born free around 1790 but became a servant to a Quaker couple and endured "harsh fieldwork on an early nineteenth-century farm."[26] She was one of the few black women during her time to proclaim the gospel in the midst of great adversity from both women and men because of her gender and race. Elaw appeared at least on one occasion with her fellow sister preacher, Jarena Lee.[27] In her autobiography, in which she describes her call to preach and her subsequent ministry, she adopts and adapts Paul's language.[28] Throughout her narrative she describes various supernatural encounters with God; what some today would call mystical experiences. Elaw repeatedly depicts her call and her ministry in terms of Paul and his ministry. As he was chosen by God, so was she (Gal 1:15).[29] Her own revelatory experience echoes that of the apostle, for she too does not know whether or not she was in or out of the body when she had her divine encounter (2 Cor 12:2–3).[30] Just as the apostle is an earthen vessel so too is Elaw (2 Cor 4:7), and as an effectual door was opened for Paul God likewise opened the door for her to preach when she traveled (1 Cor 16:9).[31] In addition, Paul's weakness that displays the excellency of God's power is similar to Elaw's weakness carried in her "poor-coloured" frame that allows God's strength to prevail in her (2 Cor 4:7).[32]

Elaw chronicles the astonishment among whites of seeing a black woman teaching and preaching. In relating their amazement, Elaw acknowledges their reactions with words from 1 Cor 1:27 that God has chosen the weak things of the world to confound the mighty.[33] Moreover, she recognizes that

25. The date of Elaw's death is difficult to determine. Some historians cite 1873, whereas others argue for the late 1840s.

26. Pierce, *Hell Without Fires*, 90; cf. 89.

27. Simmons and Thomas, "Zilpha Elaw," 167.

28. Elaw, "Zilpha Elaw," 11. See also chapter 4 of this volume, where Beverly Gaventa considers the issue of gender in relation to Paul's conception of Christian ministry.

29. She writes, "It was at one of these meetings that God was pleased to separate my soul unto Himself, to sanctify me as a vessel designed for honour, made meet for the master's use" (2 Tim 2:21) (Elaw, "Zilpha Elaw," 13).

30. Elaw states, "Whether I was in the body or whether I was out of the body, on that auspicious day, I cannot say" (ibid.).

31. Elaw remarks, "A great and effectual door of utterance opened to me by the Lord. . . . Through the instrumentality of so feeble an earthen vessel . . . and the weakness and incompetency of the poor coloured female but the more displayed the excellency of the power to be of God" (Ibid., 18).

32. Ibid.

33. She comments, "Slaveholders . . . thought it surprisingly strange that a person

her words do not consist of eloquence but, in the words of the apostle, in demonstration of the Spirit (1 Cor 2:4). Like the preacher from Tarsus, she is endowed by the Spirit and has an authority and legitimacy given by the Spirit's presence. In addition, Elaw understands the two-tier nature of the conflict in which a spiritual battle is taking place, for strongholds need to be destroyed so that the gospel may reach many (2 Cor 10:4).[34] Elaw therefore portrays herself in an apostolic role: people are turned from darkness to light and from the power of Satan to the power of God, which are all words that God speaks to Paul in Acts 26:18.[35] Elaw's ministry is affirmed because what God promised would happen through Paul's ministry is now happening through her ministry.

Not only does Elaw use Paul to characterize her call and to show that her ministry has authenticated authority, she also employs the apostle's language to resist racism. Elaw declares,

> The Almighty accounts not the black races of man either in the order of nature or spiritual capacity as inferior to the white; for He bestows his Holy Spirit on, and dwells in them as readily as in persons of whiter complexion. . . . Oh! That men would outgrow their nursery prejudices and learn that "God hath made of one blood all the nations of men that dwell upon all the face of the earth."[36]

Echoing Acts, Elaw appeals to the experience of the Spirit in which the Spirit falls upon gentiles as well as Jews, indicating gentile inclusion in God's salvific plan. Similarly, Elaw proclaims that just as God's Spirit makes no distinction between whites and blacks, having been granted to both races, human beings should not employ such differences either.

In her article "Prophesying Daughters," Chanta Haywood calls Zilpha Elaw—along with Jarena Lee, Maria Stewart, and Julia Foote—the prophesying daughters of Joel 2:28–29, who in the midst of great opposition from

---

(and a female) belonging to the same family stock with their poor debased, uneducated, coloured slaves, should come into their territories and teach. . . . But God hath chosen the weak things of the world to confound the mighty" (ibid., 18–19).

34. She explains, "For my speech and my preaching were not with enticing words of man's wisdom, but in demonstration of the Spirit, and in power; it was mighty through God, to the pulling down of strongholds; and became the power of God to the salvation of many" (ibid., 19).

35. It is important to note that these early interpreters did not make a distinction between the Paul of Acts and the Paul of the Epistles as is the case in biblical scholarship today. Similarly, the modern distinction between Pauline and Deutero-Pauline did not exist for them either.

36. Ibid., 17. Scripture quotation from Acts 17:26.

both women and men, black and white, continued to preach and prophesy. She writes that when these women used their pens to record their journeys as black women preachers they were "writing themselves into existence."[37] This statement by Haywood is significant, for as illustrated in Elaw's re- counting of her life she was indeed "writing herself into existence," and it is noteworthy, for our purposes, that *she utilized Pauline language to do so*. She saw her existence as intricately connected to the apostle: her call was tied to his call; his mandate from God became her mandate from God; and the gospel he proclaimed became hers as well. In the act of writing herself into existence Elaw laid claim upon the apostle's words and his experiences, and by doing so she demonstrated that these were not limited to him alone but were events that transcended time, space, and gender. What is more, Elaw offered alternative readings of Paul that challenged and resisted the dominant oppressive interpretations of him.

James Pennington, 1807–1870

James Pennington spent his first twenty-one years as a slave before escaping. In 1841 he published the first African American history, *A Textbook of the Origin and History of the Colored People*. In "The Great Moral Dilemma," a section of his autobiography, Pennington highlights another aspect of the effect of slavery upon African Americans by presenting a contextual ethic in which the slave must choose whether to submit to whites or to be subject to a higher power, which is God who grants all people the right to be free.[38] During his escape from slavery Pennington is found by white men who ask him two questions that become the focal point of this part of the essay: "Who do you belong to and where did you come from?"[39] Pennington im- mediately realizes that he has three options:

> I knew according to the law of slavery, who I belonged to and where I came from, and I must now do one of three things—I must refuse to speak at all, or I must communicate the fact, or I must tell an untruth. . . . What will be the consequence if I put them in possession of the facts. In forty-eight hours, I shall have received perhaps one hundred lashes, and be on my way to the

37. Haywood, "Prophesying Daughters," 356. Pierce, *Hell Without Fires*, also calls Zilpha a prophesying daughter (87).

38. Pennington, "Great Moral Dilemma," 81. See Sernett's introduction to this es- say; cf. also Pennington, *Fugitive Blacksmith*.

39. Pennington, "Great Moral Dilemma," 82.

Louisiana cotton fields. . . . I resolved, therefore, to insist that I was free.[40]

At the end of the narrative, Pennington relates that he was taught by his slave parents to tell the truth always, but at this moment in his life he could see no other way to escape except by telling an untruth. For to tell the truth would mean that he would be returned to certain torture, possibly death. The "moral dilemma" of that day inspired him "with a deeper hatred of slavery."[41] Slavery, he laments, not only takes one's freedom, one's body, and one's life but it also places a slave in moral conundrums that may cause him to die "with a lie upon his lips."[42] Pennington, then, is not proud of the fact that he lied. In his final remarks in this part of the narrative, he highlights that the system of slavery causes blacks to do things they do not want to do and to engage in acts that are contrary to their faith. Using Paul's words from Rom 7:21, where the apostle writes, "I find then a law, that, when I would do good, evil is present with me," Pennington characterizes the slave's plight: "How, when he [the slave] would do good, evil is thrust upon him."[43] Pennington makes an important change to this text, transforming it from one in which evil is present within the self to one in which evil comes from outside the self. One could argue that in this verse the apostle depicts a struggle that involves a person wrestling with inner evil. But for the slave, the text is about evil being thrust upon blacks, making them engage in sinful acts that they would not normally do. The evil is not within, Pennington insists, but without. That evil, the white's slavery system, has inherent in it an anti-moral, anti-ethical impetus. When blacks desire to live a life of goodness, their white slave masters and the larger white society will not allow them to do so. Evil is forced upon the slaves, giving them no choice but to act in ways contrary to what they desire.

Here the use of Paul for resistance occurs in what I label as reformulation. This reformulation takes place in light of the slave's continual existential crisis. In this reformulation Pennington resists the white definition of evil as his body, his origin, or his skin color and declares that slavery itself is what is evil and generates evil; it is the system that is wicked, not him. Such a statement undercuts the notion during this time that blacks—as indicated by their skin color—were malevolent beings. Pennington resists such views and denounces the system for its intrinsic immorality. Slavery is the culprit, Pennington announces to his audience, not my black body.

---

40. Ibid.

41. Ibid., 87.

42. Ibid.

43. Ibid.

Implications for Christian Ministers and Laypeople

How do these interpreters shed light on Paul in regard to race? First, one of the central tenets of the slaves' petition was "[b]ear one another's burdens." For far too long the burden for racial justice has fallen upon African Americans, who have marched, protested, written books, signed petitions, given presentations, preached, prayed, sang songs, and even died in the quest for equality. Thankfully, many white Christians have been part of this struggle as well, but too many still do not see racism as a problem or not their problem. These early interpreters urge white believers in their time and in ours to answer the call for justice by sharing the burden of their sisters and brothers of color.

Second, and in a similar vein, these writers view Paul as a resource for liberation. Despite how Paul was used against them, they refused to jettison the apostle, choosing instead to find life and freedom, not enslavement or death, in his words. Remarkably, black women, like Zilpha Elaw, claimed Paul as their own companion in the struggle for recognition of their call. Thus, these authors compel us to oppose scriptural readings that dehumanize and subjugate others and beckon us to preach and teach the gospel in a liberative way, affirming the dignity of every human being. They also challenge us to address issues of race and racism in our sermons and Bible studies and not to steer clear of the subject. Likewise, they encourage us not to be afraid to name racism as sin and to confront it when we see it. These writers took extreme risks in speaking out and in daring to claim that Pauline Scripture speaks to them and for them to others. Their boldness should inspire us as well.

Third, the vestiges of the "Josiah Priest mentality" continue to plague American society and I dare say American Christianity. To many people, black and brown skin equals danger, criminality, inferiority, and threat. The sustained unjust treatment of people of color in all levels of society continues today, ranging from racial profiling to mass incarceration to racial disparities in education. As discussed above, the seeds for such views were planted by faulty scriptural interpretation and reinforced by churches and governmental laws. Believers have inherited a racist legacy and too often have participated in this legacy, which has become part of American culture, including the culture of the church. Can we as believers refuse to renounce the chains of oppression and racism that permeate our society? The words of Paul, echoed in Haynes's denouncement of the slave trade, are divine words to us as well. God forbid!

And finally, along the same lines, part of Christian formation involves recognizing the ways in which Scripture, in this case Pauline Scripture, has been used to justify the unjustifiable. Too often in small groups or Sunday school lessons this aspect of Scripture is not discussed, which leads to a naïve understanding of Christian history in this country and results in unintended but dangerous consequences such as the perpetuation of a disjunction between Scripture and lived experience.

Our brief examination of the writings of these African Americans who lived in the eighteenth and nineteenth centuries illustrates that these early interpreters knew the power of Paul's words to shape reality and to give voice to the voiceless. Although Paul was constantly being used to silence, dehumanize, and subjugate them, these explicators reappropriated Paul as a figure of protest and resistance in opposition to the powers of oppression, evil, and slavery. Paul, these writers insisted, did not belong to the white slaveholder or to the white minister but to the slaves and even to women preachers. He was their companion, and likewise can become our companion, in the fight for freedom and the struggle for justice.

Bibliography

Braxton, Brad. *No Longer Slaves: Galatians and African American Experience.* Collegeville: Liturgical, 2002.

Cannon, Katie. "Slave Ideology and Biblical Interpretation." *Semeia* 47 (1989) 9–23.

Douglass, Frederick. "Narrative of the Life of Frederick Douglass, an American Slave, Written by Himself." In *I Was Born a Slave: An Anthology of Classic Slave Narratives*, edited by Yuval Taylor, 536–99. Chicago: Lawrence Hill, 1999.

Elaw, Zilpha. "Zilpha Elaw." In *Can I Get a Witness? Prophetic Religious Voices of African American Women, an Anthology*, edited by Marcia Riggs, 11–20. New York: Orbis, 1997.

Haynes, Lemuel. "Liberty Further Extended: Or Free Thoughts on the Illegality of Slavekeeping; Wherein Those Arguments that Are Useed in its Vindication Are Plainly Confuted. Together with an Humble Address to Such as Are Concearned in the Practice." In *Black Preacher to White America: The Collected Writings of Lemuel Haynes, 1774–1833*, edited by Richard Newman, 17–30. Brooklyn: Carlson, 1990.

Haywood, Chanta M. "Prophesying Daughters: Nineteenth-Century Black Religious Women, the Bible and Black Literary History." In *African Americans and the Bible: Sacred Texts and Social Textures*, edited by Vincent Wimbush, 355–66. New York: Continuum, 2000.

Klauck, Hans-Josef, et al., eds. *Encyclopedia of the Bible and Its Reception.* 15 vols. Berlin: Walter de Gruyter, 2009.

Pennington, James. *The Fugitive Blacksmith or, Events in the History of James W. C. Pennington, Pastor of a Presbyterian Church, New York, Formerly a Slave in the State of Maryland, United States.* London: Charles Gilpin, 1849.

———. "Great Moral Dilemma." In *African American Religious History: A Documentary Witness*, edited by Milton Sernett, 81–88. Durham: Duke University Press, 1999.

Pierce, Yolanda. *Hell Without Fires: Slavery, Christianity, and the Antebellum Spiritual Narrative*. Florida: University Press of Florida, 2005.

Powery, Emerson B. and Rodney S. Sadler. *The Genesis of Liberation: Biblical Interpretation in the Antebellum Narratives of the Enslaved*. Louisville: Westminster John Knox, 2016.

Priest, Josiah. *Slavery as It Relates to the Negro or African Race*. Albany: C. Van Benthuysen and Co., 1843.

Raboteau, Albert. *Slave Religion: The "Invisible Institution" in the Antebellum South*. New York: Oxford University Press, 1978.

Saillant, John. "Origins of African American Biblical Hermeneutics in Eighteenth-Century Black Opposition to the Slave Trade and Slavery." In *African Americans and the Bible: Sacred Texts and Social Textures*, edited by Vincent Wimbush, 236–50. New York: Continuum, 2000.

Simmons, Martha and Frank Thomas, eds. *Preaching with Sacred Fire: An Anthology of African American Sermons, 1750 to the Present*. New York: W. W. Norton & Company, 2010.

Smith, Abraham. "Paul and African American Biblical Interpretation." In *True to Our Native Land: An African American New Testament Commentary*, edited by Brian K. Blount, 31–42. Minneapolis: Fortress, 2007.

Thurman, Howard. *Jesus and the Disinherited*. Richmond, IN: Friends United, 1981.

Venable-Ridley, C. Michelle. "Paul and the African American Community." In *Embracing the Spirit: Womanist Perspectives on Hope, Salvation, and Transformation*, edited by Emilie M. Townes, 212–33. New York: Orbis, 1997.

Walker, David. "Our Wretchedness in Consequence of the Preachers of Religion." In *African American Religious History: A Documentary Witness*, edited by Milton Sernett, 193–201. Durham: Duke University Press, 1999.

6

Timely Pastoral Response to Suffering: God's Time and the Power of the Resurrection[1]

L. Ann Jervis

Talking About Suffering

P AUL THOUGHT ABOUT TWO kinds of suffering: suffering *in* Christ and suffering *with* Christ. The former is the kind of suffering that all humanity will experience and that believers go through while being in Christ. The latter is unique to believers who are in Christ. Suffering with Christ is taken on voluntarily for the sake of relieving the suffering of others.

Paul does not think that suffering is what God wants. It is what sin wants. Sin, for Paul, is the uninvited power that entered God's creation—causing all kinds of suffering—and brought with it another enemy of God: death. Suffering is sin's work.[2]

Paul's project to open believers' eyes to their location in Christ and apart from the flesh (Rom 8:1–9), where they must consider themselves dead to sin (Rom 6:11), is a radical rejection of suffering. For sin and death inhabit and use the sphere of the flesh in order to increase destructive and death-dealing behaviors. While being in Christ/the Spirit and not in the flesh (Rom 8:9) does not protect believers from suffering, Paul believes that

1. I am an enthusiastic admirer of Susan Eastman's exceptional scholarship on Paul, particularly because it is combined with the integrity of her pastoral concerns. This essay is written in her honor and was significantly strengthened by comments offered by my graduate student, Rob Walker.

2. See Jervis, *At the Heart of the Gospel*. For further discussion of the entrance of sin and death into human experience and the created order, see chapter 11 by Burroughs in this volume. For reflections on preparing for and facing death with patience and faith, see chapter 15 by Philip Ziegler.

it does give them remarkable resources both to handle involuntary suffering and to act voluntarily in opposition to sin and death.

The pains associated with living in a creation that is marred by the invasion of sin and death are shared by believers. Those in Christ can, however, endure these pains with the companion of joy. Paul also thinks that believers' requisite opposition to sin requires suffering—suffering with Christ. In what follows I will not make a distinction between these two kinds of suffering.

Suffering and Time

When we suffer, or those we care for do, the question of time is immediately present: how much longer will this go on? For Christians a secondary question may arise: how much longer will there be suffering in God's creation? Is there a time limit to suffering? When will the hope for no more sorrow or sighing be realized? In particular, given the scholarly and vocational focus of this volume's honoree, can the pastoral response to suffering be strengthened by setting it in the context of Paul's understanding of time?

The standard readings of Paul's understanding of time are salvation historical and apocalyptic. The salvation historical view understands that time and God are distinct, yet God directs and reveals Godself in time. Typically, such revelation is thought of in terms of progressives phases.[3] Apocalyptic scholars claim that time is separate from God, and God has invaded it with the new creation.[4]

While these two interpretative views see themselves in competition with each other, they do agree that time is an entity distinct from God and

---

3. Ireneaus organized his theology around the concept that God has progressively revealed Godself to humanity, culminating in Jesus Christ (*AH* 2.102, 1:424). More recently, Cullmann speaks of the phases of redemptive history (219) and of the early Christians' linear understanding of time (Cullmann, *Christ and Time*). See also Cullmann, *Salvation in History*, 249, where he argues that the apostle understood there to be a historical unfolding of a divine plan. James D. G. Dunn continues Cullmann's position (Dunn, *Theology of Paul*, 463). Currently, the most prolific and influential proponent of a version of salvation history interpretation of Paul is N. T. Wright, *Paul in Fresh Perspective*; Wright, *Climax of the Covenant*.

4. Several scholars paved the way for the present shape of apocalyptic Pauline interpretation, in particular, Kabish, *Die Eschatologie*; and Schweitzer, *Paul and His Interpreters*. Karl Barth's 1922 Romans commentary claims that Paul thinks that eternity has intruded time and in so doing has annihilated it while also establishing it (Barth, *Epistle to the Romans*, 498–99). Beker, *Paul the Apostle*; Martyn, *Theological Issues*; Martyn, *Galatians*; Gaventa, "Cosmic Power," 229–40; Gaventa, "Interpreting the Death," 125–45; and Campbell, *Deliverance of God*, are among the most powerful voices in current apocalyptic interpretation.

that when God either directs it (salvation history) or invades it (apocalyptic), the result is that time is "already/not yet."[5] Though salvation historical and apocalyptic scholars do not always use the "already/not yet" tag, I believe it adequately summarizes their thinking: the Christ event is the presence of the future, although the future partially. There is more future to come when Christ returns. In the current state of affairs, before Christ's return, believers live in the overlap of the ages. In regards to suffering, both the salvation historical and apocalyptic views of Paul's understanding of time consider that suffering and death are aspects of the continued existence of the old age.

Pastors seeking to comfort and encourage sufferers may find inspiration from the salvation historical and apocalyptic views of time by emphasizing both Paul's conviction that there will be an end to suffering and death and that the future is here in part. When death is finally terminated at the *telos*, "the end" (1 Cor 15:24–26), there will exist only the "already" of the new creation. In light of the coming glory, present suffering can be relativized (Rom 8:18). Pastoral consolation reflecting the concept "already/not yet" says: while we suffer now we may do so in full assurance that suffering and death have a shelf life. They will end.

Moreover, the salvation historical and apocalyptic claim that Paul thought that the suffering-free/death-free future is partially here may strengthen that conviction. Since the new creation is here in part, in the midst of sufferings believers can see, albeit dimly, the glorious future liberated from suffering and death. This partial presence offers consolation and, indeed, guarantees that eventually all creation, including humanity, will be forever relieved from suffering.

An alternative understanding of Paul's view of time—one that I am in the process of exploring—may also provide consolation and relief. That alternative understanding is that by virtue of being in Christ believers are already in God's time. This is not the place to argue for my understanding. However, for the purpose of this essay I here summarize some of the opinions I have come to in my previous work on Paul's conception of time.[6]

5. See, for example, the salvation historical scholar Cullmann, *Salvation in History*, 248–68, esp. 257, and the apocalyptic scholar Martyn, *Theological Issues*, 122; Martyn, *Galatians*, 104–5. In chapter 10 of the present volume, Emily Peck-McClain provides a practical example of how the apocalyptic view of the already/not yet can influence and guide church leaders in addressing the forces of sin in this time before the end.

6. See Jervis, "Time in Romans"; Jervis, "Promise and Purpose," 1–26. Also two papers presented orally: Jervis, "Enough Already/Not Yet," and Jervis, "No End in Sight."

Paul's Conception of Time

God Lives Non-Tensed Time

Paul understands God to live time. Paul's conviction that God is eternal (Rom 1:20) is not also a conviction that God lives eternity, understood as non-time.[7] When Paul prays that God's glory and blessedness would continue forever,[8] he does not conceive forever-ness as an atemporal eternity. The best clue of what eternal meant for Paul is found in 2 Cor 4:18 "we look not at what can be seen but at what cannot be seen; for what can be seen is temporary, but what cannot be seen is eternal,"[9] where Paul juxtaposes the adjective *aiōnia* (eternal) with the adjective *proskaira* (temporary or transitory). On the one hand, there are things that last only a short while (*proskaira*), and on the other hand, there are things that are eternal (*aiōnia*). "Eternal" appears to be for Paul an endless quantity of time.[10]

Such time is, however, not tensed, that is, it has no past tense, present tense, or future tense. It is all at once. Clearly, Paul does not think that God lives in tensed time. That the apostle conceives that God can pass over formerly committed sins indicates this (Rom 3:25).[11] And, the fact that God's

7. It is to be noted that Paul never states that God lives eternity.

8. Paul uses the phrases *eis tous aiōnas, eis ton aiōna,* or *eis tous aiōnas tōn aiōnōn.* Apart from 2 Cor 9:9 these phrases occur in doxologies. As a human glorifying (Rom 11:36; [16:27]; Gal 1:5; Phil 4:20) or blessing God or Christ (Rom 1:25; 9:5; 2 Cor 11:31), Paul prays that such glory and blessing would continue forever—into eternity. The apostle endorses endless (forever) human devotion to God. In the other occurrence of the phrase (2 Cor 9:9) Paul quotes Ps 111:9: "his righteousness remains forever."

9. All scriptural quotations are from the NRSV, unless otherwise indicated.

10. While Cullmann was partially correct in his suggestion that "primitive Christians" understood eternity (which Cullmann understood to be designated by the term *aeon*) "carried a time meaning" (Cullmann, *Christ and Time,* 47), we must note that Paul does not state that God lives eternity. Moreover, in regards to Paul, we should resist Cullmann's suggestion of linearity. In *Christ and Time* Cullmann speaks of the "consistently rectilinear line of the ages" (49). *Christ and Time* synthesizes the New Testament writers and so does not offer a special study of Paul. In Cullmann, *Salvation in History,* where Cullmann spends time on Paul alone, he comes to a more sophisticated understanding of the apostle's view of the relationship between the past, present, and future (see esp. 263).

Note that in Paul's undisputed letters there is no indication that the apostle thought of the ages (to which he refers in the plural only once in 1 Cor 10:11 [Eph 2:7 is part of a disputed letter]) in a sequential linear fashion.

11. Paul's presentation of *tēn paresin tōn progegonotōn harmtēmatōn* assumes that though in human time the sins are committed prior to God's setting forth the *hilastērion* (that is, from the human vantage point the sins fit in a sequential tensed time), this is not the case for God. In the human temporal present God passes over sins that are in the past in our time. God does this because God is not limited by tenses.

time is forever—that there is no end to God's time—implies that God's temporality is not lived in tenses. Tenses only exist when there is at least an end (if not also a beginning) to time. That is, without at least an end there is nothing for tenses to work with, to be in relation to. Without an end, tenses are not—there is only duration. The events in 1 Cor 15:20–28 have a tensed sequence ("then," 15:23, 24; "until," 15:25) because there is a *telos*, "end" (15:24). That *telos* is the *telos* of the *telos*—the end of ending. The consequence of the end of death, which Paul spells out as God being everything to everyone (15:28), is also the end of time determined by an end and so of time lived in tenses. The *telos* is the end of all tensed time, which is at once the wonder of God's time—time without tenses, *tota simul* (all at once)—time that has no end and so no tenses. Paul, I suggest, thinks that God's eternal existence is lived in time: time that is non-tensed and so all at once. Paul does not describe God as living a non-time eternity. We must import that idea to find it in the apostle's writings.

Moreover, it is critical to take note of the fact that Paul speaks regularly of God's activity. On the premise that activity requires time, God's activities (of which Paul mentions many, e.g., choosing Israel, raising Christ from the dead, etc.) are indications of divine temporality. While Paul sees God acting in the human experience of tensed time, Paul conceives of God's actions as sourced in God's life.

For instance, in the first verse of Romans Paul writes that he was set apart—*aphōrismenos* (Rom 1:1). The unarticulated subject of this passive participle is surely God. Paul manifestly understood that he was set apart in the context of the human experience of time, but he believes that that action is sourced in God's life. Since for Paul God is eternal (and so does not act in tenses), it seems right to understand that the apostle did not think there was a particular moment in God's own life when God set Paul apart. That does not, however, negate that something took place in God's life. And with that being the case, God acts in human time from a divine tense-less time.

In the next verse, Paul writes that the gospel was announced before the fact through God's prophets in the holy writings (*proepēngeilato*, Rom 1:2).[12] God's prophets in the Holy Scriptures have prior knowledge of the Christ event and announced it before it occurred in human history. Presumably Paul thought that what the prophets knew came from God. They announced what God gave them to announce: the prophets' announcement is God's action.[13] God determined that the gospel would be announced. The

---

12. Though it is typically translated as "promised beforehand," this rare word, which occurs only elsewhere in the New Testament at 2 Cor 9:5, should be translated "announced in advance." See Jervis, "Promise and Purpose," 13–14.

13. Dunn, *Romans*, 10; and Jewett, *Romans*, 103 make a similar point. The emphasis

result is activity in human time that is sourced in activity in God. As with Paul being set apart, this pre-announcement of the gospel by the prophets in the holy writings is initiated by God who lives *tota simul* (all at once). There was no specific moment, such as a moment in human time, in which God determined this. Nevertheless, that God acted in initiating this announcement speaks to a divine life that is temporal in an eternal sort of way.

Consequently, God's activity, taking place in time that is *tota simul*, does not involve change in God's life. That is, Paul's conception of activity in God's life does not also mean that Paul thinks that there is change in God's life. Because our time is in tenses, humans may experience God's activity as change; however, God's activity of choosing Israel, of sending God's Son, of raising God's Son from the dead, of revealing God's Son, and so on, are not indications of new moments in God's life.

God acts in God's time. Humans experience God's actions in the framework of our tensed time, and so Paul remembers what God did, acknowledges what God does, and hopes for what God will do. However, I propose that Paul understands God's time to be simultaneity, and so God's activities always simply are.[14]

Humans Live Mortal/Tensed Time

Tensed time may also be described as mortal time—time that has an end. What makes God's time and tensed time categorically distinct is precisely this fact: God's time has no end (and presumably no beginning),[15] whereas tensed time has an end and also a beginning.

That tensed time has an end is manifest in individual human lives at the death of our bodies. Furthermore, since Paul expects the end of death (1 Cor 15:26), such time itself will end. Death is intrinsic to tensed time. Death, which manufactures endings, creates the conditions for tenses. Mortal time, then, is another way to speak of tensed time.

I have decided not to refer to "created time" as the kind of time that humans live. Paul does intimate that markers of time (for example, "let light shine out of darkness," 2 Cor 4:6; "things present and things to come," Rom 8:38) are created by God. Yet, while Paul seems to think that God created

---

on God is evident also in the pronoun *autou* in the phrase *dia tōn prophētōn autou*.

14. In "Promise and Purpose" I observe that Paul does not connect fulfilment with God's promise, and I propose that for Paul the divine promise is simply in the life of God.

15. Paul's understanding of God as eternal likely means that the apostle thinks that God's time has neither end nor beginning.

time for humans, the apostle intimates that the defining feature of the human experience of time is death—the uninvited power that ends the time of individual lives (Rom 5:12–15) and the enemy God will destroy at the *telos* (1 Cor 15:26). The time that humanity lives since the entrance of sin and death is not, then, what God created. It is rather created time misshapen by sin and death—entities that Gaventa calls anti-god powers.[16]

Believers Live Christ's Time

Paul's central conviction that believers are in Christ and in the Spirit and that Christ and the Spirit are in them (Rom 8:9–11) is also a conviction about the kind of time believers live. I take Paul's stated conviction about the mutual indwelling of Christ/Spirit and believers to imply that the apostle thinks that believers live Christ's time, which is, of course, God's time. This does not mean that Paul thinks that believers are translated out of the tensed time of human temporal experience—believers experience time as having a past, a present, and a future. However, believers can recognize that our human experience of time is embraced by, surrounded by, and infused by God's all-at-once time. Believers exist in a different temporal medium than they were in before being in Christ. Our tensed time is transformed by our knowledge that it is time within God's all-at-once time. We experience time in tenses, but the endless simultaneity of God's time embraces that experience. By being in Christ we exist in God's time: *this* is the truth of our temporality. Though we experience it otherwise, our life is not actually tensed, for in Christ time has no end.

We may see Paul working with this conception of time in Phil 3:9–11. After he describes all that he has thrown away for the surpassing value of knowing Christ, Paul continues that he easily counts those things as garbage "in order to gain Christ and be found in him, not having a righteousness of my own, based on the law, but that which is through the faith of Christ/through faith in Christ, the righteousness of God that depends on faith; that I may know him and the power of his resurrection, and may share his sufferings, becoming like him in his death, that if possible I may attain the resurrection from the dead" (3:8–11, author's translation). The curious placement of "the power of his resurrection" prior to the reference to Christ's sufferings and death has, of course, been adequately explained based on the "already/not yet" framework for Paul's view of time. G. W.

---

16. E.g., Gaventa, "Cosmic Power," 229–40.

Hansen, for instance, speaks of the "dynamic polarity between the present experience of Christ and the future consummation in Christ."[17]

My understanding of Paul's view of time suggests, rather, that Paul's prioritizing the power of Christ's resurrection indicates that the apostle understands that among the wondrous gifts Paul discovers in Christ (3:9)[18] is access to the temporality of Christ—that is, the power of Christ's resurrection. In Christ, Paul discovers time that, because of Christ's resurrection, has no end. The apostle finds himself in time that is God's time—the temporality lived by the risen Christ in whom Paul lives.

Paul's reference to "the power of the resurrection" may not, then, evidence tension between the present and the future—a common concept in the "already/not yet" framework for understanding Paul on time. Rather, "the power of the resurrection" may indicate Paul's awareness that the defining feature of the human experience of time—namely, death—has been overpowered by God's raising Jesus from death.

This becomes clear in Paul's remarkable and strange idea that his knowledge of Christ (3:8) makes it possible for him to gain Christ and be found/discovered in Christ, where he can seek to know Christ (3:10), and that the crucial aspects of such knowledge are sharing in Christ's suffering and being conformed to Christ's death. Evidently, Paul does not conceive of Christ's suffering and death to be in the historical past. They are *now*, which is why Paul can share them and be conformed to them. Christ's sufferings and death exist in the all-at-once time of God. They are not in the past— they are. Christ's sufferings and death exist simultaneously with Christ's resurrection. And Paul, living in Christ's time, may participate in them now.

The Function of Hope in God's Time

My proposal about Paul's view of time offers a particular framework for Paul's expressions of hope for release from suffering and death—when mortal bodies will be spiritual bodies and so released from the pains attached to materiality subject to death (Phil 3:21). The apostle knows that he is not yet perfect (3:12), but once he has known Christ and is found in him Paul understands his human experience of time to be released into Christ's time. Paul describes himself as having been "grabbed" (*katelēmphthēn*) by Christ

---

17. Hansen, *Letter to the Philippians*, 244. Hansen continues: "the present knowledge of the resurrection of Christ guarantees the future promise of the complete knowledge of Christ by participation in his glorious resurrection life."

18. Paul highlights God's righteousness.

(3:12).[19] His life is lived in the condition of Christ and consequently the purpose of his life is to make that condition his own (*katalabō*, 3:12). Paul regards himself (3:13) and other believers (3:16) as in the process of attaining that which they have been seized by—the being and life of Christ.

This challenging thought indicates that Paul considered that his human temporality, which he manifestly experiences in tenses (and so he understands mortal time as a process and even an athletic endeavor [3:13–14]), takes place in Christ. My proposal is that Paul thought that being in Christ—and so in time without end—transforms the mortal time he lives. Paul expresses a similar thought at Phil 3:20—the place to which believers belong is heaven.

For Paul, believers live in Christ and so in the time of Christ—time that is categorically different from mortal time, for it is time that does not end. Though believers are in mortal bodies and experience time in tenses, living in Christ means the real time they live is God's time; they have eternal life despite the inevitable death of their bodies.

Paul expresses the wonder of this—amazement at it. The words *ei pōs* (3:11) have regularly been understood to express Paul's uncertainty—"if possible."[20] I hear the words rather expressing wonder.[21] While Paul elsewhere boldly states the truth that Christ will change/redeem believers' mortal bodies (Phil 3:21; Rom 8:11; 1 Cor 15:42–44), at Phil 3:11 Paul gives voice to the marvel of this. The phrase *ei pōs* signifies not Paul's uncertainty about being raised from the dead but wonder that he will be—"if, wondrously, somehow."

Mortal Time Within God's Time

As a human in a mortal body, Paul experiences his striving for the goal in tenses (Phil 3:12–14), yet, since this striving takes place in Christ (3:9, 14), it takes place in Christ's time. This is the power of the resurrection. The resurrection has transformed time by establishing endless life. Because of the resurrection, time has no end for those in Christ.

Paul's conviction about and amazement at the truth he knows—that his life is not lived in mortal time, for the Spirit of the one who brings life from the dead will bring life to his mortal body (Rom 8:11)—is at once conviction and amazement that the tenses he experiences no longer have the power or meaning they did before his knowledge of Christ's resurrection.

---

19. CEB translation.

20. NRSV. See Reumann, *Philippians*, 525.

21. cf. O'Brien, *Epistle to the Philippians*, 411–14.

Knowing Christ and the power of his resurrection is knowing that there is no end for anything except creation's bondage to decay (Rom 8:21) and God's enemy, death (1 Cor 15:26).

Because of being in Christ and because of the indwelling of the one who raised Jesus from the dead, Paul knows himself and all believers to be living in God's time, with bodies that are porous to God's time (which is why they will be made alive). It is as if, by being in Christ, believers are transformed into creatures able to breathe and live a categorically different kind of time. Already/now believers, being in Christ, are in God's time. The power of the resurrection changes the temporal reality of believers (whether or not they recognize it).

Consequently, Paul acknowledges that he has not yet obtained the resurrection of the dead while at the same time having complete confidence that he is living in the resurrected one. He looks ahead in human time aware that God's time surrounds him. The effect of this for him and others in Christ is that we may actually see and know in the deepest sense of knowledge that the decay and eventual death of our bodies, and the tenses of mortal time, are already now transformed.

We wait in mortal time for what we know already: all-encompassing life that is conclusively stronger than decay and death. The power of the resurrection has already/now transported believers into the time of God—time that does not have an end; time that is all at once.

Paul says both "now is the day of salvation" (2 Cor 6:2) and "salvation is nearer to us now than when we first believed" (Rom 13:11). He can speak both of knowing the glory of God in the face of Jesus Christ (2 Cor 4:6) and that now he knows in part, as if in a mirror dimly (1 Cor 13:12), but "then" (when the perfect comes) he will see face to face (1 Cor 13:9–12).

He is not speaking out of both sides of his mouth, trying to hold together the "already" with the "not yet." Rather, Paul sees mortal time from the vantage point of life in God's time. If the apostle only saw God's time from the vantage point of mortal time he would have written only about the partiality of his vision or about his hope for salvation. But the apostle does more than that. He gives clear confirmation of completeness—now is the day of salvation.

These two claims of hope and completeness are neither contradictory nor indications of tension between the old age and the new. Paul, living God's time, can see the presence and the advent of salvation simultaneously. From the perspective of God's time Paul recognizes the presence of salvation and can see that in mortal time this salvation is still to come. This insight, given to the apostle as he lives in Christ and so in God's time, is not fraught with tension.

Suffering and Dying in God's Time

Paul manifestly acknowledges that we still live in mortal bodies and in a creation subjected to decay and death, but he believes that decay and death do not rule our temporal experience. For we are found in Christ and know the power of his resurrection. Death has no more dominion over us.[22] Believers know that our bodies will be liberated (Rom 8:23). The power of Christ's resurrection transforms our relationship to the suffering and death intrinsic to mortal bodies.

We may, along with many eminent interpreters of Paul, conceptualize that transformative power in an "already/not yet" temporal framework. I suggest, however, that Paul is working with another understanding of time. Believers' mortal life is already transformed because we know the power of Christ's resurrection. Consequently, Paul experiences waiting for his body to be changed as so inconsequential that he can rejoice in sufferings (Rom 5:3). He knows the joy of the Holy Spirit during affliction (1 Thess 1:6). Paul became so deeply aware of Christ's life (and its time) that the apostle saw that he was not confined to mortal time. He understood believers to live mortal time that is porous to and transformed by God's time.

Paul believed that those who had in them the Spirit of the one who raised Christ from the dead now live in the glory of God's time: the death of our bodies is not the end of us. The effect of this is that mortal time for believers is *already* transformed. We see that time has no end. This is a radically and categorically different kind of time than mortal time. As a consequence of the power of the resurrection and our life in Christ we know and see the eternal dwelling (2 Cor 5:1–2) that is there in the heavens for us. Believers are already able to fix their attention (4:18) on the things that have no end; that is, they already know God's time.

I do not hear Paul conceiving of tension between two kinds of time, which, in the "already/not yet" view are the present age and the new age/new creation. Rather, I hear the apostle claim that believers are liberated from the present evil age (Gal 1:4; see also Col 1:13).[23] This is not realized eschatology—Paul is clear that the end of death and all that challenges God has not occurred in mortal time. There is a *telos* coming. But that end is the end only of mortal time. Paul and all those in Christ already/now live God's

22. Paul writes this explicitly about Christ (Rom 6:9), yet his subsequent command to "consider yourselves dead to sin and alive to God in Christ Jesus" (6:11) indicates that the apostle believes that those in Christ are enabled also to be liberated from death's tyranny.

23. I regard Colossians as an authentic letter of Paul's. Gratitude to Douglas for his convincing work in this regard (Campbell, *Framing Paul*).

time. And, in the simultaneity of God's time, the *telos* is, since all the events of mortal time are in God *tota simul*.

Suffering in God's Time

Taking this view of Paul's understanding of time offers the potential of a rich though demanding pastoral response to suffering. Paul may be understood to model the possibility of awareness of God's glory in the midst of suffering and death. God's glory is, for Paul, the antidote to and the opposite of suffering and death (Rom 8:18; Phil 3:21; Rom 5:2). Paul offers the truth that because believers are in Christ we are now the glorious and free children of God, even though the revelation of our condition has not happened in mortal time (Rom 8:19–21), and in mortal time we wait for the redemption of our bodies (Rom 8:23). God's time surrounds, embraces, and infuses believers in our mortal bodies.

Rather than conceptualizing believers as living in the overlap of the ages—a time partially the old age and partially the new; a time tense with expectation for resolution of the tension at the eschaton—believers may be encouraged to see that the mortal time we live (in which we experience suffering and death) is already changed. Life—and not death—now conditions our bodies and the time connected to our mortality. The power of the resurrection has transformed the time we live, and so as we suffer and die we may see and live the eternal life we now have (Rom 6:23).[24] The condition of our lives as we endure suffering and pass through death is in Christ Jesus where we know the exquisite and all-powerful love of God (Rom 8:39).

For Paul, the task of those in Christ is to wake up (Rom 13:11) and see where they are. Believers are citizens of heaven (Phil 3:20); we are now raised with Christ and our life is hidden with Christ in God (Col 3:1–3). This recognition not only gives assurance that God will end suffering and death, but insight into the truth that now suffering and death have lost their power to intimidate and rule.[25] Believers are invited to see the glory of God that surrounds us as we suffer and pass through death.

While this invitation may sound heartless, and so it must be offered by the pastor with sensitivity to the real pain of suffering and death, it may also be wondrously transformative. For Paul this vision was a truth that

---

24. De Boer, *Galatians*, 389: "'eternal life' can describe the life of the new age after the last judgment, yet also the quality of life for those who are now 'in Christ' (cf. Rom 5:21; 6:23)."

25. In chapter 3, Charles Campbell illustrates this truth by portraying the courageous, apocalyptic preaching of Oscar Romero.

determined his own response to his various and severe sufferings and to the threat of his own death. As Paul writes Philippians he is in great discomfort from his chains[26] and has looked the death of his body straight in the eye (Phil 1:20–23). In these circumstances the apostle directs his Philippian church to do what he models—to rejoice always in the Lord, for the Lord is near (Phil 4:4–5). Joy and its companion—lack of anxiety (Phil 4:6)—mark Paul's life as he suffers and faces death. For he does all things in Christ, including his mortal suffering.[27] Paul lives now/already in the life of God. He is not waiting for his death to transport him from mortal life into heaven/eternity. Now Paul knows himself to be a citizen of heaven. As he lives "in the flesh" he truly and really lives Christ's life (Gal 2:20). He lives God's time. In Christ Jesus Paul knows—now—eternal life.

Paul rejoices as he suffers not only because he recognizes that suffering and death have an endpoint, but because he knows that, being in Jesus Christ, God's time surrounds him as he suffers. From within God's time Paul sees that all the things of this world are passing away (1 Cor 7:31), including the egregious existence of sin and death (and so of suffering). He recognizes that in this contracted time[28] even his suffering and his mortal body have become porous to God's time—now. Before the terminus of mortal time at the eschaton, now Paul lives forever time. And awareness of God's temporality opens him to breathing life untainted by death while he suffers. The apostle waits in mortal time, but in the truth of his temporality—God's time—he rejoices.

Paul does not accept suffering as the status quo. His life is given to the abolishment of it—as was Christ's. Knowledge of God's time liberates Paul from holding onto his mortal time. The apostle's capacity to give his life for the sake of combating sin's influence and so also the spread of suffering is a response to living God's time in Christ. Paul regards his personal sufferings—whether caused by being human in creation as it is, or by suffering with Christ—to be of little account due to his intense and actual awareness of living eternal life.

Perhaps the most transformative help pastors may offer sufferers is to follow Paul's example and open believers' eyes to the wonder of their location in Christ. They may share with sufferers the job of staring down sin and death, thereby diminishing suffering's power. This is the work of love, as Christ Jesus reveals—the one who loved us and gave himself for us.[29]

---

26. Jervis, *At the Heart of the Gospel*, 40.

27. Ibid., 48–49.

28. 1 Cor 7:29, translating *sunestalmenos* as "contracted."

29. I have, of course, paraphrased here Gal 2:20.

Bibliography

Barth, Karl. *The Epistle to the Romans*. Translated by E. C. Hoskyns. London: Oxford University Press, 1933.

Beker, Johan Christiaan. *Paul the Apostle: The Triumph of God in Life and Thought*. Philadelphia: Fortress, 1980.

Campbell, Douglas. *The Deliverance of God: An Apocalyptic Rereading of Justification in Paul*. Grand Rapids: Eerdmans, 2009.

———. *Framing Paul: An Epistolary Biography*. Grand Rapids: Eerdmans, 2014.

Cullmann, Oscar. *Christ and Time: The Primitive Christian Conception of Time and History*. Translated by Floyd V. Filson. Philadelphia: Westminster, 1950.

———. *Salvation in History*. Translated by S. G. Sowers. London: SCM, 1967.

De Boer, Martinus C. *Galatians*. Louisville: Westminster John Knox, 2011.

Dunn, James D. G. *Romans 1–8*. WBC 38A. Dallas: Word, 1988.

———. *The Theology of Paul the Apostle*. Grand Rapids: Eerdmans, 1998.

Gaventa, Beverly Roberts. "The Cosmic Power of Sin in Paul's Letter to the Romans: Toward a Widescreen Edition." *Interpretation* 58 (July 2004) 229–40.

———. "Interpreting the Death of Jesus Apocalyptically: Reconsidering Romans 8:32." In *Jesus and Paul Reconnected: Fresh Pathways into an Old Debate*, edited by Todd D. Still, 125–45. Grand Rapids: Eerdmans, 2007.

Hansen, G. Walter. *The Letter to the Philippians*. Grand Rapids: Eerdmans, 2009.

Jervis, L. Ann. *At the Heart of the Gospel: Suffering in the Earliest Christian Message*. Grand Rapids: Eerdmans, 2007.

———. "Enough Already/Not Yet, Already." Paper presented at Society of Biblical Literature, University of Toronto, June 9–10, 2016.

———. "No End in Sight: Towards Understanding Paul's View of Time." Paper presented at Society of Biblical Literature, University of Toronto, June 9–10, 2016.

———. "Promise and Purpose in Romans 9:1–13: Towards Understanding Paul's View of Time." In *God and Israel: Providence and Purpose in Romans 9–11*, edited by Todd D. Still, 1–26. Baylor: Baylor University Press, 2017.

———. "Time in Romans 5–8." In *The Unrelenting God*, edited by D. Downs and Matt Skinner, 139–49. Grand Rapids: Eerdmans, 2013.

Jewett, Robert. *Romans: A Commentary*. Hermeneia. Minneapolis: Fortress, 2007.

Kabisch, Richard. *Die Eschatologie des Paulus: in ihren Zusammenhängen mit dem Gesamt Begriff des Paulinismus*. Göttingen: Vandenhoeck & Ruprecht, 1893.

Martyn, J. Louis. *Galatians*. AB 33a. New York: Doubleday, 1997.

———. *Theological Issues in the Letters of Paul*. Nashville: Abingdon, 1997.

O'Brien, Peter T. *The Epistle to the Philippians*. Grand Rapids: Eerdmans, 1991.

Reumann, John. *Philippians*. New Haven: Yale University Press, 2008.

Schweitzer, Albert. *Paul and His Interpreters*. London: Black, 1912.

Wright, N. T. *The Climax of the Covenant: Christ and the Law in Pauline Theology*. Edinburgh: T. & T. Clark, 1991.

———. *Paul in Fresh Perspective*. Minneapolis: Fortress, 2005.

7 _____

Prayer in Paul's Letters: Theology and Practice[1]

Robert E. Moses

The study of prayer in Paul's letters remains a fertile ground for exploring Paul's conception of his ministry and theology. The letters of the Apostle Paul contain numerous references to prayer. But the reader looks in vain to find a formal definition of prayer in them. Paul does not define prayer; he assumes it. We can infer from his letters that prayer for Paul is communication with God the Father through Christ Jesus with the help of the Holy Spirit, which is offered in trust that a certain result may be effected.[2] Prayer can be an individual practice or a communal practice; though, as we will see below, Paul thinks the latter is more effective.

Scholars commonly classify prayers in Paul's letters as either "prayer reports" or "wish prayers."[3] The "prayer reports" inform readers—who are addressed in the second person—that Paul has offered prayers on their behalf and sometimes includes what Paul prayed for (e.g., Rom 1:9–10; 2 Cor 13:9; 1 Thess 1:2–3; Phil 1:4–5; Col 1:9; 2 Thess 1:11; Phlm 4). The

1. It is an honor and a privilege to contribute to this volume honoring the exceptional work of Dr. Susan Eastman. I consider Susan to be both a teacher and a friend. She has always been a model for all of us of how to blend extraordinary critical scholarship with an intense love for the church and sensitivity to ministry. My own scholarship has been enriched because our paths crossed. This is a small token of my enormous appreciation to her. Of course, all the deficiencies in this essay are my own.

2. See, for example, Rom 1:8, which contains a classic formulation of how Paul understands prayer: "I thank my God through Jesus Christ for all of you" (see also 2 Cor 1:3; Col 1:3; cf. Eph 1:3). At Rom 8:26, to which we will return later in this essay, we discover that it is the Holy Spirit who aids the believer in prayer (cf. Eph 6:18). In a "wish prayer" in 2 Thess 2:16–17, Paul invokes both Jesus Christ and God. All biblical quotations are taken from the NRSV, unless otherwise indicated.

3. For further discussion see Harder, *Paulus*; Schubert, *Form and Function*; Wiles, *Paul's Intercessory*; Longenecker, "Prayer," 203–27.

"wish prayers" address the readers using "may" while speaking to God in the third person about what Paul desires for the recipients (e.g., Rom 15:5–6, 13; 2 Cor 13:14; 1 Thess 3:11–13; 5:23; 2 Thess 2:16–17; 3:5; 3:16). This essay proceeds with the assumption that the constantly emphasized theme of prayer in Paul's letters forces the reader to ask about the theological rationale of prayer in Paul's ministry. It is the aim of this essay to show that while the prayers reported and discussed in Paul's letters may operate within the limits of ancient epistolary practices, there still emerges a theology of prayer in his letters. Comparing Paul's prayer reports with ancient examples, we will show that, unlike what we encounter in ancient letters, prayer for Paul is not a one-sided affair—it is a two-way street whereby one offers petitions and thanks on behalf of others and receives the same from them. Prayers are also best offered in community. In addition, prayer is a practice whereby the church embodies how in Christ God has broken down enduring walls of separation and inequities that are built into the structures of society. Finally, Paul demonstrates in his own life and writings that human weaknesses, limitations in knowledge, and the mystery of God's will characterize human prayer.

Prayer Reports: Formulaic or Integral to Ministry?

There has been considerable discussion on how to evaluate Paul's prayers in light of ancient epistolary conventions. The debate has often centered on Paul's prayers of thanksgiving, which is a good place to begin, since the issues raised in this debate are relevant for our discussion of Paul's prayer reports. Paul often offers thanks to God in the opening (Rom 1:8; 1 Cor 1:4; Phil 1:3; 1 Thess 1:2; Col 1:3–4; Phlm 4–5; see also Eph 1:6) and the body (Rom 6:17; 1 Cor 1:14; 14:18; 2 Cor 4:15; 9:11; 1 Thess 2:13; 3:9) of his letters. Scholars often situate Paul's thanksgiving prayers within ancient epistolary conventions.[4] His thanksgiving prayers are often traced back to Greco-Roman (and Jewish) epistolary traditions.[5] However, Peter Arzt has

---

4. In the words of Paul Schubert, "The papyri convincingly attest a wide-spread conventional use of an epistolary, religious or non-religious, introductory thanksgiving" (Schubert, *Form and Function*, 180). See also Schubert, "Form and Function," 71–82; Sanders, "Transition," 348–62; Jewett, "Epistolary Thanksgiving," 40–53; Doty, *Letters*; Berger, "Apostelbrief," 190–231; O'Brien, *Introductory Thanksgivings*.

5. For examples of thanksgivings in ancient letters, see P. Mich. 1.23 (ca. 257 BCE); P. Cair. Zen. 1.59032 (ca. 257 BCE); P. Cair. Zen. 2.59160 (ca. 255 BCE); P. Cair. Zen. 3.59426 (ca. 260–250 BCE); P. Cair. Zen. 3.59526 (3rd century BCE); BGU 2.43 (2nd century CE); P. Giss. 17.6–7 (2nd century CE); P. Oslo. 3.1555.1–2 (2nd century CE); P. Oxy. 1.113.13 (2nd century CE).

argued against the view that ancient epistolary practices of thanksgiving to gods provide comparative backgrounds to Paul's own practice of offering thanks to God.[6] Having surveyed evidence from letters written on papyrus (ancient documents labeled "papyri" for short) prior to and contemporary with Paul, Arzt concludes, "There are no formal 'introductory thanksgivings' in the prooemia [introductions] of letters contemporaneous with the Pauline and other New Testament letters; hence, any reconstruction of such an 'introductory thanksgiving' shatters on the lack of evidence."[7]

Engaging all of Arzt's arguments would take us beyond the aims of this paper.[8] However, one of his assumptions raises important questions for our study of prayer in Paul's letters. Arzt argues that Paul's thanksgivings do not follow any cultural convention, because they "arise from Paul's personal feeling," while those contained in the papyrus letters are "expressed in the way that meets best the perception and the requirements of the writer."[9] Arzt's reasoning implies that prayers that "issue from the spontaneous and well-founded desire of the writers"[10] are not formulaic; conversely, those prayers that are formulaic do not express the writer's legitimate desires and personal feelings. The issue is even more pressing for Paul's numerous prayer reports since scholars generally agree that these reports *do* reflect ancient conventions and so may be considered formulaic.[11] Can we maintain, therefore, that Paul's reports of prayers reflect his genuine feelings?

What should we make of Paul's numerous claims in his letters that he not only remembers his congregants in his prayers but that he does so constantly? Paul often stresses the continual nature of his prayers for his letter recipients. A brief sample will be apt:

1. Rom 1:9: For God, whom I serve with my spirit by announcing the gospel of his Son, is my witness that without ceasing (*adialeiptos*) I remember you always (*pantote*) in my prayers.

2. Phil 1:3–5: I thank my God every time I remember you, constantly (*pantote*) praying with joy in every one of my prayers for all of you, because of your sharing in the gospel from the first day until now.

6. Arzt, "Epistolary," 29–46.

7. Ibid., 44.

8. For a helpful review, see Reed, "Are Paul's Thanksgivings," 87–99.

9. Arzt, "Epistolary," 35.

10. Ibid., 33.

11. See ibid., 38–44.

3. Col 1:9: For this reason, since the day we heard it, we have not ceased (*ou pauometha*) praying for you and asking that you may be filled with the knowledge of God's will in all spiritual wisdom and understanding.

4. 1 Thess 1:2–3: We always (*pantote*) give thanks to God for all of you and mention you in our prayers, constantly (*adialeiptos*) remembering before our God and Father your work of faith and labor of love and steadfastness of hope in our Lord Jesus Christ.

5. 2 Thess 1:11: To this end we always (*pantote*) pray for you, asking that our God will make you worthy of his call and will fulfill by his power every good resolve and work of faith.

6. Phlm 4: When I remember you in my prayers, I always (*pantote*) thank my God.[12]

Paul's prayer reports are not unique, for it is common to find reports of prayers for recipients in ancient letters. Ancient authors of letters also often claimed to be praying continually on behalf of the recipients. For example, in a letter written in the second century BCE, Isias writes to her brother Hephaestion about her hardships in having to raise his child alone in hard economic times. She expresses frustration that Hephaestion has no intentions of returning home (especially after his release from detention) or sending her financial assistance for his child. Before expressing her frustrations to him in the body of the letter, however, Isias reminds her brother that she constantly prays for his health before the gods:

> Isias to her brother Hephaestion greeting. If you are well and other things are going right, it would accord with the prayer which I make continually (*diatelō*) to the gods. I myself and the child and all the household are in good health and think of you always.[13]

In another letter, a soldier named Aurelius Polion (third century CE) writes to his siblings and his mother, chastising them for not replying to his letters and apprising him of their health. He begins the letter by reminding them of his continued supplication on their behalf before the gods:

> Aurelius Polion, soldier of legio II Adiutrix, to Heron his brother and Ploutou his sister and his mother Seinouphis the bread seller and . . . lady, very many greetings. I pray that you are in good health night and day, and I always make obeisance before all the gods on your behalf. I do not cease writing to you, but

12. See also 1 Cor 1:4; cf. Eph 1:16–19.

13. P. Lond. 42. Translation in Hunt and Edgar, *Select Papyri*, 1.97.

you do not have me in mind. But I do my part writing to you always and do not cease bearing you in mind and having you in my heart.[14]

These and many other examples make Paul's prayer reports seem clichéd,[15] completely reflecting cultural practices of his Greco-Roman context.[16]

Of course, there are some differences between Paul's prayer reports and those of the Greek papyri. The most obvious difference is that Paul's letters have coauthors and are mostly sent to communities, while the examples above are written by individuals to individuals.[17] In addition, prayers in the ancient letters are often offered for the "health" of the recipient. It is the most common prayer one encounters—that the gods will grant good health to the recipient of the letter. Paul's prayer reports, however, are not about the physical health of the recipients. Rather, his prayers concern aspects of his ministry and the believers' spiritual maturity. One might say that Paul's prayers are concerned more for the recipients' spiritual health than their physical health. Nonetheless, their similarities to the formulas used in Hellenistic letters cannot be denied. The question raised by Arzt, therefore, presses upon us: Are Paul's prayer reports merely formulaic, since they are part of ancient epistolary conventions, or do they express genuine feelings and a serious prayer life?

The two options need not be mutually exclusive. One can follow a standard of writing and yet express a genuine feeling.[18] For example, my mom's Akan tribe of Ghana believes that one has not truly shown appreciation for a gift unless one offers thanks the day after receiving it. It does not matter if one said "thank you" at the moment when the gift was received. The "thank you" that matters most is the one expressed after one wakes up the next day. It is, therefore, commonplace to receive visits or phone calls from members of this tribe the day after one has given a gift. Following this tradition may seem hackneyed to the outside eye; but to those who actually follow this custom, there is no denying that genuine gratitude is being expressed when one visits or calls the gift-giver the day after. The same may be

14. P. Tebt. 2.583. The text is poorly preserved, but most of it has been recovered with the aid of infrared images by Grant Adamson (Adamson, "Letter," 79–94).

15. See, e.g., BGU 2.423; BGU 2.632; BGU 1.27; P. Giss. 1.17; BGU 3.846; *Rev. Ég, 1919, p. 204*; P. Oxy. 3.528; P. Tebt. 2.412. For Greek texts and translations, in addition to Hunt and Edgar, see also White, *Light*.

16. For Jewish examples of this practice, see 1 Macc 12:11; 2 Macc 1:2–6.

17. See Dippenaar, "Prayer and Epistolarity," 147–88, esp. 154–56.

18. Reed is absolutely correct to note that "a generic formula, just because it is conventional, may also be used in a 'sincere' and 'spontaneous' manner" (Reed, "Are Paul's Thanksgivings," 95).

said of Paul's prayer reports. His claims to offer prayers constantly on behalf of his congregations may evince a serious prayer life, even if his reports follow an epistolary convention.

Germane to the above discussion is also the recognition that there is an aspect of Paul's prayer reports that is almost nonexistent in Greek practice. This is Paul's request for prayers from his recipients:

1. Rom 15:30–32: I appeal to you, brothers and sisters, by our Lord Jesus Christ and by the love of the Spirit, to join me in earnest prayer to God on my behalf, that I may be rescued from the unbelievers in Judea, and that my ministry to Jerusalem may be acceptable to the saints.

2. 2 Cor 1:10–11: He who rescued us from so deadly a peril will continue to rescue us; on him we have set our hope that he will rescue us again, as you also join in helping us by your prayers, so that many will give thanks on our behalf for the blessing granted us through the prayers of many.

3. 1 Thess 5:24–25: The one who calls you is faithful, and he will do this. Beloved, pray for us.

4. 2 Thess 3:1–2: Finally, brothers and sisters, pray for us, so that the word of the Lord may spread rapidly and be glorified everywhere, just as it is among you, and that we may be rescued from wicked and evil people; for not all have faith.

5. Col 4:2–4a: Devote yourselves to prayer, keeping alert in it with thanksgiving. At the same time pray for us as well that God will open to us a door for the word, that we may declare the mystery of Christ, for which I am in prison, so that I may reveal it clearly, as I should.[19]

Paul's prayer reports seem to break here from the ancient conventions when he requests prayers from his recipients for himself. And this may suggest that prayer was more integral to Paul's ministry than a prayer-formula theory would allow. There is no attested convention of prayer requests in Greco-Roman letters. For Paul, then, prayer is a two-way street: he prays for his congregations, but he also expects his congregations to offer prayers on his behalf. From the passages cited above, one gets the sense that Paul viewed the progress of his ministry as very much dependent on the prayers of others (e.g., Rom 15:30–32; 2 Thess 3:1–2; Col 4:2–4a). Intercessory prayers on Paul's behalf were the means by which Paul survived and persevered through suffering and persecution (e.g., 2 Cor 1:10–11).

---

19. So also Phil 1:18b–19; cf. Eph 6:18–20.

Paul's requests for prayer may stem from Jewish liturgical practice and belief. For example, in a letter to Jerusalem, Baruch and other Jews in Babylon ask for prayer:

> Pray also for us to the Lord our God, for we have sinned against the Lord our God, and to this day the anger of the Lord and his wrath have not turned away from us.[20]

When Paul, therefore, asserts, "I *know* that through your prayers and the help of the Spirit of Jesus Christ this will turn out for my deliverance" (Phil 1:19), he is expressing an idea present in Judaism that the prayers of the many are superior to the prayers of the individual. This is the same tradition that lies behind Jesus' saying in Matt 18:19: "Again, truly I tell you, if two of you agree on earth about anything you ask, it will be done for you by my Father in heaven." Matthew connects this saying to the community's disciplining of the believer who strays (Matt 18:15–18). In other words, for Matthew, if the community stands in agreement in its "binding" and "loosing" of a "brother" on earth, this agreement will be effected in heaven. Nonetheless, as many commentators have noted, Matt 18:19–20 at one time may have had a broader application concerning the efficacy of communal prayer.[21] The idea is also present in Rabbinic literature, where the rabbis often stressed the notion that the prayers of the many are better than the prayers of one. For example, Rabbi Hanina, when pondering the question of when is the acceptable time for prayer, reasons that it is when the congregation prays.[22] Praying at the same time as the congregation, which implies prayer with the congregation, suggests that the prayers of the many outweigh the prayers of the individual.

The above should not suggest that believers cannot and should never pray alone—Paul sometimes practiced this. Nonetheless, it suggests that even individual prayers need to be done within the context of a community in which a believer belongs. That is why Paul often "remembers" his congregations during his prayers and invites the congregations to pray *with* him even as they pray *for* him (e.g., Rom 15:30–32). A number of reasons commend themselves as to why praying in and with a community may be more effective.

First, praying in community reminds believers that the Christian journey is communal in nature. It is not a journey for lone rangers—perhaps we

20. Bar 1:13.

21. For further discussion, see Thomson, *Matthew's Advice*, 175–202; Luz, *Matthew*, 448; Davies and Allison, *Critical*, 2.781–91.

22. *b. Ber.* 8a. This and other rabbinic evidence on the superiority of communal prayer over individual prayer are listed in Strack and Billerbeck, *Kommenter*, 1.793–4.

might even say that lone rangers do not make it far on the journey. Believers are surrounded by a "great cloud of witnesses," whose presence, companionship, and care make each weight a little lighter to bear; believers can, therefore, persevere together (Heb 12:1).

Second, praying in and with a community decenters the pray-er. Believers can sometimes become absorbed in their own struggles and trials, forgetting that others are also experiencing suffering and trials. When believers can utter their prayers in community and also listen to the prayers of others, it not only creates solidarity and trust, but it also allows each believer to gain a new perspective on themselves and their trials. Perhaps communal prayer may help us see the futility of certain prayer requests; for, if we hesitate to bring them before the community in boldness, the requests may in fact be self-centered in nature.

Finally, praying in and with a community can serve as encouragement and inspiration to all, for communal prayers would inevitably include thanksgivings for answered requests or new perspectives gained. In Paul's own words, the communal prayers of believers will cause "many [to] give thanks on our behalf for the blessing granted us through the prayers of many" (2 Cor 1:11).

An Equalizing Practice?

To characterize Paul as a "man of prayer" may be a fairly accurate description of his life and ministry.[23] Paul believed that prayer should be a frequent occurrence in the life of all believers. What Paul implies in his letters about his own prayer practices—continually offering prayers for others—is precisely what he recommends for his churches. For example, Paul encourages believers in Thessalonica to "pray without ceasing" (1 Thess 5:17), he admonishes the Roman believers to "persevere in prayer" (Rom 12:12), and to the Colossian believers he says, "Devote yourselves to prayer" (Col 4:2). Paul wanted to cultivate a habit and character of prayer among all believers, because he strongly believed that followers of Jesus ought to wrestle in prayer continually. His prayer requests are, therefore, petitioned from *all* believers and offered on behalf of *all* believers. The emphasis on *all* is significant here, for it implies no exclusions—no matter one's ethnicity, class, or gender.

23. This image of Paul as a person in constant prayer is confirmed by Luke's account in Acts. See, e.g., Acts 13:2–3; 14:23; 16:25; 20:36; 21:5; 22:17; 28:8.

The extent to which Paul challenged and/or supported the gender, economic, ethnic, and social hierarchies of his day continues to be debated.[24] Paul preached a message that sought to move away from what he deemed to be the particularity of Jewish identity. For Paul, God's new creation in Christ meant followers of Jesus could no longer claim their connection with ethnicity as essential to their identity as the people of God.[25] In Paul's complex theology, the faithfulness of Jesus and believers' grateful response of faith in Jesus are the only necessities for sharing in the family of God (see, e.g., Gal 2:15–21; 6:15).[26] The extent to which this belief transformed the gender and economic hierarchies of Paul's day is a complex question and one that is a matter of ongoing lively discussion. To what extent did Paul himself and his congregations live out his extraordinary claim in Gal 3:26–28?

> For in Christ Jesus you are all children of God through faith. As many of you as were baptized into Christ have clothed yourselves with Christ. There is no longer Jew or Greek, there is no longer slave or free, there is no longer male and female; for all of you are one in Christ Jesus.[27]

In what areas was this ideal realized in the life of the believing communities, despite the enduring hierarchies of their surrounding culture? In this section, I show how Paul's call for prayer from all believers informs this discussion. Perhaps prayer was one area in which the church could live out this essential emphasis to abolish inequality. The role of women and enduring economic stratification within the Pauline congregations provide two areas of ancient inequality that intersect with Paul's teaching on prayer in unique ways.

Evidence shows that women held important positions in the early Pauline congregations and that Paul supported the ministries of these women,

24. Compare two contrasting conclusions reached by two prominent Pauline scholars: Martin, *Corinthian Body*, 231, and Aune, "Galatians 3:28," 182.

25. For example, see Paul's furious reaction to Peter's refusal to eat with gentile believers in Antioch when Jewish-Christian missionaries favoring Jewish ritual regulations for gentile believers arrive from Jerusalem (Gal 2:11–14). Compare Paul's reaction to an early Jewish text, *Jubilees* 22:16, in which Abraham articulates to Jacob Jewish attitudes toward eating with gentiles: "And you also, my son, Jacob, remember my words, and keep the commandments of Abraham, your father. Separate yourself from the gentiles, and do not eat with them, and do not perform deeds like theirs. And do not become associates of theirs. Because all their deeds are defiled, and all of their ways are contaminated, and despicable, and abominable." Translation by O. S. Wintermute, "Jubilees," in *OTP* 2.98.

26. See Hays, *Faith*.

27. See also 1 Cor 12:13; Col 3:9–11.

an argument also set forth by Beverly Gaventa in chapter 4 in the present volume.[28] Phoebe is described as a "deacon" (Rom 16:1–2),[29] Junia is counted among the prominent "apostles" (16:7),[30] and Nympha is the leader of a church that meets in her home (Col 4:15).[31] Yet this evidence must be viewed alongside other evidence in the Pauline letters that suggest that Paul sometimes wrestled between the notion of living out God's new creation and accepting traditional gender roles of his surrounding culture.[32] Among the most contested passages is the command for women to be silent in churches (1 Cor 14:33–36). I have not been persuaded by arguments that 1 Cor 14:34–35 or 14:33b–36 is a non-Pauline interpolation[33] or that Paul is quoting a Corinthian view that he opposes.[34] My rejection of the former view is based not only on the lack of manuscript evidence that omits these verses entirely, but also because these verses use similar vocabulary and themes contained in the surrounding verses of 14:25–40 (e.g., "speak" [14:27, 28, 29, 30, 34, 35]; "silence" [14:28, 30, 34]; "be subject" [14:32, 34]; "church" [14:28, 35]);[35] and my rejection of the latter position stems from the lack of any indications from Paul that 14:34–35 are a quotation.

What, then, is the significance of this passage for our discussion of prayer? At issue in 1 Cor 14:33–36 is a certain kind of speech.[36] Paul does not ban all forms of speech by women in the church. This is evident from 1 Cor 11:1–16, where Paul allows women in the church to engage in what Caroline Vander Stichele calls "vertical" speech, that is, communication

28. See Heine, "Diakoninnen-Frauen," 213–27.

29. cf. Pliny, *Ep.* 10.96.8. See Sherwin-White, *Letters of Pliny*, 708.

30. Scholarship is divided as to how the name *Iounian* should be accented. Some argue that the name should be masculine *Iounian* ("Junias") while others argue that the name is feminine ("Junia"). In a detailed study of the name, Eldon J. Epp has shown persuasively that the name intended by Paul is the feminine "Junia" (Epp, *Junia*).

31. Acts also mentions other women leaders of household churches: Mary the mother of John Mark (Acts 12:12) and Lydia (Acts 16:14–15). To the discussion of Paul's support of women in ministry should be added Paul's use of maternal imagery in his letters. On this, see Eastman, *Recovering*; Gaventa, *Our Mother*; and Gaventa, chapter 4.

32. On this see 1 Cor 11:1–16 and the household codes of Colossians (3:18—4:1).

33. For proponents of this view, see Schmiedel, *Der Briefe*, 2.181–82; Weiss, *Der erste Korintherbrief*, 342–43; Fee, *First Epistle*, 700; Munro, "Women," 26–31; Hays, *First Corinthians*, 244.

34. On this position, see Odell-Scott, "Let the Women," 90–93; Allison, "Let Women," 27–60.

35. For further discussion, see Collins, *First Corinthians*, 515–17, 520–21; Thiselton, *First Epistle*, 1151–55.

36. Stichele, "Is Silence," 241–53.

with God, either through prayer (wherein humans communicate with God) or prophecy (wherein God communicates with humans).[37] It is important to emphasize that according to 1 Cor 11:1–16 women are permitted to pray and prophesy in church, though Paul recommends that they do so with their heads covered. Thus, only about three centuries after Paul wrote 1 Corinthians, Theodore of Mopsuestia was correct to observe of 1 Cor 11 that "not only men but also women prophesied. At the time the baptized received spiritual gifts in a more obvious way, and various forms of prophecy were prominent, according to the needs of the church."[38] The notion, therefore, that Paul sanctioned women to be silent in church assemblies with respect to all forms of speech, including prayer and prophecy, must be repudiated. Perhaps we might say Paul's instructions to women to cover their hair before engaging in "vertical" speech and banning them from engaging in "horizontal" forms of communication during worship suggest that Paul had not completely broken away from his participation in the enduring hierarchical structures of his time. And yet in the congregations' communal practice of prayer, we catch a glimpse of a community living out its Christian countercultural stance against the male-dominated hierarchical structures of the surrounding culture.

The above claim can also be made when it comes to issues of class in the Pauline congregations. The question of the economic status of Paul's congregations is a complex one that continues to be debated. Addressing these debates would take us beyond the aims of this chapter.[39] Germane to our topic, however, is the question of what sort of contribution those who lived in poverty could make to the Christian community.[40] In his important book on the economic profile of the Pauline congregations, Bruce Longenecker explains that within a typical Pauline congregation roughly 65 percent of its members existed at subsistence-level.[41] A significant number of these members would be continually destitute.[42] According to Longenecker, this group was so desperate to survive everyday harsh realities that they

37. Ibid., 251–52.

38. Theodore of Mopsuestia, *Commentary on 1 Corinthians*, translated in Kovacs, *1 Corinthians*, 179.

39. On this topic, see Deissmann, *Light*; Theissen, *Social Setting*; Meeks, *First Urban*; Meggitt, *Paul, Poverty, and Survival*; Meggitt, "Sources," 241–54; Friesen, "Poverty," 323–61; Longenecker, *Remember the Poor*.

40. The topic of poverty in Paul's churches is also addressed by John Barclay in chapter 2 and Colin Miller in chapter 9 of the present volume.

41. Longenecker, *Remember the Poor*, 294–97.

42. Longenecker estimates the percentage of the destitute to be about 28 percent (ibid., 296).

would be entirely dependent upon the community's resources with nothing to offer in return. Thus, when Paul advises his congregants to set something aside weekly for the collection (1 Cor 16:1–2), Paul would not be addressing those living below the subsistence level, because they "would have nothing to put aside."[43] Again, when Paul advises the Thessalonians to "work with [their] own hands" so that they might gain the respect of outsiders "and be dependent on no one" (1 Thess 4:11–12), such advice excludes the destitute, for they "were in real need and were wholly dependent on others."[44] Even if we grant that Longenecker has given us an accurate picture of the economic profile in the Pauline communities and of those living below a subsistence level, would it be accurate to say that the latter would have nothing to contribute to the congregation and were merely dependent on the congregation's resources? Even if Longenecker is correct that they were in a dire economic situation and were in constant need of assistance,[45] his analysis seems not to take seriously Paul's attempt to create communities bounded by systems of reciprocity in which all members of the community mutually benefitted each other.

Second Corinthians 8–9 is crucial to this debate.[46] Here, Paul appeals to the Corinthians to make a generous donation to the collection by invoking the grace of God that has been at work in the congregations in Macedonia; for out of their afflictions and "extreme poverty" (2 Cor 8:2), these churches have demonstrated a "wealth of generosity" by giving voluntarily to the collection ministry. This began, however, with the Macedonians first giving themselves to God (2 Cor 8:5). This claim is crucial, for it establishes the act of generosity among believers as an act of grace that is only possible when believers first give themselves to God. It is a reenactment of God's generous act in Jesus, who, though rich, became poor for others' sakes, so that they might become rich (2 Cor 8:9). It suggests that, for Paul, when believers first give themselves to God, the grace of God would be experienced

43. Ibid., 253.

44. Ibid., 255.

45. For Longenecker to be correct would require two important assumptions to be true: first, those "who work with their hands" could not be below subsistence level; and second, Paul's claim that the Macedonians had given generously to the collection despite their "extreme poverty" (*hē kata bathous ptōcheia autōn*; 2 Cor 8:2) is false. I am not sure that both of these assumptions would hold up to scrutiny, especially the latter. In a letter (2 Corinthians) where Paul spends tremendous amounts of energy defending his own integrity, making a claim about the Macedonians that could easily be refuted by a trip to Macedonia undermines Paul's efforts and aims in this letter.

46. We cannot address here the debates about the literary integrity of 2 Cor 8–9. On this see, Young and Ford, *Meaning and Truth*; Thrall, *Critical and Exegetical*, 1.20–43, 2.503–20; Mitchell, "Paul's Letters," 307–38.

in such a way that the resources ("abundance," 2 Cor 8:14) of some will meet the needs of those in need, who in turn—by virtue of divine grace—would have an abundance that will meet the needs of those who had given to them (2 Cor 8:14). What is not clear at this point is whether the blessings offered to the rich by the poor are purely spiritual or if Paul also conceives of some material blessings as well; both could be implied here.[47]

It is at this point that discussion of Paul's teaching on prayer may be relevant, for Paul explicitly states in 2 Cor 9 that one of the ways in which the poor confer blessings upon the rich is through prayer. Paul explains,

> You will be enriched in every way for your great generosity, which will produce thanksgiving to God through us; for the rendering of this ministry not only supplies the needs of the saints [in Jerusalem] but also overflows with many thanksgivings to God. Through the testing of this ministry you glorify God by your obedience to the confession of the gospel of Christ and by the generosity of your sharing with them and with all others, while they long for you and *pray for you because of the surpassing grace of God* that he has given you. (2 Cor 9:11–14, emphasis added)

The poor believers in Jerusalem pray for those who have the means to give generously to them out of their abundance. But the entire process—from start to finish—is the working of God's grace.[48] That is why the poor do not give thanks to the rich for their gifts or attempt some payback to the rich (as one would expect in the ancient system of benefaction).[49] It is with thanksgiving that the receiving party prays, not necessarily for the gift itself, but for the surpassing grace of God that has allowed the community to walk in a relationship of mutual benefit. In light of the above discussion, it is, therefore, important to emphasize that Paul's call for believers to pray was a call made upon *all* believers. Prayer is a contribution everyone can make, whether in public or private, whether the pray-er is rich or poor.

In Paul's teachings on prayer, then, we may find one of those unique practices in the body of Christ that helped the community live out its egalitarian ideal. Prayer unites the body of Christ; and in prayer each member can contribute to the body of Christ—whether Jew or gentile, male or female, slave or free, rich or poor. If the modern church has created

---

47. See the discussion in Windisch, *Zweite Korintherbrief*, 259–60.

48. For further discussion on grace in 2 Cor 8–9 in particular and Paul's letters in general, see Barclay, "Manna," 409–26; Barclay, *Paul and the Gift*; and Barclay, chapter 2 in the present volume.

49. On the ancient system of benefaction, Seneca, *De beneficiis*.

hierarchies within its congregations, in which only a select elite is allowed to offer prayers in the assembly of the congregations, then we have lost the spirit of Paul's teachings on prayer. We have also lost the transformative power that this egalitarian practice can have on our congregations and the culture around us.

The Limitations (or Mystery) of Human Prayer

As noted above, Paul constantly offers prayers on behalf of his congregations and requests prayers on his own behalf. The contents of these intercessory prayers and prayer requests are sometimes very specific in nature. For example, in Rom 1:9–10 Paul prays that he may succeed in his plans to visit Rome. At the end of the same letter, he requests prayers for deliverance and protection from the unbelievers in Judea and that the saints in Jerusalem would express approval toward his ministry (15:30–32). In Colossians, Epaphras prays for the maturity of the Colossians and their steadfastness in God's will (Col 4:12). And in Phlm 22, Paul requests prayers that he would be released from prison and join the congregation.[50] In each of these examples, the prayer requests are specific, whether made on behalf of the congregations or requested by Paul. There is virtue in being specific about one's requests in prayer. This accords with the teachings of Jesus that warn against excessive verbiage during prayer (Matt 6:7–8).

Nonetheless, in a couple of places in his letters, Paul leaves room for the mysterious nature of prayer. This is necessary in light of the recognition of human finitude. Humans have their weaknesses, and this often clouds their judgment during prayer. In Paul's own words, because of our weakness, "we do not know how to pray as we ought" (Rom 8:26).[51] Peter O'Brien identifies two aspects of our weakness: "first, [the believer] may be 'quite at a loss' to know what to ask for, since he [sic] is unclear regarding the will of God in the matter. On the other hand, he may know precisely *what he wants* in the situation, but whether this desire is in line with the purposes of God may be questionable."[52] These two options need not be mutually exclusive; rather, they are two sides of the same coin expressing human inability to know and see God's purpose for the whole created order (8:18–25).[53] As

50. See also 2 Cor 13:9.

51. Theodor Zahn's argument that what is at issue in this verse is that believers have not been instructed properly on how to pray cannot be correct, since Paul will not exempt himself from this weakness. See Zahn, *Der Brief*, 412.

52. O'Brien, "Romans," 67. Emphasis in the original.

53. See further discussion in Byrne, *Romans*, 266–74.

a result, the spirit helps us in our weakness, interceding for us with "sighs too deep for words" (8:26).[54] The Holy Spirit, who knows the mind of God, offers intercession on behalf of believers in accordance with God's will when believers pray (8:27).[55]

This human weakness and limitation is demonstrated in Paul's own life when he pleads with God to take away a thorn in his flesh (2 Cor 12:7). The nature of this thorn is a moot point.[56] Whatever the thorn was, it is evident that Paul was displeased with it and wanted it to be removed. He repeatedly prayed that God would remove the thorn: "Three times I appealed to the Lord about this, that it would leave me" (2 Cor 12:8). Here is a classic example of how in our weakness, we as humans "do not know how to pray as we ought" (Rom 8:26), for as it turns out the thorn in Paul's flesh was a blessing in disguise. God refused to grant Paul's request, reminding him that "my grace is sufficient for you" (2 Cor 12:9). Through this thorn, Paul experienced the grace and power of God, learning in the process not to be ashamed of his weaknesses but to be content in them (12:10).

The above passages caution us against turning prayer into a simple practice that can become ritualized. Prayer is a mystery, for there is more to prayer than meets the eye. Because of sin, human knowledge of the good has been compromised (cf. Rom 1–2; 6–7). Thus, the Spirit needs to aid us in our prayers. Out of weakness, we could offer selfish prayers that request God to take from us what are actually blessings in our lives. For this reason, the notion that prayer is a means by which believers can impose upon God to grant their requests—a theology that has been popularized in prosperity gospel circles with phrases such as "name it and claim it," "believe it and receive it," "tap it and grab it"—should be deemed as unfaithful to the biblical witness. Paul teaches that not all prayer requests are granted by God.

This raises a question, then: why should believers pray since we do not know how we ought to pray or whether our prayer requests will be granted? Why heed Paul's admonishments to "pray without ceasing" (1 Thess 5:17) and to "persevere in prayer" (Rom 12:12; see also Col 4:2)? The evidence suggests that, for Paul, there is a God-given "peace" that overshadows

54. There is a history of interpreting Paul's words here as a reference to speaking in tongues. See, e.g., Käsemann, "Cry for Liberty," 122–37; Käsemann, *Commentary on Romans*, 241–42; Stendahl, "Paul at Prayer," 244. For a refutation of this position, see O'Brien, "Romans," 70–71.

55. The tradition of interceding angels in Jewish apocalyptic literature seems to lie behind this verse and Rom 8:34 (e.g., Tob 12:11–15; 1 En 9:3; 99:3, etc.). For further discussion of this tradition, see Moses, *Practices of Power*, 112–15; Moses, "Tangible Prayer," 118–49.

56. For detailed discussion of the various proposals concerning Paul's "thorn," see Thrall, *Critical and Exegetical*, 2.806–18.

believers when they present their requests to God (Phil 4:6–7), whether or not God grants the requests:.

> Do not worry about anything, but in everything by prayer and supplication with thanksgiving let your requests be made known to God. And the peace of God, which surpasses all understanding, will guard your hearts and your minds in Christ Jesus.

Paul pens these words while under arrest. He is unsure of whether, and when, he might be released to join the Philippians. He is unsure if God will even grant his and the Philippians' prayers for his deliverance (1:19). It seems that Paul is also unsure whether he will come out of this ordeal alive (1:21). Perhaps he has not known "how to pray as [he] ought" (Rom 8:26) as he weighs the benefits of being alive and of going to be with Christ (Phil 1:20–24). In fact, Paul does not know which of the two he prefers (1:22–23). Paul, then, likely toils in prayer in hopes that the Holy Spirit will shape his will to align with God's will.

Prison, treading in the shadow of death, and confusion about what God's will is are all good recipes for worry and despondency. And yet Paul rejoices (4:4) and keeps praying about everything with thanksgiving (4:6). The key to this kind of hope is the peace of God—one that surpasses all human understanding. And this peace is promised to all who pray, whenever they pray. God's peace "guards" the hearts and minds of believers, like an army guarding a base. Paul's claim that we "do not know how to pray as we ought" is both daunting and discouraging (Rom 8:26). It should shake every believer's confidence to approach God in prayer. Yet what should be the believer's response to the knowledge that our prayers are often out of line with God's will and that our prayers may not be granted? Paul replies, "Prayer!"

Bibliography

Adamson, Grant. "Letter from a Soldier in Pannonia." *Bulletin for the American Society of Papyrologists* 49 (2012) 79–94.

Allison, Robert W. "Let Women Be Silent in the Churches (1 Cor. 14:33b–36): What Did Paul Really Say, and What Did it Mean?" *JSNT* 32 (1988) 27–60.

Arzt, Peter. "The 'Epistolary Introductory Thanksgiving' in the Papyri and in Paul," *NovT* 36 (1994) 29–46.

Aune, David E. "Galatians 3:28 and the Problem of Equality in the Church and Society." In *From Judaism to Christianity: Tradition and Transition: A Festschrift for Thomas H. Tobin, S. J., on the Occasion of His Sixty-Fifth Birthday*, edited by Patricia Walters, 153–83. NovTSup 136. Leiden: Brill, 2010.

Barclay, John M. G. "Manna and the Circulation of Grace: A Study of 2 Corinthians 8:1–15." In *The Word Leaps the Gap: Essays and Scripture and Theology in Honor of Richard B. Hays,* edited by J. Ross Wagner, Christopher Kavin Rowe, and A. Katherine Grieb, 409–26. Grand Rapids: Eerdmans, 2008.

———. *Paul and the Gift.* Grand Rapids: Eerdmans, 2015.

Berger, K. "Apostelbrief und apostolische Rede. Zum Formular frühchristlicher Briefe." *ZNW* 65 (1974) 190–231.

Byrne, Brendan. *Romans.* Sacra Pagina 6. Collegeville, MN: Liturgical, 1996.

Collins, Ramond F. *First Corinthians.* Sacra Pagina 7. Collegeville, MN: Glazier/ Liturgical, 1999.

Davies, W. D., and Dale C. Allison. *A Critical and Exegetical Commentary on the Gospel According to Saint Matthew.* ICC 1. Edinburgh: T. & T. Clark, 1991.

Deissmann, Adolf. *Light from the Ancient East: The New Testament Illustrated by Recently Discovered Texts of the Greco-Roman World.* Rev. ed. London: Harper and Brothers, 1922.

Dippenaar, M. Christoffel. "Prayer and Epistolarity: The Function of Prayer in the Pauline Letter Structure." *Taiwan Journal of Theology* 16 (1994) 147–88.

Doty, William G. *Letters in Primitive Christianity.* Philadelphia: Fortress, 1973.

Eastman, Susan. *Recovering Paul's Mother Tongue: Language and Theology in Galatians.* Grand Rapids: Eerdmans, 2007.

Epp, Eldon J. *Junia: The First Woman Apostle.* Minneapolis: Fortress, 2005.

Fee, Gordon D. *The First Epistle to the Corinthians.* New International Commentary on the New Testament. Rev. ed. Grand Rapids: Eerdmans, 2014.

Friesen, Steven J. "Poverty in Pauline Studies: Beyond the So-Called New Consensus." *JSNT* 26 (2004) 323–61.

Gaventa, Beverly Roberts. *Our Mother Saint Paul.* Louisville: Westminster John Knox, 2007.

Harder, Gunther. *Paulus Und Das Gebet.* Gütersloh: Bertelsmann, 1939.

Hays, Richard B. *The Faith of Jesus Christ: The Narrative Substructure of Galatians 3:1–4:11.* 2nd ed. Biblical Resource Series. Grand Rapids: Eerdmans, 2002.

———. *First Corinthians.* Interpretation. Louisville: Westminster John Knox, 1997.

Heine, Susanne. "Diakoninnen-Frauen und Ämter in den ersten christlichen Jahrhunderten." *IKZ* 78 (1988) 213–27.

Hunt, A. S., and C. C. Edgar, trans. *Select Papyri: Private Documents.* Loeb Classical Library. Cambridge: Harvard University Press, 1932.

Jewett, Robert. "The Epistolary Thanksgiving and the Integrity of Philippians." *NovT* 12 (1970) 40–53.

Käsemann, Ernst. *Commentary on Romans.* Grand Rapids: Eerdmans, 1980.

———. "The Cry for Liberty in the Worship of the Church." In *Perspectives on Paul,* edited by Ernst Käsemann, 122–37. London: SCM, 1971.

Kovacs, Judith L., trans. and ed. *1 Corinthians: Interpreted by Early Christian Commentators.* The Church's Bible. Grand Rapids: Eerdmans, 2005.

Longenecker, Bruce. *Remember the Poor: Paul, Poverty, and the Greco-Roman World.* Grand Rapids: Eerdmans, 2010.

Longenecker, Richard N. "Prayer in the Pauline Letters." In *Into God's Presence: Prayer in the New Testament,* edited by Richard N. Longenecker, 203–27. Grand Rapids: Eerdmans, 2001.

Luz, Ulrich. *Matthew 8–20: A Commentary.* Hermeneia. Minneapolis: Fortress, 2001.

Martin, Dale B. *The Corinthian Body.* New Haven: Yale University Press, 1995.

Meeks, Wayne A. *The First Urban Christians: The Social World of the Apostle Paul*. 2nd ed. New Haven: Yale University Press, 2003.

Meggitt, Justin J. *Paul, Poverty, and Survival*. Studies of the New Testament and its World. Edinburgh: T. & T. Clark, 1998.

———. "Sources: Use, Abuse, Neglect: The Importance of Ancient Popular Culture." In *Christianity at Corinth*, edited by Edward Adams and David G. Horrell, 241–54. Louisville: Westminster John Knox, 2004.

Mitchell, Margaret M. "Paul's Letters to Corinth: The Interpretive Intertwining of Literary and Historical Reconstruction." In *Urban Religion in Roman Corinth: Interdisciplinary Approaches*, edited by Daniel N. Schowalter and Steven J. Friesen, 307–38. Harvard Theological Studies 53. Cambridge: Harvard University Press, 2005.

Moses, Robert Ewusie. *Practices of Power: Revisiting the Principalities and Powers in the Pauline Epistles*. Emerging Scholars. Minneapolis: Fortress, 2014.

———. "Tangible Prayer in Early Judaism and Early Christianity." *JSP* 25 (2015) 118–49.

Munro, Winsome. "Women, Text, and the Canon: The Strange Case of 1 Corinthians 14:33–35." *BTB* 18 (1988) 26–31.

O'Brien, Peter Thomas. *Introductory Thanksgivings in the Letters of Paul*. Leiden: Brill, 1977.

———. "Romans 8:26–27: A Revolutionary Approach to Prayer." *RTR* 46 (1987) 65–73.

Odell-Scott, David W. "Let the Women Speak in Church: An Egalitarian Interpretation of 1 Cor 14:33b–36." *BTB* 13 (1983) 90–93.

Reed, James T. "Are Paul's Thanksgivings 'Epistolary'?" *JSNT* 61 (1996) 87–99.

Sanders, Jack T. "The Transition from Opening Epistolary Thanksgiving to Body in the Letters of the Pauline Corpus." *JBL* 81 (1962) 348–62.

Schmiedel, Paul W. *Der Briefe an die Thessalonischer und an die Korinther*. Tübingen: Mohr Siebeck, 1892.

Schubert, Paul. *Form and Function of the Pauline Thanksgivings*. Berlin: Alfred Töpelmann, 1939.

———. "Form and Function of the Pauline Thanksgivings." *ZNW* 20 (1939) 71–82.

Sherwin-White, A. N. *The Letters of Pliny: A Historical and Social Commentary*. Oxford: Clarendon, 1966.

Stendahl, Krister. "Paul at Prayer." *Int* 34 (1980) 240–49.

Stichele, Caroline Vander. "Is Silence Golden? Paul and Women's Speech in Corinth." *LS* 20 (1995) 241–53.

Strack, Hermann L., and Paul Billerbeck. *Kommenter zum Neuen Testament aus Talmud und Midrasch*. Munich: C. H. Beck'sche, 1922.

Theissen, Gerd. *The Social Setting of Pauline Christianity*. Philadelphia: Fortress, 1982.

Thiselton, Anthony C. *The First Epistle to the Corinthians*. NIGTC. Grand Rapids: Eerdmans, 2000.

Thomson, William G. *Matthew's Advice to a Divided Community: Mt. 17.22–18, 35*. Rome: Biblical Institute, 1970.

Thrall, Margaret. *A Critical and Exegetical Commentary on the Second Epistle to the Corinthians*. ICC. London: T. & T. Clark, 1994–2000.

Weiss, Johannes. *Der erste Korintherbrief*. 2nd rev. ed. Göttingen: Vandenhoeck & Ruprecht, 1910.

White, John L. *Light from Ancient Letters*. Foundations and Facets. Philadelphia: Fortress, 1986.

Wiles, Gordon P. *Paul's Intercessory Prayers: The Significance of the Intercessory Prayer in Passages in the Letters of St. Paul*. Cambridge: Cambridge University Press, 1974.

Windisch, Hans. *Zweite Korintherbrief*. KEK. Göttingen: Vandenhoeck & Ruprecht, 1924.

Wintermute, O. S., trans. *Jubilees*. Vol. 2 in *The Old Testament Pseudepigrapha*, edited by James H. Charlesworth. New York: Doubleday, 1985.

Young, Frances M., and David F. Ford. *Meaning and Truth in 2 Corinthians*. Grand Rapids: Eerdmans, 1988.

Zahn, Theodor. *Der Brief des Paulus an die Römer*. 3rd ed. Leipzig: Erlangen, 1925.

Painting Hope: Formational Hues of Paul's Spiritual Warfare Language in 2 Corinthians 10–13[1]

LISA BOWENS

The painter shows or allows the seeing of "something" that without him, without his intervention, would not be seen. He manifests through his work a possibility of seeing that would otherwise remain latent. In other words, painting is an art that reveals or unveils the world from an angle that the world itself does not present to us. . . . Painting allows us to see that which without it would never be seen.

—MARCEL PAQUET[2]

Writing is the painting of the voice.

—VOLTAIRE

1. It is my pleasure to offer this essay in honor of Susan Eastman, who opened my eyes to the layered dimensions of apocalyptic thought in Paul. Susan, a brilliant Pauline scholar, combines this brilliance with pastoral sensitivity, insight, and a deep love for the church. She is my former professor, whom I am now privileged to call a colleague and friend.

2. Paquet, *Botero*, 23.

Introduction: Painting a Graphic Portrait

THE FIRST QUOTATION ABOVE, taken from Marcel Paquet's insightful discussion regarding the work of the Latin American artist Botero, acknowledges the power of painting and its ability to reveal or unveil a perspective of the world that would otherwise remain hidden. The painter discloses realities that are concealed but nevertheless real. In doing so, the artist provides a new way of seeing because she opens up the world from a different angle and reveals the imperceptible, offering a revelation which differs from the world's own view. Voltaire's words bring together the power of writing and the power of painting so eloquently described by Paquet. Writing, like painting, uncovers, reveals, and allows the seeing of something not previously envisioned.[3] Writing bestows sight to what is often unseen, providing glimpses into realities hidden from view, and vocalizes the silence by granting the power and ability of speech to say what is often unspoken. Utilizing military language in 2 Cor 10–13 Paul paints a graphic portrait for his Corinthian audience that *reveals* and *unveils* the world to them from a perspective that differs from their own. He repeatedly attempts to make plain to them what they could not otherwise perceive without his intervention—the reality of a cosmic contest and the dangerous power behind the emissaries in their congregation (11:13–15). On the surface, all that the Corinthians see are eloquent, persuasive preachers (11:4, 6), but Paul's martial imagery beckons them to look beneath the surface and see that a cosmic battle is underway. His language unveils the Corinthians' participation in this ongoing struggle and that the power behind the emissaries derives from a different spirit (11:4, 13–15).

The apostle's martial imagery is significant, for it points to God's war in and for the world to rescue humanity and the cosmos from anti-God powers.[4] In other words, Paul's portraiture depicts the existence of spiritual warfare with vivid and deep resonances, tracing an epistemic, cosmic, and anthropological landscape. At the same time Paul paints this picture of intense combat he augments the picture by depicting himself as unqualified for the task of warfare. This unexpected portrayal of himself, which I term antiphonal dissonance, in which he renders himself both as an equipped soldier and a deficient participant, reinforces his emphasis upon the spiri-

---

3. In tyrannical regimes, written propaganda seeks to conceal truth rather than reveal and uncover it. For the purposes of this essay we will focus on the positive aspect of writing and its ability to enlighten. For further discussion of political forms of communication and their implications for Christian life, see chapter 3 by Charles Campbell and chapter 13 by Douglas Harink in the present volume.

4. For the language of anti-God powers see Martyn, *Galatians*, 370–73.

tual dimension of the war and God's power in it. This essay argues that Paul's martial imagery 1) occurs throughout chapters 10–13 and not only in 10:3–6; 2) recapitulates warfare rhetoric while simultaneously subverting it; and 3) aims to unveil an embattled reality. In light of Paul's extensive use of martial language in these chapters, what might it mean for us as pastors, ministers, and laypeople to read Paul with a spiritual warfare lens? Can this language be formative and constructive for believers today or should it be discarded due to its violent undertones? Taking the former stance, the fourth prong of this essay's thesis describes the constructive formational aspect of this warfare language and its ability to shape in a positive manner the perceptions and perspectives of those who dare to hear the apostle's voice and to see the world that he captures with his words.[5]

The Layered Contours of Martial Imagery in 2 Corinthians 10:3–6 and Mind Language in 4:4; 10:5; and 11:3[6]

The military terms in 10:3–6 are well-known: *strateuō*, "wage war" (10:3);[7] *hopla*, "weapons" (10:4);[8] *strateia*, "warfare" (10:4);[9] *ochyrōma*, "stronghold" (10:4);[10] *hupsōma*, "exalted entity, raised entity" (10:5);[11] *aichmalōtizō*, "capture" (10:5);[12] and *hetoimō echontes*, "standing ready."[13] However, the connection of this language to the mind or thoughts and the persistence of this martial terminology in the rest of the letter have not been sufficiently exam-

---

5. Regarding the integrity of 2 Corinthians some interpreters opt for a two-letter theory (chapters 1–9 and chapters 10–13), whereas others posit as many as five. Our discussion will assume that the chapters belong to the same letter, with chapters 10–13 exhibiting a heightened tone with regard to military imagery. For a thorough analysis of the various partition theories see Harris, *Second Epistle*, 8–51.

6. All translations of primary texts are the author's unless otherwise noted.

7. Luke 3:14; 1 Cor 9:7; 2 Tim 2:4; Arrian, *Anabasis of Alexander*, 7.8.3.

8. Asclepiodotus, *Tactics*, 12.10; 12:11; Arrian, *Anabasis of Alexander*, 7.10.2; 7.11.7; Dionysius of Halicarnassus 6.27.3; 6.29.4; Onasander, *The General*, 42.20.

9. Xenophon, *Agesilaus*, 6.3; Dionysius Halicarnassus 6.26.1; 6.29.1.

10. Xenophon, *Hellenica*, 3.2.3; Polybius 4.6.3; Ps 88:40 LXX; Prov 10:29; 21:22; Nahum 3:12, 14; 1 Macc 1:2; 14:42; 2 Macc 8:30; 10:15; Philo, *De Confusione Linguarum*, 129–30.

11. *Hupsōma* is a debated term. See Malherbe, "Antisthenes and Odysseus," 144–45; Thrall, *Second Epistle*, 612–13.

12. Aeneas, *Tacticus*, 4.11; Diodorus Siculus 13.24; 14.37.3; Plutarch, *Moralia*, 233c; Onasander, *The General*, 35.4; Josephus, *Ant.* 10.153; 1 Macc 5:13; 10:3; in reference to captives see *Plutarch's Lives*, Book 5, Pompey, 45.4.

13. Polybius 2.34.2; Philo, *Leg. Ad Gaium* 259; Dionysius Halicarnassus 8.17.1. See also Brink, "General's Exhortation," 191–201, 74–89.

ined.[14] With these terms Paul asserts that he does not wage war according to the flesh and that his weapons are mighty in God (10:4). His language points to a realm beyond the human sphere and his divine weapons destroy "reasonings," "strongholds," and "every high or exalted entity," and they *capture every mind or thought (noēma)*" for the obedience of Christ. Paul's focus on *noēma* in 10:5 and in other parts of the letter (4:4; 11:3) indicates that minds and thoughts are central to the conflict.

Earlier in 4:4 Paul states that the god of this age blinds the minds (*noēmata*) of unbelievers from the gospel. The phrase "god of this age" refers to Satan and the word *noēma*, which occurs in 10:5 and appears also in 4:4, suggests that Paul connects the minds that are blinded by the god of this age with the minds or thoughts that his divine weapons capture.[15] In other words, the minds being blinded in 4:4 are included in the minds the apostle's weapons rescue in 10:5. Hence, the "spirit-ual" dimension of the war—Paul fights against a spiritual power, Satan, the god of this age, and this enemy's tactics to blind and deceive. Paul's divine mission comprises rescuing the unbelievers in 4:4 and his Corinthian audience since they, too, are in danger as he explicitly states in 11:3: "I am afraid that as the serpent deceived Eve with his craftiness, your minds [*noēmata*] may be led astray from sincerity and purity which is in Christ." Just as unbelievers' minds experience blindness from the god of this age, the Corinthians' minds encounter the danger of being led astray through deceit. The use of *noēma* language coupled with martial imagery in 10:5 illustrates the epistemological dimension of the conflict.

The apostle's depiction of the mind as susceptible to the spirit world aligns with some Jewish traditions. In the book of Jubilees, after he destroys the temple of idols and moves with his father to Haran, Abram prays:

My God, my God, God most High,

You alone are my God.

You have created everything;

Everything that was and has been is the product of your hands.

You and your lordship I have chosen.

Save me from the power of the evil spirits who rule the
thoughts of people's minds.

14. I argue for this perspective more fully in my monograph (Bowens, *An Apostle*), from which some material in the following paragraphs have been taken. See also Bowens, "Investigating," 3–15.

15. The phrase "god of this age" denotes Satan and is similar to other expressions used in the New Testament to refer to Satan such as "the ruler of this world" in John 12:31 and 16:11 (cf. 1 Cor 2:6, 8). This language also corresponds to the apostle's view of the present age as evil (Gal 1:4).

> May they not mislead me from following you, my God.
>
> Do establish me and my posterity forever.
>
> May we not go astray from now until eternity.[16]

Here Abram acknowledges the power of evil spirits to rule humanity's minds and thoughts. The anthropological perspective of this text is that human beings are vulnerable to outside forces that desire to control them and lead them away from following God's path. This prayer of deliverance, which asks for God's assistance, recognizes God's power to deliver and rescue humanity from these evil beings. At the same time, this human susceptibility to evil forces does not negate human agency, for Abram declares that he has chosen God's lordship. Thus, the prayer illustrates the existence of an epistemological, cosmological, and anthropological nexus in which divine and human agency are dynamically interrelated.

In 1QH[a], an ancient Jewish text from Qumran also known as the Hodayot, the Teacher declares God to be a God of knowledge and recognizes the holy spirit as a source of knowledge. He writes, "And I, the Maskil, I know you, my God, by the spirit which you have placed in me. With faithful devotion have I listened to your wonderful secret counsel. By your holy spirit you have opened up knowledge within me through the mystery of your wisdom."[17] Here the writer asserts that he knows God because of the spirit God has placed within him. As Jason Maston writes, "God intervenes in the human's life and not only alters one's being, but also actually imparts a new spirit, his own spirit, that leads the human into knowledge and teaches him how to obey God."[18] For the writer of this ancient text, the holy spirit provides knowledge and insight, which cannot be achieved by a human being but must be granted by God.[19] A few lines later, the writer understands God to be the source of insight: "What can I say unless you open my mouth? How can I understand unless you give me insight?"[20] Here the Teacher's reliance upon God's granting of understanding and his inability to have knowledge apart from God's assistance comes to the forefront.

These passages demonstrate a relationship between anthropology, cosmology, and epistemology. Whether it is evil spirits that rule people's minds,

---

16. 12:19b–20. All translations of Jubilees are from VanderKam, *Book of Jubilees.*

17. 1QH[a] 20.14–16. Hebrew text, column, and line enumeration used for this translation comes from Schuller and Newsom, *Hodayot,* but all translations are the author's unless otherwise noted.

18. Maston, *Divine and Human,* 106.

19. My translation takes the phrase "[b]y your holy spirit" to begin a new sentence, whereas Maston, *Divine and Human Agency,* believes that it modifies "I listened" (116).

20. 1QH[a] 20:35c–36.

a holy spirit who provides understanding, or humanity's dependence upon God for knowledge, these excerpts foreground an epistemic element to the relationship between the human and the suprahuman. Within this religious context, Paul's statements about the god of this age blinding unbelievers' minds as well as the apostle's participation in God's mission to rescue minds is understandable. As Abram saw God as the one who could save minds from the powers of evil, so too does Paul, who views himself as fighting alongside God to liberate those deceived and blinded by the enemy.

Tracing the Continuity of Martial Terminology in 2 Corinthians 11–13

In the previous section, we discussed the presence of warfare terminology in 2 Cor 10:3–6. However, Paul's martial imagery does not end with these verses but persists in the final chapters. "Standing ready" (*hetoimō echontes*) reappears in 12:14 and can denote military preparedness. In 13:2 Paul employs the term *pheidomai*, which can refer to sparing persons or things in war.[21] In 11:8, Paul utilizes the word *opsōnion*, pointing to the pay soldiers receive or a soldier's rations (cf. 1 Cor 9:7). *Ekkoptō* and *aphormē* appear in 11:12 and allude to military combat. *Ekkoptō* means "to beat off, to cut off, destroy," whereas *aphormē* can refer to an opportunity or base of operations.[22] With such vocabulary, the apostle insists that he will "cut off the opportunity" of the opponents who have come into the Corinthian congregation. Although Paul uses these terms in other letters (for example, 1 Cor 7:28) with no martial connotation, the specific martial context of this portion of the Corinthian correspondence, especially highlighted by the way he begins chapter 10, suggests that here the military resonances of these words should not be dismissed.[23]

Paul's depiction of himself as engaged in military action continues in his hardship catalog (11:23–33), a list similar to the adversities encountered by generals and soldiers during military training and combat.[24] For example,

21. Herodotus 1.80.19; Polybius 20.5.9; Josephus, BJ, 1.352. Paul uses *pheidomai* in 12:6, but the context there does not suggest a military connotation.

22. *Ekkoptō*: Diodorus of Sicily, 14.115.6; Plutarch, *Caesar*, 26.2.11; Xenophon, *Hell.* 7.4.26; *aphormē*: Polybius, *The Histories of Polybius*, 3.69.8–13; Philo, *Flaccus* 47; Dionysius of Halicarnassus, *The Roman Antiquities*, 6.25.3; Onasander, *The General*, 42.15; Cassius Dio, 37.52.3. Barnett, *Second Epistle*, also notes that *aphormē* is a military term for a base from which to launch a military operation (515, n. 18).

23. For the martial imagery in Romans see Gaventa, "Rhetoric of Violence," 61–75.

24. Sallust, *Bell. Jug.* 85.29–30, 33–34; Arrian, *Anabasis*, 7.10.1–2; Onasander, *The General*, 10.5. Other hardship catalogues in 2 Corinthians occur in 4:8–12; 6:4–10; 12:10.

in this list the apostle refers to being stoned, to suffering from hunger and thirst, and to enduring the cold, all of which appear in hardships encountered on or in training for the battlefield.[25] Furthermore, Paul closes the epistle with the terms *katartisis* (preparation) in 13:9 and *katartizō* (training, equipping, preparation) in 13:11, which can also have martial overtones.[26] In these verses, Paul calls upon the Corinthians to recognize their role in the conflict, and he prays for their preparation. Thus, in his use of martial language throughout these final chapters Paul describes himself as fighting alongside God and against Satan and demonic powers (11:4, 14–15; 12:7), and he portrays himself as standing ready, sparing no one, receiving a soldier's pay, and cutting off the enemy's assault. His words paint a solemn portrait for his audience.[27]

Yet in the middle of his sustained martial portrait Paul inserts two surprising aberrations. In 11:6 the apostle writes, "And even if I am untrained in speech, I am not untrained in knowledge but in every way and in all things this has been revealed to you." Also, in 11:29 he asks, "Who is weak? And am I not weak?" These statements alone are not necessarily alarming but the astonishing nature of such remarks arise from the broader context since Paul, who makes a point to depict a cosmic clash and to emphasize his role in the cosmic struggle, admits his deficient speech skills and his weak state, admissions that do not bode well for one who seeks to convince his audience of his military prowess in this cosmic fight.

In his military treatise on generals, Onasander includes the ability to speak well as one of the necessary qualities. The following quotations represent this viewpoint:

> We must choose a general, not because of noble birth as priests are chosen, nor because of wealth as the superintendents of the gymnasia, but because he is temperate, self-restrained, vigilant, frugal, hardened to labour, alert, free from avarice, neither too young nor too old, indeed a father of children if possible, a ready speaker (*hikanon legein*), and a man with a good reputation.[28]

---

25. Arrian, *Anabasis*, 7.10.1–2; Onasander, *The General*, 10.5; Sallust, *Bellum Jugurtha*, 85.33–34. See Bowens, *Apostle in Battle*, for discussion of specific texts. For different views than what is presented here consult Fitzgerald, *Cracks in an Earthen Vessel*, and Glancy, "Boasting of Beatings," 99–135.

26. Diodorus Siculus, *Bibliotheca Historica*, 12.84.2, 13.38.5, 13.70.2, 13.80.5, 13.97.1, 16.16.3, 19.61.5, 19.62.8; Polybius, *Histories*, 1.47.6, 3.95.2; Plutarch, *Alex.* 7.1; Herodotus, 9.66. So also Brink, "General's Exhortation," 84.

27. See also the discussion of *ekphrasis* (word paintings) in Mitchell, *Heavenly Trumpet*, 101–4, 118–21. My thanks to George Parsenios for alerting me to this source.

28. Onasander, *The General*, 10.1.

A ready speaker (*legein d'hikanon*); for I believe that the greatest benefit can accrue from the work of a general only through this gift. . . . No city at all will put an army in the field without generals nor choose a general who lacks the ability to make an effective speech (*oude dicha tou dunasthai legein hairesetai stratēgon*).[29]

As Onasander indicates, a common expectation of an effective general included the gift of oration. Paul's acknowledgement of his lack of training in speech is significant in light of the way he has represented his martial credentials. Paul disrupts his military portrait by admitting that one of the important attributes a general should have he lacks. This admission, however, serves the apostle's purpose, for from the beginning of chapter 10 Paul states that power belongs to God, not him, in this cosmic struggle. Consequently, his inability to speak well indicates that the strategy for the conflict is not about him, his eloquence, or his lack thereof, but is about God who ultimately triumphs over all opposition.

Additionally, Paul's declaration that he is weak (11:29) appears at the end of his list of struggles on the battlefield in which he highlights the bodily price of this cosmic conflict. Akira Satake mentions the possibility that the Corinthians may have perceived the apostle's hardship catalog (11:23–33) as a sign of his heroism.[30] That Paul may have been identified as a hero by the Corinthians at this point in the letter accentuates the next statement he makes regarding his weakness, for it disrupts his military cavalcade in a sobering way. The last thing a soldier general wants to concede is weakness. Once again, Onasander sheds light on Paul's statements through his assertion that weakness is a despised quality in a military leader, a characteristic that is displayed when a general begins an expedition and then ceases to follow through with it: "For while everyone laughs at folly and rashness, we despise weakness, and the enemy—whoever they may be—even if they experience no harm, have good reason to hate the would-be invaders, as men who have not lacked the will but lacked the ability to put a matter through."[31] Onasander indicates that weakness, in the context of martial life, was considered a loathsome quality and, therefore, it was not a deficiency a general would have admitted openly. Weakness meant a "lack of ability" to follow through. Also, Onasander insists that generals should not be too young or too old. If one is too old, then physical weakness may hinder the fulfillment of his duties: "The old man is weak, and neither [the young man or the old

---

29. Ibid., 10.13, 16; cf. Cicero, *Philippic*, 4.11; Caesar, *The Gallic War*, 2.21.

30. Satake, "Schritt für Schritt," 289.

31. Onasander, *The General*, 4.4.

man] is free from danger, the young man lest he err through reckless daring, the older lest he neglect something through physical weakness."[32]

For Onasander, bodily strength is important, which is why old men are not good choices for generals due to their frailty. Onasander's comments affirm that important traits for a general are physical strength and stamina. These selections demonstrate that weakness, whether defined as lack of ability or as a weakened physical state, was considered a liability. For Paul to claim weakness, then, is unusual on several levels.

Rather than seeing his hardship catalogue as an indication of hero status or as a signifier of his strength and endurance, Paul calls these experiences weaknesses (*astheneia*), underscoring his perception of his bodily suffering, for this list is about human weakness, not human strength. Moreover, his afflictions reflect the sufferings of his Lord and his body becomes "a sign of Christ crucified."[33] The apostle links his battle-ridden body with that of Jesus when he writes that Jesus was crucified out of weakness (*astheneias*) (13:4), thereby connecting the weaknesses he experiences with his Lord's crucifixion. Even his anguished queries in 11:29—"Who is weak? And am I not weak?"—convey such a relationship. To claim weakness, then, simultaneously subverts expectations for a general and signals that this is a different kind of warfare. Paul sees himself in the next phrase of 13:4 as well. As Jesus lives by the power of God, so too does the apostle. Susceptible to the rigors of the conflict, his body endures through God's power that tents over him and preserves him.[34]

What is more, Paul's willingness to describe a supernatural battle with terminology from the human martial arena but at the same time to disrupt this description speaks volumes. Spiritual warfare includes humanity, both believers and unbelievers, but human abilities and strength do not determine the outcome. While human skill and strength carry significance in human wars, in the battle that Paul describes and in which he takes part, these qualities do not carry weight. In fact, Paul's description of himself as inept undercuts the emissaries in Corinth who do seem to believe that these attributes matter, signifying their misunderstanding of the cosmic struggle underway and their transference of human rules to the cosmic battlefield. These emissaries and their Corinthian followers give undue import to eloquence and strength, indicating that they operate in the old age schema. Paul, in disrupting the martial résumé of the general, exemplifies antiphonal

32. Ibid., 1.9 (modified translation).

33. Eastman, *Recovering Paul's*, 183.

34. Following Young and Ford, *Meaning and Truth*, I use the image of a tent that is highlighted in their translation of 2 Cor 12:9b: "Gladly then will I take a pride in weaknesses, *that the power of Christ may be pitched like a tent over me*" (274, emphasis mine).

dissonance: his subversive speech illustrates that the struggle underway no longer operates in the old age paradigm. The intensified struggle between the old and the new age means that the contours of the battlefield and the strategies of the conflict have been transformed. Paul's lack of credentials in speech and his admission of weakness bolster his qualifications in God's economy, for God, as Paul informed the Corinthians in earlier correspondence, chooses the weak things of the world to shame the strong (1 Cor 1:27). By extension, God uses the inarticulate to silence the eloquent.

Christian Formation through Martial Imagery in Broad and Fine Strokes

Can Paul's military language positively shape believers today? Is a spiritual warfare lens appropriate, can it be applied in a modern context, or should it be abandoned? Several ways exist in which we might answer such questions, but to do so we must revisit the text.

In 11:20 Paul describes the emissaries' actions with the following language: *katadouloō* (enslave), *katesthiō* (devour or exploit), *lambanō* (take in by deceit or violence, take advantage of), *epairō* (lift oneself over), and *derō* (strike or beat). In short, these expressions depict an atmosphere in the Corinthian congregation of domination, oppression, exploitation, and subjugation. For Paul, such actions exhibited by these so-called *diakonoi dikaiosynēs* (servants of righteousness), which the Corinthians tolerated so well and originate from a different spirit (11:4), denote a way of being that is antithetical to the gospel. By inserting martial imagery into these chapters Paul inserts resistance language in order to oppose those who would oppress God's people. For believers today the apostle's warfare imagery provides a language of resistance against oppression. Thus, the martial terminology in these chapters is about resisting oppression, not producing it.

Indeed, Paul's statements in these verses reveal the struggles of a pastor trying to protect a congregation as a parent protects a child (11:1–3; cf. 12:14–15). The gospel, Paul proclaims, is liberating, and any gospel that denies this reality is no gospel at all but rather something "different" (11:4). The apostle intervenes in the lives of his congregants by helping them see that they are being exploited and by urging them to resist. Likewise, pastoral leaders need to encourage those entrusted in their care to resist oppression—whatever form that oppression may take, and pastors must aid them in the process. Martial terminology, then, depicts God's liberating movement into the human sphere, for God refuses to abandon humanity to

enslaving and oppressive powers. Like Paul, believers are called to participate in God's liberative mission.

Furthermore, Paul's language in these chapters does not justify human war, although such language has been used in the past to do so and
with disastrous consequences. Despite such misappropriations, however,
the apostle's insistence that his weapons are not *kata sarka* (according to
flesh), but mighty in God, asserts that human weapons do not pertain to
the war he describes even though the human body suffers in this spiritual
engagement. In Corinth, the supernatural battle involves the mind, the
body, and the proclamation of the gospel.[35] The reality of struggle appears
in the opposition to the gospel as indicated by the apostle's hardship catalogues (11:23–33). His body becomes the canvas that vividly and graphically displays his war wounds. To borrow the language of John Barclay, the
apostle's body becomes "the critical site of resistance."[36] For example, Paul's
use of *errabdisthēn* in 11:25 highlights imperial resistance to the gospel
since *rhabdizō* means to be beaten with rods and was a notable Roman
punishment. Although Roman citizens were usually excused from this
penalty, there is evidence that Roman citizens did receive this sentence,
and to these instances Paul adds his own testimony.[37] By utilizing martial
imagery Paul proclaims that the liberating gospel he preaches faces ob-
struction and resistance, and he alerts us to the reality of antagonism to the
gospel message. This viewpoint resonates with many believers today who
suffer persecution and even martyrdom for their Christian faith. Those
who proclaim the word must be prepared for challenge from all sorts of
authorities, including the government.

Additionally, this warfare terminology is neither about dominating or
killing human enemies nor about a Christian triumphalism that says "we're
right, you're wrong, God's on our side." Rather, Paul fights from a position
of weakness, a place of dependence, not entitlement. The cosmic conflict
demonstrates to believers the fragility of humanity and the need to depend
on God. This stance of weakness shields us from pride and helps us to see a
common weakness—namely, susceptibility to evil—that binds all humanity.

35. To say that this cosmic conflict involves the mind and the body is not to posit an
anthropological dualism, such as the mind vs. the body. Instead, Paul's focus on both
underscores a holistic assault.

36. Barclay, *Paul and the Gift*, 505.

37. Acts 16:19–24; Cicero, *The Verrine Orations*, 2.5.139–140; Josephus, BJ, 2.308,
Plutarch, *Caesar*, 39.2. Although Paul does not explicitly mention his Roman citizen-
ship in his letters, many commentators assume the veracity of Acts regarding this point.
For example, Furnish, *II Corinthians*; Harris, *Second Epistle*; Martin, *2 Corinthians*. But
see the important discussion in Barreto, *Ethnic Negotiations*, 139–80.

Paul highlights that Satan blinds unbelievers and can deceive believers, which underscores everyone's vulnerability. Such recognition compels compassion and understanding for the other.

As noted above, Paul focuses on the mind and thoughts in these chapters and, by doing so, provides us with a glimpse into one of the focal areas of the cosmic conflict. To combat the deception taking place in Corinth, Paul re-"minds" the Corinthians of their identity in Christ by re-"minding" them of the gospel they received in the past and their previous experience with the Spirit (11:4). He also affirms who they are in the present and that God is still powerfully at work in them (13:3). Like the Corinthians, believers today have to be re-"minded" of who they are and to whom they belong. Society often imposes contrary identities upon believers, forcing them to find their identities in careers, money, success, political parties, and even in denominations, but the cross remains the definitive source of identity formation.

Likewise, a major concern of Paul's discussion centers upon the Corinthians' adherence to a different gospel (11:4) through deception (11:3). Today, the church faces similar struggles with the appearance of "different gospels" vying for reception among the faithful. Such "gospels" range from attaching the appellation Messiah or Savior to a political leader to proclaiming that Jesus died so that all would be millionaires. Such "gospels" are not good news at all but evidence of deception, and Paul's martial imagery points to the necessity of active defiance of any news that purports to be the gospel but is really *kata sarka* (according to flesh).

Equally important, the apostle's martial imagery exposes the myth of human autonomy. One of the oft-repeated critiques of Paul's cosmological language is that it is no longer an option for moderns, especially in the age of smartphones, Twitter, and all of the technological and medical advances of our time. But a quick glimpse at the news or the scanning of a magazine article demonstrates that with all the technological advances that permeate our societies, hatred, poverty, racism, sexism, and other ills still exist. Paul's martial imagery depicts a humanity that is up against forces with which it cannot contend alone. As the apostle well understood anti-God powers are also anti-human, and these forces use human beings to engage in activity opposed to God's redemptive will for the world. The apostle's repeated emphasis on God's power, not his human strength, as well as the antiphonal dissonance he exhibits by characterizing himself as weak and an ineffective speaker, underscore the need for dependence on God not human vessels.

At the same time the apostle accentuates God's power, he highlights the interrelationship between human and divine agency, for Paul has weapons that are mighty through God, and his sufferings display the power of

God. Similarly today, believers cooperate with God's actions in the world by proclaiming the liberating gospel of Jesus Christ. A contemporary example of the dynamic correlation of divine and human agency comes to the fore in Martin Luther King Jr.'s essay, "Paul's Letter to American Christians," in which he takes on the persona of the apostle to address believers in the United States. In the following excerpt, he accentuates a divine-human partnership. He writes,

> May I just say a word to those of you who are the victims of the evil system of segregation. You must continue to work passionately and vigorously for your God-given and constitutional rights. It would be both cowardly and immoral for you patiently to accept injustice. . . . But as you continue your righteous protest always be sure that you struggle with Christian methods and Christian weapons. Be sure that the means you employ are as pure as the end you seek. Never succumb to the temptation of becoming bitter. As you press on for justice, be sure to move with dignity and discipline, using love as your chief weapon. Let no man pull you so low that you hate him. . . . Even if physical death is the price that some must pay to free their children from psychological death, then nothing could be more Christian. . . . The end of life is not to be happy nor to achieve pleasure or avoid pain, but to do the will of God, come what may.[38]

King's letter brings together human participation with God's liberating war for humanity. He echoes Paul's understanding of Christian weapons and emphasizes the need for believers to take part in God's call for righteousness. The human and the divine cooperate to reveal and enact God's emancipating purpose in the world.[39]

Paul's use of martial imagery is "reality depicting" language, portraying the "real world" where the presence of inimical powers exist, which seek to devour and destroy all that God has created.[40] Paul's own testimony to his afflictions bear witness that the life of one who follows a crucified Messiah is a cruciform existence filled with pain, struggle, and anguish (see also Gorman, chapter 1 of the present volume). Jesus's death was a violent one,

---

38. King, "Paul's Letter," 131–32.

39. In *Becoming the Gospel*, Michael Gorman's description of the *missio Dei* captures this partnership well: God "is seeking not just to save 'souls' to take to heaven some day, but to restore and save the created order: individuals, communities, nations, the environment, the world, the cosmos. This God calls the people of God assembled in the name of Christ—who was the incarnation of the divine mission—to participate in this *missio Dei*, to discern what God is up to in the world, and to join in" (53).

40. The expression "reality depicting" comes from Soskice, *Metaphor*, 145, 148.

for he was crucified by the hand of the Roman Empire. One can assume that this fact was not lost upon the apostle. To follow a Lord who succumbs to death at the hands of the Romans is to follow a Lord who enters into a reality in which spiritual and political rulers often intertwine with dangerous consequences (1 Cor 2:6, 8). But Paul assures the Corinthians and us that Jesus was crucified out of weakness but lives by the power of God (2 Cor 13:4). God's power, despite the level of opposition, whether human or cosmic, always prevails.

In sum, Paul appropriates martial terms from the human arena, but he arguably destabilizes this language in four ways: 1) by applying it to a cosmic war, he makes it clear that human weapons do not apply; 2) by depicting himself as a weak, unqualified general, he relativizes human skill; 3) by employing it to describe satanic powers and the emissaries' false gospel, he provides language that resists and challenges oppressive entities; and 4) by depicting God as the ultimate victorious general behind the warfare, he directs our focus on the all-powerful God who fights with a Messiah crucified out of weakness, indicating that this warfare language is not about destruction but instead about hope.[41] Paul's martial language paints a counter-portrait of rescue from the cosmic powers who are creating the abusive atmosphere in the Corinthian congregation and assaulting all of humanity.

The apostle's military imagery ultimately paints a portrait of hope, for God has not abandoned humanity to powers that enslave, oppress, and devour. This warfare language not only exposes the fallacy of human autonomy but also portends the end of human domination of each other. It proclaims that God is at work in the world, freeing, rescuing, and redeeming God's creation. Such language heralds that the new age has broken into the old and that a divine interruption of the demonic is taking place, an interruption that will prevail. And this is a message that forms and shapes believers' lives and ministries, providing critical hope in this present evil age (Gal 1:4).

Paul, War, and Monet

In 1886 Guy de Maupassant published his eyewitness account of Monet at Étretat:

"The artist walked along the beach, followed by children carrying five or six canvases representing the same subject at different times of the day and with different effects. He took them up and put them aside by turns according to changes in the sky and

---

41. For different perspectives than what is presented here see Roetzel, "Language," 77–99; Lampe "Can Words."

shadows." Monet painted the dramatically arched projection in the cliff at Étretat six times from this angle: twice during each of three visits to the Normandy coast in 1883, 1885, and 1886. He refined the pictures in his studio.[42]

Maupassant's observations of Monet shed light on Paul's use of martial imagery in 2 Cor 10–13. Like Monet's repeated return to the same subject, Paul revisits again and again in these chapters the existence of cosmic warfare through his recurrent use of military terms. The purpose of Monet's return was to paint the same subject at "different times of the day and with different effects." Paul, too, returns to the same subject painting a picture of cosmic warfare for the Corinthians in its various contours. This warfare, Paul insists, involves both the body and the mind, both the human and the suprahuman. "Now is the day of salvation," Paul declares in 2 Cor 6:2. Yet it is clear that in this day of salvation a battle still rages on. The existence of the battle is vividly displayed upon Paul's body and in the contest for the minds of believers and unbelievers. Like Monet who wanted to paint his subject at different times of the day, Paul sketches for his audience a view of the battle from several vantage points. Apostles and believers are on the battlefield fighting at the same time they live in the day of salvation.[43] For Paul the "different times of day" have intersected: the day of salvation is also the day of battle. Battle and victory occur simultaneously, for at this present moment one cannot exist without the other.

There is something provocative about looking at the same subject at different times of the day because one does perceive the subject differently. New shadows and new perspectives arise. Paul acknowledges that the battle he portrays affects the *sarx* (flesh) and the *noēma* (mind), the unbeliever and the believer, even the entire cosmos, but it is still the same struggle, the same contest, and the same subject. Yet the shadow of the cross looms large over all of Paul's depictions, including the canvas of his body, signifying God's indefatigable power to triumph over all evil—blindness, deception, affliction, and the ultimate enemy, death.[44]

42. This paragraph is from the Monet exhibit as seen on March 3, 2014 in the New York Metropolitan Art Museum.

43. See also chapter 6, where Ann Jervis considers the complexity of suffering that Christians experience in God's time by means of Jesus' resurrection.

44. My thanks to Stephanie Bowens, Beverly Gaventa, J. Ross Wagner, and the Princeton Theological Seminary New Testament Research Colloquium for reading earlier drafts of this essay and offering comments and suggestions.

Bibliography

Barclay, John. *Paul and the Gift.* Grand Rapids: Eerdmans, 2015.

Barnett, Paul. *The Second Epistle to the Corinthians.* NICNT. Grand Rapids: Eerdmans, 1997.

Barreto, Eric. *Ethnic Negotiations: The Function of Race and Ethnicity in Acts 16.* Tübingen: Mohr Siebeck, 2010.

Bowens, Lisa. *An Apostle in Battle: Paul and Spiritual Warfare in 2 Corinthians 12:1–10.* Tübingen: Mohr Siebeck, 2017.

———. "Investigating the Apocalyptic Texture of Paul's Martial Imagery in 2 Corinthians 4–6." *JSNT* 39 (2016) 3–15.

Brink, Laurie. "A General's Exhortation to His Troops: Paul's Military Rhetoric in 2 Cor 10:1–11." *BZ* 49 (2005) 191–201.

———. "A General's Exhortation to His Troops: Paul's Military Rhetoric in 2 Cor 10:1–11." *BZ* 50 (2006) 74–89.

Eastman, Susan. *Recovering Paul's Mother Tongue: Language and Theology in Galatians.* Grand Rapids: Eerdmans, 2007.

Fitzgerald, John T. *Cracks in an Earthen Vessel: An Examination of the Catalogues of Hardships in the Corinthian Correspondence.* SBLDS 99. Atlanta: Scholars, 1988.

Furnish, Victor P. *II Corinthians.* AB 32A. New York: Doubleday, 1984.

Gaventa, Beverly Roberts. "The Rhetoric of Violence and the God of Peace in Paul's Letter to the Romans." In *Paul, John, and Apocalyptic Eschatology: Studies in Honour of Martinus C. de Boer,* edited by Jan Krans et al., 61–75. Leiden: Brill, 2013.

Glancy, Jennifer A. "Boasting of Beatings (2 Corinthians 11:23–25)." *JBL* 123 (2004) 99–135.

Gorman, Michael. *Becoming the Gospel: Paul, Participation, and Mission.* Grand Rapids: Eerdmans, 2015.

Harris, Murray J. *The Second Epistle to the Corinthians: A Commentary on the Greek Text.* NIGTC. Grand Rapids: Eerdmans, 2005.

King, Martin Luther, Jr. "Paul's Letter to American Christians." In *Strength to Love,* 127–42. New York: Harper & Row, 1963.

Lampe, Peter. "Can Words Be Violent or Do They Only Sound That Way? Second Corinthians: Verbal Warfare from Afar as a Complement to a Placid Personal Presence." In *Paul and Rhetoric,* edited by J. Paul Sampley and Peter Lampe, 223–40. New York: T. & T. Clark, 2010.

Malherbe, Abraham. "Antisthenes and Odysseus, and Paul at War." *Harvard Theological Review* 76 (1983): 143–73.

Martin, Ralph P. *2 Corinthians.* WBC 40. Waco, TX: Word, 1985.

Martyn, J. Louis. "From Paul to Flannery O'Connor with the Power of Grace." In *Theological Issues in the Letters of Paul,* 279–97. Nashville: Abingdon, 1997.

———. *Galatians.* AB 33A. New York: Doubleday, 1997.

Maston, Jason. *Divine and Human Agency in Second Temple Judaism and Paul.* Tübingen: Mohr Siebeck, 2010.

Mitchell, Margaret. *The Heavenly Trumpet: John Chrysostom and the Art of Pauline Interpretation.* Tübingen: Mohr Siebeck, 2000.

Paquet, Marcel. *Botero: Philosophy of the Creative Act.* Translated by Susan Resnick. New York: Mallard, 1985.

Roetzel, C. J. "The Language of War (2 Cor. 10:1–6) and the Language of Weakness (2 Cor. 11:21b—13:10)." *Biblical Interpretation* 17 (2009) 77–99.

Satake, Akira. "Schritt für Schritt: Die Argumentation des Paulus in 2Kor 10–13." In *Der Zweite Korintherbrief: literarische Gestalt—historische Situation—theologische Argumentation. Festschrift zum 70. Geburtstag von Dietrich-Alex Koch,* edited by Dieter Sänger, 283–99. FRLANT 250. Göttingen: Vandenhoeck & Ruprecht, 2012.

Schuller, Eileen M., and Carol A. Newson. *The Hodayot (Thanksgiving Psalms): A Study Edition of 1QH^a.* SBLEJL 36. Atlanta: Society of Biblical Literature, 2012.

Soskice, Janet. *Metaphor and Religious Language.* Oxford: Clarendon, 1985.

Thrall, Margaret E. *The Second Epistle to the Corinthians.* ICC 47:2. Edinburgh: T. & T. Clark, 2000.

VanderKam, James C., ed. *The Book of Jubilees: A Critical Text.* CSCO 511. Lovanii: E. Peeters, 1989.

Young, Frances M., and David F. Ford. *Meaning and Truth in Second Corinthians.* Eugene, OR: Wipf and Stock, 1987.

9

Paul the Personalist: Why the Poor Matter to the Church

Colin Miller

Although I have been asked to contribute a piece about Paul's thoughts on economic justice and ministry to the dispossessed, I don't think the apostle cared about either of these issues. This will come as no shock to Susan Eastman, whom I got to know when I was the Episcopal priest in charge of a Catholic Worker House in Durham. During that time, I had the honor of having Susan on my dissertation committee. She, too, knows the Worker well, having served a community outside of Pittsburgh similar in many ways to mine. So I've been privileged to trade thoughts with her about many things important to both of us: the priesthood, Paul, and the poor.

When I consider Paul and the poor, I find no indication that he concerned himself with economic justice or ministry with the dispossessed. This is not just because he didn't know these categories, but that, if he did, he would have positively opposed them as "another gospel" (Gal 1:6) that makes it difficult to believe in Christ. This is because St. Paul, like Peter Maurin and Dorothy Day, is a personalist. As such, to seek economic justice or a ministry to the oppressed cannot but reinforce Pauline scholarship's penchant to make "Christ" an abstraction.

The argument to reach this conclusion is a wide-ranging one, so I had better give an indication where we are headed. In the first section I use the thought of John Henry Newman to help us see that, for Paul, the church provides the tangible, concrete activities that make *faith* in Christ possible. I ground this reading of faith—what Newman calls *real assent*—in Paul's account of the sacraments. In part two I argue that the other principal component of the church's imaging of Christ is our *neighbor's face*. This is why Paul is a *personalist*: our neighbor's irreducibly particular face helps make possible real assent to Christ. I argue that this principle is behind Paul's otherwise inexplicable obsession with relations between people and unity in the church: faith in Christ depends on it. Finally, in part three, I suggest that it is because of their particular ability to enable faith that Paul is concerned about the poor. The faces of these neighbors make the poor Christ present to us, which keeps him tangible and concrete.

This way of seeing things came to me by my experience at the Catholic Worker House. The idea of the house was simple. A bunch of Christians would live together, being the church going about ordinary church things, centered around the house chapel where we had daily Mass and the Liturgy of the Hours. This was our simple ministry, and it was certainly not particular to us. The other clergy, divinity school students, and poor people who lived in the house were there because they were friends wanting a place to stay, and so, as Christians, we tried to find them room. We also had to eat, and so most days we all had breakfast and supper together, and people from the neighborhood, poor and rich, often came by to pull up a chair and load up a plate. We just thought we were common Christians being the church.

Yet we found ourselves routinely faced with others' perception that we were doing something else; namely, that we had what they often called a "ministry to the poor" that the rest of the church did not share. I was often asked well-meaning but at first bewildering questions like, "How can I get involved in your hospitality ministry?" or, "What are the criteria for getting a space at your shelter?" People, including the poor, wanted to know what sort of "services we provided" (to which I would usually reply, "Matins and Vespers"), when we were going to be "feeding" (to which another priest responded, "Y'aint cattle, but we're gonna have supper in a minute"), and what sort of "programs" or "assistance" we tried to connect people to. After a time we learned to simply repeat the mantra of the wisest of our poor friends, "I don't run nothin'." We had run up against the widespread assumption that the poor were a discrete group that "the church should help." So this essay tries to show why, following Saint Paul, I have come to think this is a dangerous way to frame the matter. As strange as it may seem, the church is not for the poor as much as the poor are *for the church* and an important aid to her faith.

A Tangible Faith

There is no doubt that Christ, for Paul, is the center of everything: "To live is Christ" (Phil 1:21).[1] "I consider all things rubbish compared with the surpass-

1. The translations below are the author's, made mainly from the 27th edition of the Nestle-Aland in Greek in comparison with the *Nova Vulgata* and the *Douay-Rheims*. If

ing eminence of the knowledge of Christ" (Phil 3:8). It is also clear that *faith* or *belief* is the normal way that Paul thinks Christ is encountered: "We live by *faith*" (2 Cor 5:7). The centrality of both *Christ* and *faith* are axioms of Paul's letters: "I have been crucified with Christ, I no longer live, but Christ lives in me. The life I live now in the flesh I live by faith in the Son of God" (Gal 2:20). It might seem a strange question, but *why* is this so?

One disciple of Paul, who also highlighted the centrality of faith, is eminent nineteenth century theologian (Blessed) John Henry Newman (1801–1890). Newman's own account of faith, I suggest, can help us see why it is so central to Paul's thought, and why we cannot understand what Paul says about other people without it. Faith, for Newman, as he develops his position in his *Essay in Aid of a Grammar of Assent*, is what he calls *real assent*. To give real assent to something is the shorthand way of naming what we do when we think and live like something is *true*. As such, faith or belief, for Newman, is assent to a truth as a *forcible, vivid object of experience*, which lives in us by *tangible images* that represent the object to our minds as a concrete reality. He contrasts this with the logical, purely abstract kind of thinking in a subject like mathematics.[2] He calls this *notional assent*. Notional assent is not bad. In fact, *most* of our judgment, our assents—and we hold a vast variety of them—are notional. It's just that there is nothing of *experience* in notional assents—say math—just as there is nothing of experience in most of our judgments—say, that England is an island, or what happened in most of the history of the United States. Real assent, on the other hand, encompasses a narrow range of things that we know very deeply. We assent to our spouses' love for us by a thousand different practical experiences. Its claim to truth is real to us in a way that most claims are not.

Both notional and real assent, he thinks, are unconditional—this is why he says they are both "assent."[3] The popular claim today that all things are matters of probability, for Newman, cannot do justice to the facts of the way that we go about our ordinary lives. We do not go about our daily lives by first calculating a variety of probabilities and *then* acting. We simply act, and this is precisely because we assent to a thousand things as unconditionally true. On this point, Newman is concerned to attack a certain skepticism that would call all things into question. His point is that such skepticism is defeated by simply looking at human beings. We receive most things on faith—we learn to speak, who our parents are, what the basic furniture of the world is, what has happened, and what we should do, without ever ask-

there are important differences between these two, I have noted them.

2. See Newman, "Notional and Real Assent," 49–92.

3. Ibid., 135–72.

ing any questions about most of it. Newman's point is that this is the way that it should be—or at least it is the only human way that these things can be. We humans thus *rightly* claim to know a whole host of things that we have simply been *told* and taken on the *authority* of others. We quite rightly *assent* to most of these things.

Christian faith then, for Newman, is this kind of real assent applied to Christ.[4] On the one hand, this means that such faith is not less reasonable than any of those other claims that we hold but never go about proving. We *may* go about proving them, and using such reason is not insignificant, but faith itself does not require it any more than does assent to who our parents are. Moreover, this faith is not cognitivist, it is not a *mere* assent to a proposition as true, but as a living, present reality. Faith in Christ for Newman is always living faith. Making heavy use of *memory*, real assent is cultivated by being variously touched by the concrete object it intends, so that such belief is much more likely to lead to action in accord with it than is notional assent. In this way, it is more intense and practical than notional assent.

> Belief, on the other hand, being concerned with things concrete, not abstract, which variously excite the mind from their moral and imaginative properties, has for its objects, not only directly what is true, but inclusively what is beautiful, useful, admirable, heroic; objects which kindle devotion, rouse the passions, and attach the affections; and thus it leads the way to actions of every kind, to the establishment of principles, and the formation of character, and is thus again intimately connected with what is individual and personal.[5]

As such, real faith requires a vivid imagination constituted by the memory of sensible, material objects.

In the case of faith in Christ, the images, experiences, and memories by which this faith lives have their source in the church. This part of his account of faith comes out most clearly in his *Essay on the Development of Christian Doctrine*. For Newman, the primary way that we come to real assent is through "the church system," which is "at once dogmatical, devotional and practical"—a seamless garment.[6] It gives us all the vivid practical experiences we need in order for our faith in its claims to be real. This, in fact, is one of the main points of the *materiality* of the incarnation. The center of Christianity is not any abstract or notional claim. Christianity is

4. Ibid., 93–124.

5. Ibid., 97.

6. Newman, *Essay on the Development*, 29, 36.

founded upon a concrete, living, divine person who has come into the orbit of our *senses* as a human being.[7]

But since most of us live far from first century Palestine, the church takes over the incarnation where the ascension left off and, with its own tangible reality, makes possible faith in Christ. The extension of the logic, practices, and materiality of the incarnation by the church's various means Newman calls *the sacramental principle*.[8] Christ's flesh, as it were, unfolds into the sacraments, which extend his presence to the church through space and time. Thus, the *sources* of real assent—the tangible images and activities that engage our senses—ultimately cluster around the church, and especially the liturgy, principally the Eucharist. It is there that all the senses are engaged and we receive a sort of picture of Christ. The priest, the altar, the bread, wine, incense, kneeling, icons, crosses, the readings, and the church building itself are all an unfolding of the incarnation into the present, and they give to the imagination the sources upon which to rest its faith in the one Christ at the heart of it all.[9]

I think that, not in the same terms, but one way or another, the apostle would agree. Given space, we could show this in detail, but here we can be content to recall that, in terms of the concrete sources of faith for Paul, pride of place must go to the dominical sacraments. I assume that the celebration of these made up the majority of what Paul's churches did together.[10] In other words, Paul's congregations were primarily concerned with worship. We can gather this even from the surface of his letters. Nearly the whole of 1 Corinthians treats the liturgical assembly in one way or another (see esp. 1 Cor 8–14), including a long discussion of the Eucharist (1 Cor 10–11). Second Corinthians 3 talks about reading of the Scriptures, which we may presume is a liturgical event. The apostle uses baptism to illustrate the Christian life in multiple places (e.g., Gal 3:27; Eph 4:5; Col 3:12), and especially in Rom 6, with the long exposition of dying to sin and rising in righteousness. I even think, in company with a few others, that there is a direct reference to the Eucharist in Rom 12:9, and that the rest of the letter from there is concerned with this sacrament. In fact, wherever Paul talks about "thanksgiving" (e.g., Phil 4:6), there is good reason to hear at least an allusion, if not a direct reference, to "the Great Thanksgiving"—the Eucharist. These examples demonstrate that the images of the liturgy—as the sourcing of the faith—are not ancillary to, but constitutive of, Paul's doctrine.

7. Ibid., 93–95.

8. Ibid.

9. Ibid., 169.

10. See Miller, *Practice of the Body*, 136–96.

Encountering Christ through Each Other

All this, so far, has been but a necessary preliminary to what I shall now designate as St. Paul's "personalism." The latter has all sorts of different definitions and aspects, and I will elaborate the precise one I mean in reference to Paul below. But it is enough to start to say that, for Paul, people are not just made in the image of God, not just siblings in Christ, and not just full of dignity. They are a further instance of the sacramental principle. The sacraments in the first place and the human being in the second are the twin sources of belief for Paul. They mediate the reality of Christ, making him concretely present, so that he can be believed in as a real object. Without these, the church could not exist. But with these, the church—at whatever stage of its development—has the basic images it needs for its faith to thrive.

The basic text relating Paul's personalism is 2 Cor 3:18. There Paul says that when the law is read to the Jews today they are unable to see Christ in it—it is veiled to them. "*We* all," however, "with unveiled faces behold the glory of the Lord—his very *image*—and are transformed from glory to glory" (2 Cor 3:18). At first this might seem as if Paul is saying that Christians see the *Lord's glory* face to face, since the veil has been removed. But that does not square with what Paul says in 1 Cor 13:12: "we see *now* in a mirror, darkly, but then we *shall* see face to face." Moreover, in this age, even Christians "live by faith, not by sight" (2 Cor 5:7). We cannot see Christ now because "he dwells in inaccessible light, whom no human has seen nor is able to see" (1 Tim 6:15). The time of seeing the Lord face to face is not yet.

So 2 Cor 3:18 must mean something else. I suggest it means that the way we perceive the Lord's glory now, prior to the eschaton, is in the face of our *neighbor*. This *is* the kind of seeing that we do now, and, I will argue, precisely the kind that allows us to have *faith* in Christ, whom we do not yet see. The image, then, that Paul does say that we see, and which he sets apposite to his glory, is the image God planted in humanity when the Trinity said, "Let us make humankind in our image" (Gen 1:26). As God's image bearer, the human face reflects the glory of the Lord. Thus, the *face* to which Paul refers in 2 Cor 3:18 is not the *Lord's* face but the face of *another human being*. This makes good sense of the context, because in 2 Cor 3 Paul is arguing that his authority does not need letters of recommendation (3:1) since the Corinthians *themselves* are already "epistles of Christ, written not with ink but with the spirit of the living God" (3:3).

The image or icon that *is* the Christian person is related to and directly derivative of the one primary icon of God, the incarnate Lord. "For he is the image of the invisible God" (Col 1:15). This demonstrates that, for Paul, image-bearing is an extension of something like Newman's sacramental principle. Second Corinthians 3:18 thus suggests that the way the Christian sees clearly, without a veil, happens when he or she is able to perceive Christ, who is the Image of God, in the face of another person. This unveiled seeing, though it still happens through a mirror darkly, Paul elsewhere glosses as "faith."

The *face* of our neighbor, then, for Paul, is one of the concrete images that makes real assent possible—it yields a vivid sense of Christ as a present object. This is the first way that Paul is a *personalist*, by insisting on the necessity of seeing our neighbor's unveiled face. To call this personalism is entirely fitting, since *persona* is one word for face in Latin, which can translate the Greek word in this text, *prosōpon*. Here, however, the Vulgate has *facie*. To say that Paul is a personalist is to say that he is a face-ist.[11]

This is important for understanding the way that Paul refers to other people. First, Paul does not know our popular phrase "the other" as a way of naming someone else to whom he is obligated. "The other" has become a sort of abstract term of moral discourse today, even giving birth to abstract nouns like "othering." But Paul only knows two generic words for someone else: the *neighbor* and the *sibling* (*adelphos*, "brother/sister"). Both of these he uses precisely because he is a personalist. "Neighbor" in English means someone to whom you are *neigh*—it is someone who is *near* you—and this is true in Greek and Latin too. It is someone whose *face* you can see—a *persona*. The "sibling" is someone even closer—someone who shares in being a son or daughter of the Father and so shares the icon of Christ the Son (as in Rom 8:29).

Neither of these is "the other," which is a phrase that refers generically to anyone and often everyone in the world, usually someone we are encouraged to be in some way responsible for—the hungry in Africa, refugees, the marginalized, or whomever. Paul would be perplexed at our obsession with these. Groups or abstract individuals like these are not, and cannot be, near to us. We cannot see their faces, and so we cannot relate to them as icons of Christ. Surely they are important, but precisely because they are neighbor or sibling to other neighbors and siblings and ultimately siblings to Christ their brother. In this way we can specify that the *face* that Paul thinks is so important is our neighbor's face *in its irreducible particularity*. It is not a general or notional face. Seeing Christ's image requires a concrete human being, *this* human being. "Others" do not have faces.

Consonant with this personalism, I submit that relations between people occupy the practical content—the lived, concrete object in the life of the church—of nearly everything that Paul writes. Indeed, it is telling that he

---

11. *Prosōpon* can mean "mask" as well. It does not in this case.

usually writes about people *and* the liturgy at the same time. This can easily be lost behind Paul's more notional or abstract theological terms. A particular schema has often been assumed, by Catholics and Protestants alike, that the great themes of Pauline theology (justification by faith, participation in Christ, or whatever) are the leading ones, to be followed by sanctification or the "moral" sections of the letters. On the basis of these most important matters, Paul then lays out, from time to time and mostly at the end of the letters, how people should behave if these theological themes are true. Yet this is very much a scholar's view: abstract theological questions come first, then we "apply" theology to the moral life, and then we further apply the moral life to life with other people. This view has been justified, for instance, by pointing to the structure of Romans: first there is justification by faith (Rom 1–4), then sanctification (Rom 5–8), and then life in the church with other people (Rom 12–15).

But this is not right. In the first place, if what we have said so far is true, this is bad theology. It takes the sources of faith—the liturgy and other people—and makes them secondary, while, apparently, insisting that Christians have faith without any concrete instances on which to hang it. In other words, on this account Paul is preaching a gospel that asks people to have faith in something that is entirely abstract and only later gains texture. In Newman's terms, this faith could only be "notional" and as such it makes "Christ" simply a word without content—a theological abstraction. It puts the church—its liturgy and communion with other people—last, as a *conclusion* to an argument that begins abstractly. This dearth of ecclesiology is all too common in readings of Paul.

But not only is this bad theology, it also just does not square with what Paul says. Paul assumes that the church comes first, in its liturgy and face-to-face life together, which is the content of what sanctification *looks like*. Further, Paul knows no strong distinction between this sanctification and what it is to be "justified" or "made just" by faith. If this is right, faith as real assent is entirely grounded in its material sources in the church. Faith in Christ becomes rightly inseparable from participation in "his body, which is the church, the fullness of him who fills all in all" (Eph 1:22). If one wants to understand the *order of discovery* by which one comes to faith, then, one should *first* read Rom 12–15, then Rom 5–8, and then Rom 1–4. The argument that Christianity *is* begins with the experience of daily life in the church.

We can illustrate this by looking at Romans in more detail, since Paul textually links *all* the major sections of the letter together by certain key concepts, all of which have to do with our neighbors: love for neighbor in Rom 13 is part of what it means to "put on the Lord" and not "make provision for the flesh" (13:14), which is also the main topic of Rom 8:1–14.

Romans 8, in turn, illustrates the topic of Rom 1–4, the "fulfillment of the law" (Rom 8:2). All this is included in his discussion about what it is to be "justified" (Rom 5), and this is seamlessly part of being "sanctified" (Rom 6–8). We could not have better evidence than this for the inseparability of theology and ethics, of relationship with God and relationship with people. The thematic and even verbal repetition throughout Romans assures us that he has a thick ecclesial practice in mind even when he is only connoting it by more abstract terms. Love of neighbor is close to the heart, then, of everything Paul says in Romans, from beginning to end. Life with other people appears as important as it ought to be if it is one of the primary sources of the very faith Paul preaches. Once again, the point is Christ: in order to know him, it is necessary to see my neighbor.

This explains why Paul's letters are constantly preoccupied with relations among people. We may be astounded at how many of these texts there are. First, there are those that immediately echo the love commandment: "Be slaves to one another . . . love your neighbor as yourself . . . bear one another's burdens, and thus fulfill the law of Christ" (Gal 5:13–14; 6:2). This is the "freedom" for which "Christ has set you free" (Gal 5:1), the love of neighbor that sources "faith, which works through charity" (Gal 5:6). Again, this is directly connected to the rest of the moral life, namely "the fruit of the Spirit" that are contrary to the "concupiscence of the flesh" (Gal 5:14). Likewise in Ephesians, after instructing them to "put on the new man," he goes on immediately, "put away lying, and let each person speak the truth to his neighbor" (Eph 4:23–24; see also Col 3:9). The saints, in this way, show us Christ: "May Christ dwell by faith in your hearts, that you may be able to comprehend, *with all the saints*, the charity of Christ" (Eph 3:18).

Second, such personalism reveals why Paul is so obsessed with *unity* in general. This is usually accounted for by appeal to the theoretical or mystical unity of the church, which ought then be exhibited on the ground. Real as such unity may be, there is a more pressing and compelling explanation for Paul's solicitude. Without unity, the church cannot see Christ: "if you bite and devour one another watch out, you will consume each other" (Gal 5:15). "Let us do good to all while we have time, but most of all to the household of the faith" (Gal 6:9). "In as much as it is up to you, make peace with all" (Rom 12:18), but at least "have peace among yourselves" (1 Thess 5:13). For the sake of knowing *Christ* it is important to live "with humility and mildness, with patience, supporting one another in charity, careful to keep the unity of the spirit in the bond of peace" (Eph 4:2; see also Col 3:12–14), and so "let every strife and anger and wrath and indignant cry and blasphemy be removed" (Eph 4:30–31). The purpose of his famous exposition of the divine condescension in Phil 2:5–11 is that everyone "think the same things,

having the same charity, the same soul, thinking *one thing*, not in conten-
tion, nor ambition, but in humility thinking others superior to yourself"
(Phil 2:2–3).[12] If there is division, faith will be jeopardized, for people will
not look at each other's faces.

Likewise, *marriage* in the church is defined by imaging Christ to
one another. Like the other sacraments, this "great mystery" makes present the reality of "Christ and the church" (Eph 5:32). The husband images
Christ by sacrificing himself for the wife, and the wife images the church
by submitting to the husband and receiving Christ's redeeming gifts (Eph
5:22–33). The reciprocal duties involved *perform* and make Christ present
in the church by enacting his immolation, the washing he accomplishes in
baptism and the purification of the church in general. Even the *bodies* of the
spouses become the images of the one *body* of Christ, united with Christ
the head (Eph 5:23, 30). For all the symbolism, as in the Eucharist, there is
no indication that this is merely symbolic. As the Eucharist does not just
represent but in fact performs the sacrifice of Christ, so the action of the
spouses is the performance of the mystery of salvation in the midst of the
church, becoming the sources of the church's faith in Christ they cannot see
by the spouses they can see.

The Poor Christ in the Face of the Poor

So far, Paul the personalist suggests that the face of our neighbor, in its irreducible particularity, like the sacraments, makes Christ a vivid reality in
the church. And it is as a personalist that we must now understand the things
the apostle says about money, the weak, and the poor. The first thing to say is
that, because the primary function of our neighbor is to make faith possible,
the "poor saints" (Rom 15:26) are at no disadvantage in terms of contributing
to the church.[13] If they remain poor, they do not suffer lack in this regard. At
the same time, Paul is not unconcerned that their material wants are cared
for, since he insists on "a certain equality" (2 Cor 8:14–15) entirely consonant
with the communitarian vision of Acts: "they had all things in common"
(Acts 2:32). Paul assumes followers of Christ will "make the needs of the
saints common" (Rom 12:12). This is the proper context for his maxim that
"if someone will not work, he will not eat" (2 Thess 3:10), in which all receive
according to their need and not according to their ability to contribute. There

12. For further reflections on Christ's condescension in Phil 2, see chapter 1 by
Michael Gorman.

13. For similar conclusions by way of different arguments, see chapter 2 by John
Barclay and chapter 7 by Robert Moses.

is always the possibility of freeloaders, but this maxim in 2 Thessalonians underlines rather than tells against this relative equity.

Yet distribution of temporal goods is not an end in itself. Rather, the church practices this distribution of goods because it is yet another way of enacting the presence of Christ among them by performing the same act that he performed. "For you know the grace of our Lord Jesus Christ who for us became poor though he was rich, in order that you might be rich through his poverty" (2 Cor 8:9). Giving to the poor is a good work in imitation of Christ's good work in the incarnation, for Paul exhorts, "abound in every good work [of almsgiving], just as it is written, 'he scatters, he gives to the poor'" (2 Cor 9:8–9). Almsgiving is one of the primary motivations the apostle gives for the goodness of work: "labor, working the good with your own hands, so that you might have something to give to the one who lacks" (Eph 4:29). In other words, alms are part of a divine gift economy, since it is the Lord who has already given us anything that we might ever give. This means, first of all, the "gift of Christ" (2 Cor 8:9), and second, the very alms we give to the poor, so that when we give we can expect our barns to be refilled (2 Cor 9:10). When we give alms out of "carefulness of others" (2 Cor 8:8) or "offer hospitality to strangers" (Rom 12:13), we affirm that we understand that nothing we have is ours, for "what do you have that you did not receive?" (1 Cor 4:13).

Alms, then, are a "proof of charity" (2 Cor 8:8), not as a simple moralism but as a necessary performance if everything one has is always and only a gift for one's neighbor. "Give to one another just as God in Christ gave to you" (Eph 4:31). Thus, almsgiving in the church is not motivated by saccharine pity, nor does it estimate financial equality important for its own sake. Rather, it makes possible a visible enactment of the economy of salvation. This is why Paul can say that the Christians "know about fraternity" because they have been taught it by God—they are *theodoctoi*: "God-taught-people" (1 Thess 4:9). The poor thus make up a special part of the church's images, making faith tangible. With the poor in our midst, Christ cannot be an abstraction.

For the church, poverty and being associated with poverty have always been badges of honor since Christ was poor. This is the second major way the poor contribute to faith, since they image the *poor* Christ. For this reason, the church must always have the poor within it: "Do not think about lofty matters, but associate with the lowly" (Rom 12:12) and "receive the weak" (1 Thess 5:14). Riches, on the other hand, are dangerous precisely because they tempt one to place oneself outside the divine economy. So, "piety with contentedness is a great achievement. For we brought nothing into the world, and we can bring nothing out of it. But having food and clothes, let us be pleased enough with these. Those who want to be rich fall into temptation and snares and many base and harmful passions. . . . For the love of money is the root of all evils" (1 Tim 6:6–10). It is not only, then, that having more money than one needs is evil, though it is. The rich, stepping outside of God's economy by the hoarding of goods, *"are led away from faith"* (1 Tim 6:10) precisely because the image of that economy is meant to be faith's aid. To guard against this, Paul says, "Command the rich of this world not to be arrogant nor to hope in their uncertain riches but in God, who provides all things abundantly, to give alms, to lavish goods easily, to share, and to make for themselves treasure for the coming age, so that they might *receive* true life" (1 Tim 6:17–19).

This, then, is the proper place of the poor for Paul: they are not an external object of charity but an internal aid to faith. Therefore, what is really amazing and perhaps surprising about Paul's personalism is that through it we are able to see that Paul was obsessed with *God*. It is important in this regard to avoid *reducing* that obsession to an obsession *with* other people, rather than *through* them. He is not concerned with equality for equality's sake or with the poor for poverty's sake. The church and people are *signs* that fill our imaginations with the thought, not of themselves, but of the Living Person for whom it is trivial to suffer the loss of all things (Phil 3:8). Everything, in fact, for Paul, is set up to refer us and restore us to God. We *use* people to get to God (which is not the same as *abusing* them). As another disciple of St. Paul, St. Augustine, has it, "If you should not love even yourself for your own sake, but for his in whom your love finds its proper Object, no man can be angry if you love him too for God's sake."[14] This is the primary motion of salvation, since each person is estranged from God and finds his happiness in him alone and not in other people. The church, the Eucharist, the liturgy, the other sacraments, our neighbors, and the poor are all so important for Paul because these are the God-given means for knowing Christ, who is the way back to God, and there is nothing better than that. Paul is concerned with other people, not for their own sake, but for this reason. Paul's churches had no social programs; their only tangible characteristic was the worship of their Lord. The church is not about people; the church is about God.

We can now see why I said that Paul is not concerned with economic justice and ministry to the dispossessed, and this for a number of related reasons. First, the church is in the divinely appointed business of restoring people to communion with their maker, which is the only real thing they lack, by bringing them to faith, or real assent, to Christ. This is the

---

14. Augustine, *De Doctrina Christiana* I.22, A.T.

church's rather *limited* mission, and it only includes the redressing of social and financial inequalities insofar as these are an impediment to this mission. The *Lord's* providence, not the church's, extends to all the earth, to every corner, facet, and atom of the world. God is not far from anyone (Acts 17:27), and there are endless arms of politics, government, and social life that concern themselves with temporal social inequities, always with many good and faithful Christians in them. I think this is Paul's position, and not only mine. That Providence really does care for such people is the reason that "everyone ought to be subject to the governing authorities . . . for it is a service of God for your good" (Rom 13:1, 4). Within the church, the humble and poor are received and alms are distributed to them as a performance of the economy of salvation. They have themselves come to the church, not because the church should be a dispenser of temporal gifts or as a way out of financial difficulties or social exclusion, but because they have been caught up by faith in the sublime vision of Christ.

In other words, the church's social program is internal to its greater mission. This does not mean that it thinks the grave inequalities that exist in the world today are not weighty matters. Rather, the way that the church goes about addressing these is called *evangelism*. It has no social strategies to recommend other than itself. What we now call the "social gospel" cannot be divorced from the spread of the gospel itself, which is the spread of the message of the Vivifying Personality at the heart of church. It is true that wherever the church has spread and become the central force in society there has been a certain "leavening" of the people around it, even if they are not formally part of its fold. Yet this is not a formal necessity of the church being the church. Rather, if one desires to extend the features internal to the church to a greater mass of the world, there is no way to do that without extending the whole church to those masses. There is little more hope that the world outside the church will adopt the social principles and practices internal to the church than that it will begin to adorn its streets and businesses with its candles, icons, or incense. The reason for the church's economic practices, unity, and inclusion of the poor is its obsession with its otherwise invisible Lord, whom its members make present.

Finally, if this is a faithful rendering of St. Paul's doctrine, a corollary danger emerges. If the church, as the church, does become interested and involved in the project of righting the evils of societal inequalities, oppression, dispossession, and the like, it obviously undertakes an enormous and almost infinite project. If righting these external wrongs is in fact an urgent part of the church's mission, it can only hope to do so by spending most of its time dealing with hoards whose faces it cannot possibly genuinely claim to see. This may or may not be a disservice to these people. What is clear is that when these abstract "others"—the poor, the dispossessed, the power-less, the homeless, or whomever—become the objects of the believer's gaze, Paul's personalist principle is lost.

This was what was most troubling about the suggestion that the Catholic Worker House had a special mission to the poor, or that *we* were there for *them*. On the contrary, like St. Paul, we thought *they* were there for *us*. We wanted definitively to reject the temptation to be "for" a faceless abstraction, because in the end this risks allowing Christ himself to become one. "Christ" would then simply be a pious cypher for a theological project, ideology, or social or political program. It might be possible to have a notional theology *about* him, but it would not be possible to have a devotion *to* him. A church where Christ is this sort of abstraction would become a church, in the course of time, without any faith. Where the poor are only "others," Christ will cease to be what he clearly was to St. Paul—the overwhelming object of faith, an ever-living and real person, known by the sacramental practices of the church, and by our neighbor's face.

Bibliography

Miller, Colin. *The Practice of the Body of Christ: Human Agency in Pauline Theology After MacIntyre*. Eugene, OR: Pickwick, 2013.

Newman, John Henry. *An Essay on the Development of Christian Doctrine*. New York: Longmans, Green and Co., [1845] 1909.

————. "Notional and Real Assent." In *An Essay in Aid of a Grammar of Assent*, 49–172. Notre Dame: University of Notre Dame Press, [1870] 1979.

10

In Christ Together: Intergenerational Ministry and 1 Corinthians 12

Emily A. Peck-McClain

W HEN PEOPLE TALK ABOUT the church, they often speak of it as a body and as the body of Christ. In 1 Cor 12, Paul crafts this metaphor beautifully. To a divided community, Paul gives this metaphor imaging every part of the body as valued, needed, and connected. Vulnerable parts of the body need special care, and all parts of the body come together to create the whole. Beautiful, indeed. When read within the context of Paul's theological, Christological, and anthropological worldview, the body also becomes a powerful metaphor that can change the way we do ministry in our churches.[1]

---

1. Susan Eastman, in her book *Recovering Paul's Mother Tongue*, presents a helpful study on the purpose of metaphor. Looking to Janet Martin Soskice, Eastman writes that "metaphors are not a substitution for what could be said directly without metaphors, nor are they simply an emotional appeal" (22). They "point beyond themselves to invisible realities" (23). This is particularly helpful when considering the metaphor of the body in 1 Cor 12. This metaphorical language serves a purpose; it points to the reality that Christians are not living their own lives once they are baptized; they are bonded with other Christians and are "in Christ" (Paul's term for what we today might call "Christian"). Metaphor, in other words, is not *just* rhetoric or *just* imagery, it does something for Paul's letter that language lacking metaphor would be unable to do. Metaphor serves a purpose; it describes truth, invites imagination, and forms the community into a body while offering imagery through a rhetorical device. Susan Eastman uses insights like this often, crossing disciplines and seamlessly weaving them together with Paul. She has been a professor, mentor, and friend to me in my scholarship and life. It is both my honor and joy to contribute this essay to honor her as a teacher, scholar, friend, and pastor.

Gifts

A striking precursor to Paul's metaphor of the body of Christ states that to each member a gift is given. He wants his audience to be informed about gifts (1 Cor 12:1). There are different gifts and each member of the body is given a gift of the variety available. Gifts are given by the Spirit and activated by God.[2] Paul then goes on to list several possibilities of gifts. This is probably not intended to be a complete list of gifts since other gifts are listed elsewhere in Paul's letters.[3] These gifts, whatever they are, are an important part of the community at Corinth, and an important way to understand how the community comes together and what its purpose is. The gifts of the Spirit—activated (verse 11, *energei*) by God—are foundational to the body of Christ.

In 1 Cor 12, Paul begins by talking about *pneumatikōn*, usually translated as "spiritual gifts." This is not the word he continues to use though. By verse 4, he begins to use a new term: *charismata*. These gifts are, of course, connected with the Spirit (Gk. *pneuma*), though not linguistically. Instead, these gifts are connected to *charis*, grace. As Paul is talking about the giftedness of those who are in Christ, he is talking about how their gifts are grace-in-action. These various gifts, which are manifestations of the Spirit (12:7), are also grace. Paul names these gifts as the "utterance of wisdom," "utterance of knowledge," "faith," "healing," "working of miracles," "prophecy," "discernment of spirits," "various kinds of tongues," and "interpretation of tongues" (12:8–10).[4] He then launches into his metaphor about the body.

These gifts are all important, the people on whom they are bestowed and in whom they are activated are each as important as the other. No body is complete without all its parts, and no body is complete without all its members. The gifts given to the Corinthians are all they need (1 Cor 1:7). They are the manifestations of grace, ways for individuals within the body and the body itself to participate in the work of this time—namely, the defeat of sin.[5] These gifts are how every member of the body can be used by God to help usher in the new creation that Christ began. In the middle of

2. This is my paraphrase of 1 Cor 12:1–7.

3. Paul also writes about charismata in Rom 12:6–8, slightly differently than in 1 Cor 12:8–10 or 28. In Gal 5:22–23, Paul writes about the fruit of the Spirit, but not gifts. For further discussion of gift, see John Barclay's chapter 1; for reflections on both gift and the body of Christ, see Beverly Gaventa's chapter 4.

4. All scriptural quotations are from the NRSV unless otherwise noted.

5. When I refer to "sin" in this essay, it is important to note that I am not talking about individuals making poor choices, knowingly or unknowingly. Instead, I am referring to the power of sin, just as Paul does. People can participate in the power of sin through their actions and inactions, something with which Paul also agrees.

this divided community of Christians at Corinth there is important work to be done, inspired and enacted by the Spirit through these gifts. In fact, these gifts can only be understood through the Spirit (1 Cor 2:12). Paul addresses many different and specific concerns of the Christian community at Corinth in this letter but reminds them that they have work to do. There is urgency in his letter, not only for healing the divisions and settling disputes in this specific community but also because of what he knows about the time in which they are all living.

Paul knows that these gifts, working together in the body of Christ through the people upon whom they have been bestowed, are essential to the continuing work of Christ in this time between the cross and the eschaton. According to Paul's worldview, including his theology shaped by his own conversion, we are living in the time between the old age and the new creation. Many people commonly refer to this time as the "already and not yet."[6] Christ has come into the world and things have fundamentally and forever changed, yet the final and complete coming of the new creation still remains in the future. The present time is a contested time of battle between grace and sin; in fact, Paul calls it the "present evil age" in Gal 1:4.[7]

Churches today, situated in the same cosmic context, struggling alongside God against the powers of sin and death until the new creation arrives fully, are therefore charged with a similar task as that of the first-century church in Corinth. Churches—today as then—are made up of individuals given different gifts, brought together for the purposes of God, and become stewards of those gifts and their uses. Churches must both recognize and value the gifts that different people have to offer the community as a whole; they should engage their ministries as a response to that awareness.

Each person has gifts that are the manifestations of grace, given by the Spirit, and understood through that same Spirit. A community that separates its members according to their ages during worship, education, mission, and fellowship is a disconnected, dismembered body. Often this kind of generational segregation leads to a body lacking some of its parts. Consequently, parts of the body are considered "not the real church" or at least are not invited to be present for much of what the church does. These parts are often children, youth, and young adults.[8] Effectively, ministries

6. For a somewhat different take on Paul's conception of time and the already and not yet, see chapter 6 by Ann Jervis.

7. In 1 Corinthians, Paul calls the time "this age" in 1:20 and 3:18 as he compares proclaiming Christ crucified to foolishness, although it is actually wisdom for those who are in Christ. For further discussion of foolishness and apocalyptic imagery, see chapter 3 by Charles Campbell.

8. For the purposes of this chapter, I am focusing on generational segregation in the

that dis-member the body are ministries that disempower the activity of grace in the church and therefore in the world.

Common Good

In 1 Cor 12:7, Paul writes, "To each is given the manifestation of the Spirit for the common good." The referent of "the common good" is actually unclear. The common good of whom? Who makes up the "common"? Does Paul mean that all these gifts are for the common good of the body? The common good of the world? The common good of all Christians in Corinth? The common good of all Christians in the world? Certainly at least part of what Paul is talking about is the common good of the body of Christ at Corinth. This first letter to the Corinthians is all about helping them out of some messes in which they find themselves. There are divisions within the community, and there have been some activities by some members that have been unethical. The community of new Christians is unsure about how they should be relating to the larger Corinthian community. These are all reasonable concerns. And, it should be noted, ones with which church communities still wrestle today.

Paul's concerns in his letters, however localized, are also never solely about those communities. Christians, those who are baptized into Christ's death and now live in his resurrection (according to Rom 6), live as individuals in communities with other believers. But they are never *only* individuals, and their community is never *only* the church with whom they gather for worship, support, and work in the world. Paul's worldview is cosmic in scope, dealing with powers and principalities (Eph 6:12) all being defeated by Christ's action on the cross. Communities deal with many challenges in their own particular contexts. In Corinth, clearly divisions are part of those challenges. Other letters of Paul to other communities show us some of the struggles early Christian communities faced. But, each separate Christian community or church is also part of the cosmos-wide body of Christ that is fighting to bring about the new creation for the whole of the cosmos. Each individual is a member of a body of believers, each community is a member of the body. There are layers of participation for those who are in Christ— they are individually members of Christ and connected in a local Christian

---

church. It should be noted, however, that dis-membering the body happens all the time in churches in the way that people who are different in some way from the self-identity of the majority of members of a church are excluded—people who speak different languages, people of different races, people of different socioeconomic statuses, people of different physical or mental abilities, people of different sexualities or gender identities, etc.

community, and they are connected to all other Christians, all as part of Christ's inevitable final victory over sin and death. The common good, therefore, must deal with not only individuals and their local manifestation of the body of Christ but also with the cosmos-wide body of Christ, the one that is defeating the power of sin in present time battles even as the power of sin has already been ultimately defeated on the cross and the war won.[9]

Importantly, working for the common good might not always seem good.[10] Because of the nature of living in this "already and not yet" time when sin is still active, being on the side of Christ means enduring suffering in the present time.[11] For example, earlier in 1 Corinthians, Paul describes being treated like garbage (4:13). Sometimes being in Christ and working for the common good is going to mean that individuals, a community of individuals, or even the cosmos-wide body of Christ will experience suffering. The way to good for all of creation is still the way of the cross.

Connecting the Members

After Paul discusses gifts and their purpose in 1 Cor 12, he then delves into the metaphor of the body of Christ. Here is where the gifts come together. Here is where the action for the common good takes place. Here is how Christians can envision who they are and how they are connected with others who are also in Christ. Here is where we find a metaphor that challenges age segregation in churches and provides a compelling description of what it can look like when generations are together for living Christian lives, all empowered to use their gifts for the good of all and tasked with the care of other members.

All individual members in the church need other Christians whose gifts—together with their own—function for the common good. The individuals together, with their Spirit-given gifts, act in grace and as Christ in their communities and the world for the purpose of participating in Christ's defeat of the powers of sin and death. The point, then, of the exercise of these gifts is to act as Christ's body to work in the world in such a way that battles sin until it is finally and ultimately defeated when the new creation

9. Martyn, *Theological Issues*, 283.

10. Susan Eastman notes in "Double Participation and the Responsible Self in Romans 5–8" that "[l]ife in community is not always good news!" She continues in a footnote: "The idea of the self-in-relation *per se*, let alone communal solidarity or corporate identity, is no panacea for humanity's ills" (Eastman, "Double Participation," 97).

11. For example, Eastman, *Recovering Paul's Mother Tongue*, 121. For further reflections on Christian suffering, see chapter 1 by Michael Gorman, chapter 3 by Charles Campbell, chapter 6 by Ann Jervis, and chapter 8 by Lisa Bowens.

is completely established. Paul issues the charge for Christians to live connected to one another and to act in Christ; this can only happen because through their baptism Christians are already incorporated into the resurrected body of Christ. First Corinthians implores them to act like the people they already are and shows them how to do so through this metaphor of the body. There are many, and increasingly more, resources for intergenerational ministry but I know of none that take this task of participating in Christ for the common good and for the defeat of sin into consideration.

Intergenerational ministry resources often rely on sociological, psychological, historical, and educational reasons why keeping generations together in church is a good idea. For example, teenagers are more likely to have an active faith if they also connect with those who are younger than they are in the church.[12] Certainly studies based in these areas of human behavior and theories are part of the reason that intergenerational ministry is important in churches; they have much to offer. Faith formation is best when it engages all people of the church in the different ministries of the church so that Christians of all ages can grow in their faith and support others doing the same. But to what end? This is where these studies can fall short. Christian faith formation is not an end in and of itself. If a church sees its goal in forming people in the faith to be simply forming people in faith, then people will rightly wonder what the point is. Paul provides the necessary perspective for why forming Christians of all ages, together, is important. The purpose of Christians acting faithfully together is for grace's final and ultimate defeat of sin and death, in which Christians and the gifts they are given participate. Christians are formed into being members of the body of Christ, gifted to act as agents of grace, emboldened by the Spirit, and inseparable from other members because the body woven together is the strongest presence of Christ in the world.[13]

Adolescent Members of the Body of Christ

Adolescents are one segment of the contemporary church that is usually separated from the rest of the church. For years, churches have operated under the assumption that teenagers do not want to be around adults or children, that they dislike "traditional" worship, and that they are best attracted to church for its entertainment possibilities. Unlike young adults,

12. Amidei, Merhaut, and Roberto, *Generations Together*, 11.

13. In chapter 9 of this volume, Colin Miller articulates a similar perspective by highlighting the sacramental nature of the human being and our need to see the faces of our siblings in Christ in order for us to experience real faith in Christ.

who are often simply ignored by churches and are therefore completely absent, youth are often present in the community but relegated to the periphery. They have their own fellowship space and time. They have their own worship services and service activities.

In 2005, sociologist Christian Smith with Melinda Lundquist Denton published a book called *Soul Searching*, in which they collected, reported on, and responded to an extraordinary amount of qualitative research culled from interviews with thousands of teenagers in the United States. One of the main takeaways from their work is that American teenagers are mainly not religious. Instead, they ascribe to a kind of American faith, which Smith and Denton refer to as Moralistic Therapeutic Deism (MTD).[14] According to the authors, MTD holds to the following tenants:

1. A God exists who created and orders the world and watches over human life on earth.

2. God wants people to be good, nice, and fair to each other, as taught in the Bible and by most world religions.

3. The central goal of life is to be happy and to feel good about oneself.

4. God does not need to be particularly involved in one's life except when God is needed to resolve a problem.

5. Good people go to heaven when they die.[15]

Even those who do consider themselves religious according to traditional denominations and faiths ascribe to the tenants of this new "American faith." Another scholar notes, carefully and convincingly, that American teenagers have the same faith as their parents, likely the most influential people in their lives.[16] This means that teenagers in the United States tend to have faith in a self-serving and largely disinterested God who exists to help people be happy and go to heaven when they die. This is the same faith their parents hold to, regardless of whether they profess to be Christian, Muslim, Jewish, other, or "none of the above."

In the flurry of books, articles, and curriculum suggestions that has since followed the publication of that research, intergenerational ministry rather than age-segregated ministry has been emphasized.[17] According

---

14. Smith and Denton, *Soul Searching*, 162.

15. Ibid., 163.

16. Dean, *Almost Christian*, especially chapter 6.

17. Even though the research from Smith and Denton was published in 2005 and the contemporary emphasis on intergenerational ministry is fairly recent (and much of it especially when concerning adolescents is based on that research), this is not a

to many of these writers and scholars, intergenerational ministry will help young people be in relationship with those who are more developed in their faith, will raise Christians from a young age to be fully part of the church, and will keep the gifts of young people in the church rather than in the Sunday school classroom or youth building away from the rest of the congregation. For those working in youth ministry, this means that teenagers will have adults to look up to and learn from, seeing their faith tradition embodied and practiced with integrity and passion *if* the adults themselves can begin to do so. All people will see lifelong faith lived in and by people they both know and respect. Additionally, it will be harder for young people to "age out" of their church's ministry when they graduate high school or complete confirmation (a common concern in many churches). Intergenerational ministry offers more opportunities for all in the church to interact, support, and worship with each other.

According to religious educator and faith development theorist James Fowler, people may be at various stages of faith during their lives. Fowler created his theory based on a number of qualitative interviews with people with varying experiences and commitments to a religious faith. Although his research is dated, the way that he thought through the six stages of faith remains helpful in considering how, when, and why people grow or do not grow in their faith. For example, Fowler notes that the majority of religious folks will remain at a stage available to most people around adolescence for the duration of their lives.[18] In his scheme, this is Stage Three, which he terms Synthetic-Conventional Faith. There is, therefore, no guarantee that the adults with whom young people interact will have a more developed faith than the young people themselves; nor is it a guarantee that a young person will not have a *more* developed faith than the adults with whom they interact.

Intergenerational ministry means more interaction between generations, a closer community, and possibilities for intentional faith formation for the whole body together. This ministry embodies and is in theological concert with Paul's body of Christ metaphor in 1 Corinthians. The truth is that separating the Christian community based on age or life stage is an odd practice without real biblical foundation. This is not to suggest that every

completely new idea. There is plenty of research on the benefits of intergenerational ministry, especially in the field of religious education, going back to the 1970s. In fact, the separation of ages during worship is a fairly recent trend historically that scholarship and practice is now reversing (Allen and Ross, *Intergenerational Christian Formation*, chapter 2).

18. Fowler, *Stages of Faith*, 164. Fowler draws on information from developmental theorists Jean Piaget, Erik Erikson, and Lawrence Kohlberg as he develops his theory.

70 year old in a church wants to go to laser tag with the youth group. This does argue that keeping different ages apart for their religious education and worship can harm the unity of the body of Christ and leaves each age group without the gifts the other age groups have to offer the community.

The book *Intergenerational Christian Formation* makes clear that one of the most important ways to help a church embrace the paradigm shift necessary to be effective in intergenerational ministry is to be clear about the biblical reasons behind it. The authors offer several biblical examples, including the one from 1 Cor 12, although without taking into account Paul's worldview.[19] When reading Paul closely, however, especially taking his anthropology and apocalyptic perspective into account, this scriptural support of intergenerational ministry becomes even stronger.

In churches that do not embrace intergenerational ministry, adults are sought to work with young people, children or youth, usually because they are needed to fill roles young people cannot fill themselves. Children need supervision, or they are not safe. They need someone to help them use the restroom, fix snacks for them, and to make sure no one sticks their fingers in an electrical outlet. Some teenagers are not old enough to drive and cannot legally sign a contract to reserve a retreat space. Youth groups need drivers and chaperones. Churches have policies that include ratios of adults to children and males to females. Events involving young people need to be in compliance with these policies in order for the events to take place safely. These policies are designed to keep everyone (adults, children, and teenagers) safe, and they should be in place and followed.

Of course, there is also the reality that children and youth need teachers, people who know more about faith than they do. Young children who cannot read need the Bible to be read to them. If a teenager is going to join the church through baptism or confirmation, someone needs to teach them what the church says on matters of theology and something about its history.

When seeking to educate young people in the church, to form them into being Christian rather than being followers of MTD or leaving religion all together, churches also must realize that Christian education is not the sole property of adults who are passing information on to children and youth. It is simply not the case that children and teenagers have nothing to offer the church or that older adults have already given all they can give. It is also not the case that adults no longer need Christian education themselves. Young people have powerful and prophetic lenses with which they view the

---

19. Allen and Ross, *Intergenerational Christian Formation*, especially chapter 5; 1 Cor 12 is considered mainly on pp. 114–15.

world, church, and the Bible. They often naturally embody the kind of passion adults have suppressed over time.[20] They are not empty vessels waiting to be filled with knowledge about God and church—they have their own knowledge about and experience of the Holy.[21] After all, no matter what age a person is, they are still created in the image of God. Adolescents are just as capable of experiencing God as anyone of any age. As they learn information from other folks in their churches—older and not—they will interpret it differently, put it into conversation with their own lives in unique ways, and offer something back to their teachers.

Knowing about faith, however, is not the only goal of Christian education or of intergenerational ministry. Knowing information about faith does not always lead to and is not equivalent to having faith or living faith in practice. Christian education is about more than information. Faith is about who a person is and about what they do in response to their faith as much as it is about what they know.[22] Lived and embodied faith are essential parts of Christian education and the continuing development of a person's faith, neither of which can be reduced simply to knowledge about Christianity.

If we are to take Paul and the way he sees the world seriously in 1 Cor 12, we also need to look at how adults are asked to be involved in ministry with young people, how young people are asked to be involved in ministry with adults, and for what purpose. Typically when adults are asked to help with programs and events focused on young people, they are recruited as volunteers. Likewise, young people may be asked to volunteer as acolytes for a traditional worship service, to play music in a contemporary one, or to teach older adults how to use the computer. They may be volunteered to move heavy furniture in the fellowship hall. All of these are legitimate needs and roles to play in the ministries of the church, but the truth is that the church does not need *volunteers* for their programming with young people. Nor does it need *volunteers* to run the food pantry or host the homeless shelter. Nor does it need *volunteers* to come to worship or to read Scripture in worship. Nothing about the body of Christ metaphor in 1 Cor 12 calls for volunteers.

---

20. Dean, *Practicing Passion*, 25.

21. The critique of the "banking model" of education comes from Freire, *Pedagogy of the Oppressed*, chapter 2.

22. Christian educators have long been arguing that there is more to their vocation than conveying information. For example, Fred P. Edie writes in what ways Christian education is about knowing, being, and doing in his article, Edie, "Christian Educator's Imagination," 9–29; Thomas H. Groome writes that Christian education is about educating for the Christian faith as being "a way of the head, a way of the heart, and a way of the hands" (Groome, *Will There Be Faith?*, 111).

David Eagle, in a *Christian Century* article, made the point that churches are dealing with the reality of many fewer volunteer hours available to them than in previous generations.[23] People are busier. Commitments are more numerous. Households are strained in resources: financial, relational, and temporal. Many households include parents and caregivers who work long hours, sometimes at multiple jobs, and children who are busy with school and often the requisite extracurricular activities to ensure a well-rounded life (and for résumés and college applications), babysitting younger siblings, part time jobs to help with household expenses, and, lest we forget, downtime and social lives. Just ask the youth pastor of a typical mainline church trying to get a commitment from teenagers for attendance at a mission trip fundraiser or confirmation class—there is going to be a serious conflict with other things vying for teenagers' time. These are difficult realities; the church competes with all kinds of activities and demands on time.

Instead of calling for volunteers or offering strategies for competing with the demands on people's time, in 1 Cor 12 Paul talks about how connected the body of Christ is and lists gifts that those who are in Christ's body can have, all for the common good. What if instead of looking for volunteers, churches look for what gifts its members have and for the common good to which those gifts could contribute? What if churches did not separate the ages but viewed all members as intricately part of and integral to the whole and acted according to that view?

Members of the Body

Paul's awareness that Christians are not living their own isolated lives is pervasive in his writings. For example, he writes that baptism is into Christ himself, into both his death and his resurrection (Rom 6:1–11). Those who are in Christ have died with Christ and are living in his resurrection while they wait for their own—the resurrection that will come at the end time. Quite literally and also metaphorically, those who are baptized are living only because they do so in Christ. This is not only a symbolic existence. The Christian's life is a life in Christ. Living in Christ, in his body, happens with other Christians in daily life, and necessarily means participating in Christ's continuing work in the world.

Susan Eastman, in her chapter in *Apocalyptic Paul*, explains Paul's challenging and complicated anthropology. She uses the term "double

23. Eagle, "More People."

participation" to describe the place of the self in Rom 5–8.[24] By following how Paul talks about the self and others and about the world in which people find themselves, Eastman makes clear that the life lived now is one lived in two realms of existence. Those who are in Christ live both in redemption and in the reality that the eschaton, the time of final and complete redemption of creation, has not yet come. Eastman points out that the point of living this double life is that "the self is trained as a responsible agent, indeed as a soldier who is to present her bodily members as 'weapons of righteousness' (6:13) and thereby to conquer evil with good and death with life."[25] The self has responsibility because it is in Christ, freed from the grasp of sin and death. According to J. Louis Martyn in his close reading of Galatians, this existence is not as an individual but as an individual-in-community. This community is morally responsible because it is in Christ and infused with the Spirit of Christ. Martyn writes, "Every one of Paul's hortatory sentences presupposes the presence of Christ and the constant activity of Christ's Spirit, as it causes the church to be able to hear."[26] Eastman is careful to preserve the reality of the individual even as it is within the communal. She calls Paul's concept of the individual a "self-in-relationship, corporately constituted yet still a distinct self."[27] This is the individual to whom is given these various manifestations of grace that Paul lists in 1 Cor 12. He writes to a community that is likewise living in this complex web of relationship. They are living in the in-between time, and they are members of their own community; they are also and always members of the body of Christ and yet still individuals.

Dale Martin points out that Paul is up front about his purpose in writing 1 Corinthians. This letter is a "deliberative letter" in which his words are meant to convey and impress upon the hearers of the letter that they are much better together than divided. He urges the Corinthians "to do what is beneficial and what will make for the common advantage, rather than exercising their complete autonomy."[28] Throughout the whole letter, especially in chapter 12 with the compelling metaphor of the body, the Corinthians are invited to envision and imagine themselves (and to act accordingly) as a member of a body—an arm, a foot, or ear—rather than as an autonomous individual member of an organization, gathering, or group, as Christians

---

24. Eastman, "Double Participation," 107.

25. Ibid. See also chapter 8, where Lisa Bowens examines and explains Paul's imagery and its implications for the spiritual warfare that pervades Christian life.

26. Martyn, *Theological Issues*, 234.

27. Eastman, "Double Participation," 101.

28. Martin, *Corinthian Body*, 38–39.

today might be formed to think of themselves in relation to their church. In fact, the gathering of Christians at Corinth, the church, is itself a part of the universal body of Christ. They do not exist in isolation from other Christian communities, whether separated by time or space. Christians at Corinth simultaneously live in redemption yet also wait for the completion of the new creation, just as Christians in the twenty-first century do. These Christians in Corinth participate in their local community of believers and also in the universal body of Christ. Twenty-first century Christians, too, live their lives in Christ and do so both in their local churches and in the universal body of believers.

First Corinthians 12 offers another kind of "double participation." Paul points out that each individual is given a gift and that gift is always and completely part of the whole and is, in fact, given for the benefit of the whole. This is extremely counter-cultural in a society where the autonomous individual is the highest ideal. We strive for personal advancement and financial security and independence for our families. We think about our gifts, normally interchangeable with "talents," as being able to achieve those ends. We are conditioned to see our gifts as our possessions, and we decide how and when to use them. Our talents will set us apart in our college applications or résumés, at our jobs, or in our social circles. Considering our gifts as given by the Spirit, as expressions of grace, and as being given for the purpose of the common good leads to a very different way of conceiving our purpose and identities as Christians.

Intergenerational Ministry and 1 Corinthians 12

There is much the church can learn from this metaphor in 1 Cor 12. The implications are vast, extending far beyond the local church, though I do think they may begin there. Each individual member of a church is but one member of an entire body. Each church is but one member of the full body of Christ, living and acting as grace against sin and death in this world while we wait for our own resurrection. This certainly calls into question the idea of volunteerism in the local church. No one is volunteering, and in fact the "common good" extends beyond the local church or even the body of Christ as a whole. The good of the whole is good for the entirety of the creation, which is caught in and participating in this battle between grace and sin. The body of Christ, in which Christians live, is not a neutral place for folks to gather, volunteer their time, and have lock-ins. The body of Christ has a purpose in this in-between time in which sin and death are still active. The ultimate defeat of sin and death depends on the continued action of grace. Of course, members of the church may gather and give of their time and even have lock-ins. But it is essential that they (and we) not forget that the purpose is to fight against sin in whatever ways it manifests itself in the world and even within the church.

Eastman points out that, for some, lacking autonomy and finding life in community is not "always good news."[29] This is undoubtedly true, and not only because it goes against our cultural conditioning. Age-segregated ministries in the church fit much better with Western culture. Members are separated into markets, based on age and perhaps life experience. This makes it much easier for a church to consider ways to target each specific market with curriculum, activities, merchandise, and "experiences." Churches often ask new members, including teenagers through the confirmation process for example, to make an individual profession of faith. We are culturally conditioned to think in terms of the individual. If we take seriously that life in the body of Christ is life that lacks autonomy, life that is intimately and inextricably connected to others, it poses challenges to the way many Christians are used to church being done. Niche markets in the church are a thing of the past. We begin to take responsibility for the faith of other members rather than leaving it up to the individual and their personal experience. In an individual achievement-based society, what does it mean if the church radically forms people to think of themselves as a different kind of individual, one without autonomy?

Part of the challenge, too, is that every Christian community is not equal. The *kind* of community in which one lives and worships is so important. If one's identity, one's position, and one's capacity to act on the side of Christ depend on the people with whom one is connected, not just any church will do. A church must take seriously its task to fight against sin, and part of doing so is to honor each member, the gifts they have been given, and the connection all the members have, which partly means using those gifts for the good of all. Churches need to understand, discuss, and act with their awareness of the connection between each member and all the other members of the body—those local and those further away in time and/or space. At the end of chapter 12, Paul writes, "If one member suffers, all suffer together with that member; if one member is celebrated, all celebrate with that member" (12:26, author's translation). The sharing of burdens and of celebrations is a distinctive gift of being in the body, especially in an often-fractured society. Members take care of one another— something that cannot happen if members are separated from each other by age or anything else.

29. Eastman, "Double Participation," 97.

The metaphor of the body in 1 Cor 12 also shows clearly that being in Christ is being so connected with others who are in Christ that one is responsible to care for those who are weaker, less respectable or honorable than others, or inferior (all terms Paul uses in 1 Cor 12 to describe some members of the body). It's not hard to think of what parts of the body Paul might be referring to in an actual body. Our genitals, our arthritic hip, our knee that needs ice after every run, the broken bone that needs a cast, our eyes that weaken with age, our blood with cholesterol levels that need constant medication. These are all parts of the body that need extra care or attention, parts of the body we treat differently than other, stronger parts. As in many places in Paul's epistles, he is speaking on different levels at the same time. A body is an appropriate metaphor for the church, too. This is part of why the metaphor is so striking even centuries after it was written. It is not hard to think about those "inferior" members of a church's body, just as it is not hard to think about the inferior members of the human body. As it is in many churches, there are many who are left out: for example, young, squirmy children; those who suffer from physical or mental conditions that make sitting for long periods impossible; those who learn or process differently than by sitting and listening to a sermon; those who don't speak the language of the pastor; those who cannot hear.

Adolescents too, I have noticed, are probably always lumped into that "inferior" category of a congregation. Often, churches welcome with open arms children who are considered cute (at least until after the children's message, when they are expected to evaporate or suddenly become adult enough to sit quietly for the remainder of a service geared toward those who can sit still and listen to a lengthy and probably somewhat heady sermon). Then they start puberty. They are moody. Smelly. Awkward. They should shave, well, but not yet, even though that nearly-moustache is weird looking. They are not wearing clothes appropriate for worship anymore. They fall asleep during the sermon. They slouch. They grunt. They are clumsy. They are always on their phones. They use strange words all of the sudden that do not make any sense. I have heard all of this and more as congregations usher their youth out of the church and into the youth annex or youth room for their own worship and their own fellowship time. Adults and teenagers alike are told that teenagers do not like "adult worship." There is an assumption that teenagers do not want to be around adults; and, many adults are uncomfortable around teenagers.

Research, in fact, shows the opposite. Teenagers do want to be around caring adults.[30] Youth need (and want) mentors and guides who will share

30. For example, DeVries, *Sustainable Youth Ministry*, 145; Root, *Revisiting*

in their faith journeys with them.[31] And if you have ever seen young people working with children at Vacation Bible School, it is also clear that many of them have no objection to being with those who are younger than they are. Yet so often they are effectively cut off from the church until they are deemed more acceptable or manageable, by which point they may have left the church completely.

God unites the body so that there is no division—or dissension as the NRSV translates the Greek—between its members (1 Cor 12:25). All members must take care of the other members; and, in fact, there are some members who need extra care. Note, these members of the body are not to be separated from the body, punished, or ignored, but given extra care. Young people, then, including the teenagers, need extra care; they do not need to be cut off from the congregation or the larger body of Christ. Doing so is the opposite of care; it is forfeiture.

In Practice

There are many books and articles written about intergenerational ministry, including ideas for how to involve all ages in worship, mission, and fellowship activities of the local church. Paul's image of the body of Christ and its gifts given for the good of the whole calls for some different suggestions grounded in a different theology. Paul demands that we take seriously that each of us, no matter what age, is given a gift meant for the good of the whole. He demands that we take seriously that the time we are living in is a time of cosmic battle and that as a community we are responsible for ethical action in this time. This means that what the church must do, with its members united and its gifts in use, is fight against sin. Without all its members present, the body of Christ will not be as strong; it will fail to be the body it is able and empowered to be as baptized and living in the resurrected Christ.

The good of the whole body is for every member to be present and valued for who they are and the gift of grace they have been given. The good of the whole body involves every member working together to identify where sin is active and together fighting against it. When a church is not committed to these two ways of being together, it risks not being effective as the body of Christ in the world.

A concrete example is a meeting I had with pastors who wanted to know how to get "butts in the seats" for increased numbers of adults to

---

Relational Youth Ministry.

31. For example, Root, "Doubt and Confirmation," 196–7; Dean, *Almost Christian*, chapters 6–7; Amidei, Merhaut, and Roberto, *Generations Together*, 8–13.

volunteer with their churches' youth ministries. The real question is not, "How do we get adults to volunteer with our youth program?" The real question is, "How will our church be the body of Christ at this current time given how we see sin active in our community, our country, or our world?" Participation in the body of Christ is necessarily participation in the battle between sin and grace. When the church has identified a place—for there will be many—where sin is active, the next question is how to employ the gifts of the church to combat it.

If sin is present in anti-Semitic graffiti springing up in a church's neighborhood, then the gifts present in the church must combat not only the actual graffiti but also the fear, racism, and hatred behind it. The youth, children, and adults in the church must work together, using the gifts of each person, to come up with and act upon solutions. All members are essential to the body, and each member, no matter the age, brings a different gift into the conversation and into the action.

If sin is in a community's inability to find God's active presence in their daily lives, then the members of the church must turn to each other and use the gifts present there to learn together how to connect with God. This might happen through new spiritual practices the community can learn and practice together, maybe in different ways than has become the custom. If sin is showing up in the church through the stereotyping of people based on age, it is both up to and within the power of the whole community to combat this fallacy.

If, as many parents of teenagers insist, underage drinking, premarital sex, and drug use is how sin is operating in the lives of adolescents, then it is not the youth minister's job to scare teenagers away from these temptations to participate with sin or distract them with wholesome activities. Instead, it is up to the entire church, including the teenagers, to use their gifts to combat sin as it manifests in these ways. Youth need mentors who have struggled against addiction to share stories. Youth need to learn how to honor their own and others' bodies and sexualities. They need to teach adults what is different now from when they were teenagers, so that the whole body can support each other as they learn to combat heteronormativity, gender stereotyping, marketing campaigns that target young people and their hormones, and patriarchy. None of this can happen by relegating the teenagers to the "youth building" and offering them distractions. Manifestations of sin must be combated. When connected with the whole body, youth enter into these conversations and consequent actions knowing that they can and will win.

There are many resources for ways to do intergenerational ministry, some of which have already been cited in this essay. Many of them include strong theological reasoning and wise practical suggestions. There are re-sources for including all ages in every aspect of the church's life together. There are liturgies and creative suggestions for embodied worship that is more accessible not only to small children but also to anyone who does not sit still or function mainly cerebrally. Church worship services are typically geared toward those who are able to read, to sit still for at least an hour (quietly), and to listen to and find meaning in a sermon, the language of which is normally geared toward the adults in the room. Liturgy scholars and theologians have been reminding Christians for years that worship is formative when it is embodied. This is part of why rituals in the church's worship are so meaningful; they often require people to move and to act with their bodies, minds, and spirits all engaged.

Paul's image of the body of Christ in 1 Cor 12 gives churches an im-portant biblical grounding for intergenerational ministry and the purpose of it. Paul's metaphor does not stand alone, however, as an aspirational image that churches can look to as they explain and understand their inter-generational ministry goals. Instead, Paul's metaphor—placed rightly into his context and worldview—serves as an imperative not only for churches to be intergenerational in their ministries but to know that these minis-tries serve an important purpose for Christ's continuing work in the world. These ministries are part of how the church can participate in the final and complete defeat of sin and death and the flourishing of the new creation, which was promised by God, begun on the cross, and for which we all wait together and work toward now. We must be intergenerational because it is the best chance we have for embodying grace in a world so in need of grace's action. We must be intergenerational because without it we are not acting as baptized people raised together in the one body of Christ. We must be intergenerational because all our gifts are needed in this world at this time. Quite simply, we need each other, and we are only ourselves when we are with each other.

Bibliography

Allen, Holly Catterton, and Christian Lawton Ross. *Intergenerational Christian Formation: Bringing the Whole Church Together in Ministry, Community and Worship*. Downers Grove: InterVarsity, 2012.

Amidei, Kathie, Jim Merhaut, and John Roberto. *Generations Together: Caring, Praying, Learning, Celebrating, and Serving Faithfully*. Naugatuck, CT: Lifelong Faith Associates, 2014.

Dean, Kenda Creasy. *Almost Christian: What the Faith of Our Teenagers is Telling the American Church*. New York: Oxford University Press, 2010.

————. *Practicing Passion: Youth and the Quest for a Passionate Church*. Grand Rapids: Eerdmans, 2004.

DeVries, Mark. *Sustainable Youth Ministry: Why Most Youth Ministry Doesn't Last and What Your Church Can Do About It*. Downers Grove: InterVarsity, 2008.

Eagle, David. "More People, Looser Ties: Social Life in the Megachurch." *The Christian Century*, April 8, 2016. http://www.christiancentury.org/article/2016-03/more-people-looser-ties.

Eastman, Susan. "Double Participation and the Responsible Self in Romans 5–8." In *Apocalyptic Paul: Cosmos and Anthropos in Romans 5–8*, edited by Beverly Roberts Gaventa, 93–110. Waco: Baylor University Press, 2013.

————. *Recovering Paul's Mother Tongue: Language and Theology in Galatians*. Grand Rapids: Eerdmans, 2007.

Edie, Fred P. "The Christian Educator's Imagination." *Religious Education* 107 (January–February 2012) 9–29.

Fowler, James W. *Stages of Faith: The Psychology of Human Development and the Quest for Meaning*. New York: HarperSanFrancisco, 1981.

Freire, Paulo. *Pedagogy of the Oppressed*. Translated by Myra Bergman Ramos. 30th Anniversary Edition. New York: Continuum, 2001.

Groome, Thomas H. *Will There Be Faith? A New Vision for Educating and Growing Disciples*. New York: HarperOne, 2011.

Martin, Dale B. *The Corinthian Body*. New Haven: Yale University Press, 1995.

Martyn, J. Louis. *Theological Issues in the Letters of Paul*. Edinburgh: T. & T. Clark, 1997.

Root, Andrew. "Doubt and Confirmation: The Mentor as Co-Doubter." In *The Theological Turn in Youth Ministry*, by Andrew Root and Kenda Creasy Dean, 192–98. Downers Grove, IL: InterVarsity, 2011.

————. *Revisiting Relational Youth Ministry: From a Strategy of Influence to a Theology of Incarnation*. Downers Grove: InterVarsity, 2007.

Smith, Christian, and Melinda Lundquist Denton. *Soul Searching: The Religious and Spiritual Lives of American Teenagers*. New York: Oxford University Press, 2005.

11

Christlike Feasting: Attentiveness, Solidarity, and Self-Restraint in Romans

PRESIAN R. BURROUGHS

F RIENDSHIPS COMMONLY DEEPEN AROUND food. People bond over meals
while they discuss the latest issues, share personal stories, and laugh
over common foibles. Their connections strengthen through the breaking of
bread. These bonds can grow stronger and extend to even more people as
Christians partake of broken bread during Eucharist. Friendships are formed
and strengthened in the presence of good food and the good Creator.

When I was a seminary student and then her first doctoral advisee, I
had the privilege of enjoying several meals with Susan Eastman, and I offer
this essay in her honor. During those meals together, we would give thanks
to our Creator for the food before us and enter a sacred space of conversation and edification. Because of Susan's pastoral *and* academic wisdom, I
was the primary beneficiary of our lunchtime fellowship. She would listen
to me reflect on my emerging sense of vocation, my developing grasp of
Paul's thought, my concern over how to bring Pauline studies into conversation with other disciplines (especially ecology), and my questions about the
finer points of teaching and grading, and she would graciously offer her
insights. Even though our respective roles conferred unequal amounts of
power, our meals together revealed our fundamental solidarity—no matter
our differences, we both depended on nourishment from the Creator and
God's creation and benefitted from mutual encouragement and love.

Sharing meals together also played an important role in establishing
solidarity between diverse peoples in first century Rome. Although Paul's
letter to the Christians in Rome addresses a wide variety of theological and
practical issues, incompatible eating practices that threatened to divide the
Roman churches take center stage in chapters 14–15. Seeking the unity of all
God's people (whether Law-observant or not), Paul directs the Christians

not only to continue expressing gratitude to God for their food but also to exercise self-restraint in their food choices so that they, like Christ, might truly walk in love and not "destroy one for whom Christ died" (Rom 14:15b, author's translation).

Paul's call to Christlike feasting holds relevance for God's people to-day in ways that extend beyond questions of Law observance. We live in a time when most of our foods are grown by agricultural practices that pollute soils, waters, and air through the use of toxic chemicals and climate-warming fossil fuels. These practices—especially the use of pesticides and herbicides—diminish the health of farmworkers and consumers, people for whom Christ died. Without even intending to do so, we daily engage in eating habits that injure the human and nonhuman creation that Jesus came to liberate. This situation of undue destruction calls for our attention, and Paul's theology of creation articulated in Romans invites us to reorient our practices in solidarity with the suffering of all creation, to live in gratitude for creation's innumerable gifts, and to exercise self-restraint so that its suffering might be reduced.

When we read Romans with an eye toward our current ecological situation, we find that this letter provides a guide for navigating many of the difficult eco-ethical decisions we face today. Chapter 1 directs us to attend to creation's witness to God and to live in gratitude for the gifts of God's creation. Chapter 8 leads us to recognize the ways in which human sin negatively affects creation but also how human righteousness—especially of Jesus Christ and ultimately of God's resurrected and glorified children—will liberate creation from ongoing destruction. Chapters 14–15, finally, teach us to practice Christlike feasting by expressing gratitude to God for our food and exercising loving self-restraint so that we might live as people who support the flourishing, rather than the destruction, of God's human and nonhuman creation.

Romans 1: Proper Attentiveness

At the beginning of his letter to Rome, a missive in which he elaborates the theology and practical implications of God's universal gospel, Paul explains that people fail to glorify and give thanks to the Creator God (Rom 1:21–23, 25). He states,

> For what can be known about God is plain to them, because God has shown it to them. Ever since the creation of the world his eternal power and divine nature, invisible though they are, have been understood and seen through the things he has made.

So they are without excuse; for though they knew God, they did
not honor him as God or give thanks to him, but they became
futile in their thinking, and their senseless minds were dark-
ened. (1:19–21)[1]

Here in chapter 1, Paul acknowledges God as the Creator and points to
problems that exist between creatures and Creator. If God's human creatures
maintained a proper relationship with the Creator, they would both glorify
God and thank God for the gifts of creation. Glorifying God, on the one
hand, would involve a humble acknowledgment of the complete otherness
of God, the distinction between God and creation.[2] Sincere thanksgiving
to God, on the other hand, would recognize that God has given good gifts
without which life could not survive.

Undergirding Paul's indictment of humanity stands a particular theology of creation that recognizes a dynamic relationship between God and
all that is not God, what I am calling *creation*.[3] This relationship moves in
two directions simultaneously, both of which highlight the close connection
between the Creator and the creation.

In the first, initiating movement of a Pauline theology of creation, God
directs divine energies toward creation.[4] As hinted in Rom 1:20 and poeti-
cally portrayed in Gen 1–2, God made the creation, speaking the creation
and all living things into existence (according to the first creation account
in Gen 1:1—2:3) and fashioning humanity out of the fertile soil, apparently
with God's own hands (according to the second creation account in Gen
2:7). God also draws near to the creation through self-disclosure and allows
the creation itself to manifest some aspects of the Creator God, in particular God's power and divine nature (Rom 1:19–20). This is not to say that
creation reveals the full knowledge of God to sentient beings, but certainly
"God has revealed something of himself in and through the created world."[5]
Standing behind Paul's words in this passage is God's ongoing care for the

1. All scriptural quotations are from the NRSV unless otherwise indicated.

2. By glorifying God, as Robert Jewett explains, people acknowledge "the relative
status of God and humankind. This expression differentiates true worship from the
worship of the images of humans, birds, and serpents (1:23)" (Jewett, *Romans*, 157).

3. Although this chapter often refers to humans and "creation" as if these were two
distinct groups, we must always recall that humans too are creation. At times, I will
highlight this fact by using the phrase "nonhuman creation" in order to describe those
created things that are not human beings.

4. Drawing upon the rich theological insights of the Orthodox tradition, Norman Wirzba describes God's energies as "the divine operations that go forth from God
and communicate God in the world. These energies are not creatures but God himself
(though not according to God's substance)," (Wirzba, *From Nature to Creation*, 81).

5. Matera, *Romans*, 49.

creation. From beginning to end, the Bible depicts God as the loving and creating Provider, who sustains, renews, and directs creation (Ps 104:30; Job 38:41). Fundamental to a Pauline theology of creation, then, is the recognition that God is intimately involved in the creation.

The second movement within a Pauline theology of creation is creation's response, testifying to God's existence and—at least among sentient beings like humans—glorifying God for God's being. God has created the world in such a way as to display God's "eternal power and divine nature" (Rom 1:20; see also Ps 19:1; 97:6). The power of the natural world reflects God's own unbounded power and invites people to worship the One who is other than creation. As sentient beings, we humans may perceive from the wonders of creation that a powerful, divine Creator is present. This is not to say that through the creation people come to know the fullness of God's redeeming love, which is revealed in God's covenant with Israel and the renewed covenant through Jesus Christ.[6] Yet, Paul suggests that through creation itself people can know God as the generous Creator to whom they ought to render thanks (Rom 1:21; 14:6). Gratitude to God for the gifts of the earth, therefore, is always appropriate.

Unfortunately, rather than feasting their eyes on the magnificence of creation and thereby recognizing the magnificence of the Creator, people often consume creation and forget the Creator. Human sin distorts and misappropriates the creation's revelatory testimony about God's power and divinity (1:20–23). Perception—or, more rightly, misperception—is at the root of the problem since people perceive creation with a view toward satisfying selfish appetites.[7] Thus, people not only neglect the Creator God by failing to "honor him as God or give thanks to him" (1:21), but they also misconstrue creation itself. This, according to Paul, erroneously leads them into making created things into idols or gods. People "worshiped and served the creation rather than the Creator" (1:25, NET), because they imposed upon creation inordinate expectations, assuming somehow that

6. Keck, *Romans*, 63; Jewett, *Romans*, 154–5; Dunn, *Romans*, 57–58; and Moo, *Epistle to the Romans*, 105.

7. Wirzba, *From Nature to Creation*, 87–94. Influenced by the ascetic traditions of Christian monasticism, Wirzba describes the ways in which sinful human passions distort our vision of and consequent relationships with creation: "Asceticism is all about attending to customary ways of approaching others that lead to distortion because what we see is dominated by the anxiety or hubris or insecurity we so often feel" (ibid., 89). In order to counteract and correct this distortion, we must engage in a rigorous process of self-examination (with the assistance and encouragement of a community) (ibid.). This process "begins with attention to how personal ambition, fear, and boredom get in the way of seeing things for what they are, that is, expressions of God's love, and as such, the material manifestations of God's goodness and delight" (ibid., 91).

created things—whether people, animals, or inanimate objects—would deliver God-sized blessings, meaning, and results.[8] People no longer directed their adoration to the eternal God—"from [whom] and through [whom] and to [whom] are all things" (11:36)—but instead adored and served perishable and transient things. In doing so, humans interrupted the generous movement of God toward creation and creation's own movement back to God by focusing their attention on the creation itself rather than directing their gaze *through creation* onto God.

One may be inclined to conclude that the solution to this problem is to concentrate all our attention on the Creator. Yet, because we are embodied beings that depend upon the creation for air, water, shelter, and nourishment, we cannot entirely disregard creation; we must continue to toil and till the ground in order to "eat of it all the days" of our lives (Gen 3:17). The dualism in which we isolate spiritual attention from physical necessities promises to lead our spirits and the well-being of creation into grave danger. In turning all of our spiritual energies entirely away from the creation in order to concentrate solely on the Creator, we are blinded to the fact that nonhuman creatures occupy their own, unique position of value in the Creator's economy. This position of value should shape our own response of gratitude and self-restraint. To concentrate simply upon God would ignore the value of that which God has made and the divinely derived claim that it has upon us. Elevating the self at the expense of other members of creation, such a posture would lead to mutual deterioration and destruction.

Proper worship of the Creator thus requires appropriate attentiveness to creation. This means we must remain alert to the ways in which creation points toward the gracious provision of our Creator even as we acknowledge creation's limits. As Paul's theology of creation continues to unfold in Romans we also find that appropriate attentiveness to creation means remaining alert to the ways in which our activities harm creation. In chapters 5 and 8, Paul directs our attention to the ways in which our lives and purposes intertwine with the whole creation, and he calls us to live in solidarity with creation's suffering as well as its liberation.

Romans 8: Solidarity

In Rom 8:19–22, Paul depicts creation as being subjected to frustration and enslaved to destruction. These undesirable circumstances result, in part, from human sin but will be rectified when God ultimately liberates humans

8. Ibid., 48–49.

from sin at their resurrection (8:19, 21, 23).[9] This way of portraying creation's current condition and its ultimate liberation indicates an important aspect of Paul's theology of creation. Paul suggests that humanity and creation stand in solidarity, solidarity of suffering as well as liberation. Solidarity expresses the fact that humanity and the rest of God's creation are interdependent; they currently share in suffering and ultimately will share in the experience of salvation. So intertwined are they that creation's suffering goes hand in hand with humanity's slavery to sin. Since human sin inflicts devastation and destruction on both human and nonhuman creation, people hold some responsibility for the unnecessary degradation of creation. Although Jesus rectifies this situation so that people may be liberated from sin's tyranny (6:12–13), the nonhuman creation's liberation will not be realized until the presence and possibility of sin are finally and fully removed.

The twin principles of solidarity and responsibility come embedded within Paul's larger explanation of how sinful people live into their redemption, the righteousness and abundant life that the indwelling Spirit makes possible (8:1–13). Yet, even within this abundant life, Paul acknowledges that God's people continue to suffer (8:17). This acknowledgement of suffering brings Paul to address the wider creation's suffering and also its hope of liberation. The nonhuman creation now experiences slavery to destruction but will ultimately be liberated into glory, as Paul explains in 8:19–23:

> For the creation expectantly awaits the apocalypse of the sons of God. For the creation was subjected to futility, not willingly, but on account of the one subjecting it in hope that the creation itself will be liberated from the slavery of destruction into the liberty of the glory of the children of God. For we know that the whole creation is groaning and laboring together even till now. And not only creation but also those having the first fruits of the Spirit, we and they groan in ourselves while awaiting adoption, the redemption of our body. (Rom 8:19–23, author's translation)

The concepts of solidarity and human responsibility emerge in Paul's references to subjection, waiting, mutual groaning, and liberation, and they harken back to the earliest creation narratives in the Bible. To grasp the theology of creation at work here, one must unpack what Paul means by creation's subjection and its liberation.

---

9. While here I concentrate on the ways in which sin, death, resurrection, and the eschaton affect creation, Ann Jervis in chapter 6 considers these in relation to human beings, though without losing sight of the new creation. For further discussion of the new creation, also see Charles Campbell's chapter 3.

Solidarity of Subjection

Paul takes it for granted that the creation exists in a subjected state, noting, "The creation was subjected to futility, not willingly, but on account of the one subjecting it" (8:20, author's translation). But, one might ask, to whom was creation subjected? In the immediate context, the answer remains obscure. In order to fill in these gaps, we must look to the wider context of this letter, primarily chapter 5, where Paul reflects upon primeval history in order to contrast the failure of Adam with the fidelity of Christ.

According to Paul, Adam's fateful transgression introduced sin, condemnation, and death into human existence (5:12–21).[10] He explains, "Sin came into the world through one man, and death came through sin, and so death spread to all because all have sinned" (5:12). By referring to the Bible's first human, Adam, and describing the origin of sin in this way, Paul likely draws upon the creation account found in Gen 2–3. In this second creation account, God gives Adam (and thereafter Eve) one command to govern life in the Garden of Eden: "of the tree of the knowledge of good and evil you shall not eat, for in the day that you eat of it you shall die" (Gen 2:17). Death, then, would be the consequence of transgression.[11] When Adam and Eve *do* transgress God's command by feasting upon the forbidden fruit, God consigns human beings to a mortal life that will no longer find any reprieve in the fruit of the tree of life (2:9).[12]

In addition to incurring the just sentence of death, humanity's sin blights the land and places people into an antagonistic relationship with the rest of creation. God declares to Adam:

> cursed is the ground because of you; in toil you shall eat of it all
> the days of your life; thorns and thistles it shall bring forth for
> you; and you shall eat the plants of the field. By the sweat of your

10. For an insightful examination of this passage and Paul's anthropology more generally, see Eastman, "Double Participation."

11. For a detailed explanation of Rom 5 in relation to the Genesis narrative, see Cranfield, *Critical and Exegetical Commentary*, 269–81. Other Jewish interpreters around the time of Paul also drew from Gen 3 the inference that death was foreign to God's intended created order and that it intruded upon the human experience. For example, see Wis 2:24 and the Apocalypse of Moses 32 (ibid., 274). Whether death here refers to cessation of life that strikes any and all living things or humanity alone is up for debate.

12. Wenham, *Genesis*, 83. By being expelled from the garden of God and not having access to the tree of life, the man and woman "were no longer able to have daily conversation with God, enjoy his bounteous provision, and eat of the tree of life; instead they had to toil for food, suffer, and eventually return to the dust from which they were taken" (ibid., 74).

face you shall eat bread until you return to the ground, for out
of it you were taken; you are dust, and to dust you shall return.
(Gen 3:17–19)

The once fruitful land now lies cursed because of human beings.[13] As a
result, if people are to postpone the sentence of death, they must do so
through the continuous, difficult toil needed to nourish earthly life.[14]

Together Rom 5 and Gen 2–3 teach that disobedience mars the human
creature's experience in this world and blemishes the nonhuman creation
itself. When read through the lens of Gen 2–3, Rom 8:20 suggests that human sin subjects the land (and the rest of creation) to frustration. The Greek
term often translated in Rom 8:20 as "frustration" or "futility" names an
"ineffectiveness of that which does not attain its goal."[15] That goal, according
to the creation narratives of Genesis, entails being fruitful and multiplying
(Gen 1:11, 22, 24, 28), basking in the presence of God (3:8), and producing
plants that are "pleasant to the sight and good for food" (2:9). These ends
are frustrated when human sin disrupts creation's ability to produce and
support life. While it presumably matters little to the land whether it grows
vegetables or thorn bushes, it matters greatly to humans.

The land's propensity to support the flourishing of thistles and thorns
(in other words, plants that do not produce edible food for humans) rather
than fruit trees, grains, and vegetables drastically changes its relationship
with humans. In order to obtain nourishing foods, people must now tear at
and cut into the once spontaneously fecund soil. They must dig water chan-
nels, create terraces, and rip down trees. Although these activities may bring
about a certain kind of productivity, they are often attended by negative,
unintended consequences, such as erosion, flooding, and the leeching of
nutrients from the soil. Although God had placed humans in the garden in
order to till and keep it so that they might experience solidarity and mutual
flourishing (Gen 2:15), humans and the fertile soil now stand as adversar-
ies. The solidarity they do share is no longer in flourishing but in suffering.
Nevertheless, Paul suggests that another possibility exists, for the creation
was subjected *in hope* (Rom 8:20).

---

13. Ibid., 82.

14. Wenham makes a similar connection: "Man's offense consisted of eating the
forbidden fruit; therefore he is punished in what he eats. The toil that now lies behind
the preparation of every meal is a reminder of the fall and is made the more painful by
the memory of the ready supply of food within the garden (2:9)" (ibid., 82).

15. Cranfield, *Critical and Exegetical Commentary*, 413.

Solidarity of Liberation

Suffering, frustration, and destruction are not the end of the story. Just as God would not leave sinful humanity to condemnation and death (Rom 5:8–10), neither does God abandon subjected creation to perpetual futility and destruction. Instead, God seeks to liberate creation from its current condition, as Paul indicates at 8:21: "the creation itself will be liberated from the slavery of destruction into the liberty of the glory of the children of God" (author's translation). Because this verse occurs in a passage with clear eschatological overtones,[16] the future tense of "liberate" and the reference to the glory of God's children indicate that creation's liberation will take place when God ultimately resurrects the children of God.[17] Prior to that eschatological event, the nonhuman creation waits for the fullness of God's salvation that has come in and through Jesus Christ. God's people wait too as they groan in solidarity with the nonhuman creation and eagerly anticipate the consummation of salvation (8:19, 22, 23). Just as human and nonhuman creation stand in solidarity in their suffering, they also experience solidarity in their hope of God's ultimate salvation. Yet, it is reasonable to wonder what the liberation of nonhuman creation entails.[18] Three elements in verse 21 suggest an answer: the meaning of destruction, the concept of liberation, and the implications of glorification.

Paul's description of creation being enslaved to *decay* (NRSV) may conjure visions of spinach leaves in the fridge growing slimier by the day. The underlying Greek term *phthora*, however, has a broader range of

16. See, for example, Paul's reference to the "apocalypse of the sons of God" and "the redemption of our bodies" in verses 19 and 23. Many thanks to Susan Eastman, who during my doctoral studies helped me understand the apocalyptic and eschatological nature of this passage while also grasping its relevance for daily life now.

17. See my dissertation, "Liberation in the Midst of Futility," where I provide more detailed explanation of this interpretation.

18. Most theological reflection focuses on the implications of God's salvation for humanity and only rarely considers the implications for the rest of creation. When we do consider creation's salvation it is usually to imagine what sort of environment we humans will enter at the resurrection. Even more than imagining bodily resurrection, many American Christians imagine they will become semi-angelic beings that fly up to heaven. God's salvation, in this depiction, entails whisking us away from embodied life on earth so that we can enjoy an ethereal existence with the angels and God. We find these mistaken perspectives especially in hymns. See, for example, the lyrics of the following United Methodist hymns: UMH 528, "Nearer, My God, to Thee"; UMH 361, "Rock of Ages, Cleft for Me"; UMH 308, "Thine Be the Glory"; and UMH 700, "Abide with Me." But Paul's repeated emphasis on bodily human resurrection and his portrayal of nonhuman creation entering the "glorious" environment of God's children (8:21) push against these popular misconceptions.

meanings.[19] It can describe the passive processes of decomposition (thus, decay) (1 Cor 15:42) or the active practice of destruction and death (1 Cor 3:17). Since physical destruction leads to the passive processes of decomposition, "slavery of destruction" encapsulates both ideas (Rom 8:21). This phrase also aligns with the theological anthropology Paul has already articulated in Romans: because human sin is to blame for the entrance of sin and death into the human experience (5:12), human sin appears also to stand behind the nonhuman creation's inordinate experience of active destruction. Put together with Paul's understanding of creation as subjected to frustration, 8:21 further indicates that creation is not only frustrated in its divine calling to flourish but may be prevented from doing so because of humanity's destructive activities.

Liberation from anthropogenic destruction, then, suggests that creation would be freed from excessive forms of damage and the ongoing threat of destruction. Several passages in Isaiah—particularly chapters 11 and 65—articulate a similar vision of the new creation.[20] After extolling the positive social effects of Jesse's descendant who rules with righteousness and faithfulness (Isa 11:1–5), Isaiah describes the effects of the Messiah's rule on the animal world:

> The wolf shall live with the lamb,
>
>> the leopard shall lie down with the kid,
>
>> the calf and the lion and the fatling together,
>
>> and a little child shall lead them.
>
> The cow and the bear shall graze,
>
>> their young shall lie down together;
>
>> and the lion shall eat straw like the ox.
>
> The nursing child shall play over the hole of the asp,
>
>> and the weaned child shall put its hand on the adder's den.
>
> They will not hurt or destroy
>
>> on all my holy mountain;
>
>> for the earth will be full of the knowledge of the Lord
>
>> as the waters cover the sea. (Isaiah 11:6–9)

---

19. BDAG, 1054–55.

20. Isaiah 11 probably influenced Paul's own conception of creation's liberation; he at least had this passage in mind when writing to the Romans since he quotes Isa 11:10 (the verse that immediately proceeds those quoted here) in Rom 15:12.

Here, predators lie peacefully with their former prey, carnivores now eat plants, none destroys another, and the earth itself is overflowing with the knowledge of God. In fact, this knowledge of God seems to be the reason why none destroys another on God's sacred mountain.[21] Perhaps, according to this theology of the new creation, the earth will perfectly communicate the knowledge of the Lord in fulfillment of God's purposes (Isa 11:9; Rom 1:19-20). Human sin will no longer impede, and God's liberation of creation will restore it to its God-given roles of reflecting the Creator and teeming with life.

But this liberation also goes beyond the mere restoration of Eden. Creation will move *from* its current slavery "*into* the liberty of the glory of the children of God" (8:21b), enjoying its own form of glory. For humanity, glorification involves bodily resurrection and participation in God's immortality. For nonhuman creation, the experience of glory likely involves fullness of life.[22] God's liberation, on the one hand, will terminate creation's ongoing experience of destruction, which takes place under the supervision of sinful humanity; on the other hand, liberation will inaugurate creation's God-given experience of life and flourishing when humans are finally free from sinful impulses. In the eschatological future—in God's new creation—the nonhuman creation will experience the Spirit's life-sustaining and life-restoring power by entering the liberty God has prepared for Jesus' siblings (8:11, 21, 29). The solidarity in suffering brings with it solidarity in hope and liberation.

Although we must wait for our ultimate liberation from sin in order for nonhuman creation to be liberated, this does not mean we humans are

---

21. Brueggemann perceives a similar dynamic at work in Isa 11 as I see in Rom 8. Although scholars debate the connections between Isa 11:1–5 (focused on humanity) and 11:6–9 (focused on nonhuman creatures), he argues that these sets of verses stand together and inform one another so that "the new scenario for 'nature' is made possible by the reordering of human relationships in verses 1–5" (Brueggemann, *Isaiah*, 102; see also Blenkinsopp, *Isaiah*, 263–65). Brueggemann suggests that Gen 3 stands behind Isa 11 and concludes that "*The distortion of human relationships* is at the root of *distortions in creation. . . .* It is a *human* violation of God's order that produces the enemies of *nature*" (Brueggemann, *Isaiah*, 102; emphasis original).

22. Cranfield asserts that *eleutheria tēs doxēs* (liberty of glory) "is a liberty which results from, is the necessary accompaniment of, the (revelation of the) glory of the children of God. Paul's meaning is hardly that the creation will share the same liberty-resulting-from-glory as the children of God will enjoy, but that it will have its own proper liberty as a result of the glorification of the children of God. We may, however, assume that the liberty proper to the creation is indeed the possession of its own proper glory—that is, of the freedom fully and perfectly to fulfill its Creator's purpose for it, that freedom which it does not have, so long as man [*sic*], its lord (Gen 1.26, 28; Ps 8.6), is in disgrace" (Cranfield, *Critical and Exegetical Commentary*, 416).

free now to live in whatever destructive ways we please. As Paul has already exclaimed in 6:1–2, "Should we continue in sin in order that grace may abound? By no means! How can we who died to sin go on living in it?" Paul expects that those who receive new life in Christ will no longer "present [their] members to sin as instruments of wickedness" but will instead "present [their] members to God as instruments of righteousness" (6:13). Christians now "walk in newness of life" and live into the righteousness that Christ himself embodied (6:4, 11).[23] Therefore, in a creation marred by sin and destruction and during this time of waiting for God to conform us to the image of his Son (8:29), we allow God to transform our lives in line with God's future liberation of creation. In chapters 14–15 Paul fleshes out this call to transformation by pointing to two Christlike characteristics: gratitude and loving self-restraint.

Romans 14–15: Gratitude and Self-Restraint

Chapter 14 addresses a conflict happening within and between the various house churches in Rome. A chief aspect of this conflict concerns what community members might eat at their communal meals, during which they also celebrated the Lord's Supper.[24] One faction in Rome understood Christlike behavior to be specified by the Law, so they ate meat from approved animals that were slaughtered according to Jewish regulations.[25] Practically, this sometimes meant that God's people refrained from eating meat entirely, particularly when they lived in foreign lands.[26] A different faction of Jesus followers apparently considered themselves to be free from the dietary restrictions of the Mosaic Law, believing that "in the Lord Jesus . . . nothing is unclean in itself" (14:14). These Christians regarded eating meat from animals that were not Law-approved or had not been slaughtered ac-

23. Emily Peck-McClain argues in chapter 10 that by intergenerational formation the church best supports Christians as they resist the domination of sin and instead live into the new life of righteousness.

24. Jewett, *Romans*, 834–35; Barclay, "Faith and Self-Detachment," 193.

25. Barclay, "Faith and Self-Detachment," 192–93.

26. The specific identity of those who eat only vegetables is debated, but most scholars agree that these Christians refrain from eating meat in order to follow Torah. They are followers of Jesus that may be either Jewish or gentile converts to Judaism. Their diet may be practically motivated since kosher meats would be difficult to obtain, but it could also be motivated by devotional goals. As Gary Shogren illustrates, important Jewish heroes (for example, Daniel [Dan 1:8–13]; Tobit [Tob 1:10–11]; Judith [Jdt 10:5; 12:1–4, 17–19]; and Esther [Esth 14:17]) refrained from eating meat and wine in foreign lands especially when those foods were associated with imperial regimes (Shogren, "Is the Kingdom of God about Eating," 249).

cording to Jewish custom as an expression of their Christian liberty. Bringing these two factions together for a common meal would prove challenging to say the least. The vegetarians might judge (and implicitly condemn) those who lived in apparent disrespect of God's Laws (14:3b). The omnivores, in turn, might despise the vegetarians (14:3a), assuming that their conscientious eating habits flowed from outmoded dietary restraints rather than Christian liberty.

Paul's response to this conflict is complex. Fundamentally—and perhaps surprisingly to many Christians today—Paul affirmed that both factions were motivated by a desire to honor the Lord and to act in gratitude toward the Creator and Sustainer of life. He states, "those who eat, eat in honor of the Lord, since they give thanks to God; while those who abstain, abstain in honor of the Lord and give thanks to God" (14:6). Both groups, then, express gratitude to the Creator, a quality that ought always to mark the Christian's relationship to food, whether feasting or fasting.

Such gratitude—the humble recognition that we depend on powers beyond our own for which we give thanks—is central to Christlike feasting not only in Romans but elsewhere in the New Testament. The practice of thanking God for the gifts of food was modeled by Jesus (Mark 8:6; 14:23; Matt 15:36; 26:27; Luke 22:19; John 6:11; 1 Cor 11:23–26) and practiced by Paul and the early Christians (Acts 27:35; 1 Cor 10:30–31; Rom 14:6).[27] This practice of thanksgiving was and continues to be so central that it marks a key act in Christian worship, the Eucharist (*eucharisteō*, "to give thanks"), which recalls when Jesus "took a loaf of bread, and when he had *given thanks* [*eucharistēsas*], he broke it and said, 'This is my body that is for you. Do this in remembrance of me'" (1 Cor 11:23–24, emphasis added).[28] Gratitude of this sort recognizes the ways in which the lives of animals and plants and the elements that produced them support our well-being and flourishing.

Yet an "attitude of gratitude" alone does not ensure righteous, Christlike feasting and fasting. Paul provides more concrete measures of Christlike behavior in the rest of chapter 14. He exhorts the Roman Christians who eat meat to take thought for how their actions affect those around them since the choices they make—even about something as apparently innocuous as eating—can "destroy one for whom Christ died" (14:15b, author's translation). Paul's concern here is that the empowered ("strong" in the NRSV) who eat

---

27. Wolff, "Thanksgiving," 436.

28. Elizabeth Theokritoff beautifully illustrates a Pauline theology of creation by explaining: "When we offer products of the earth as Eucharist and receive them back from their Creator as the food of incorruption, we are recognizing that the creation of the world and its ultimate transformation are both part of the same movement, the same divine plan" (Theokritoff, *Living in God's Creation*, 42).

meat might put pressure on those who refrain from eating meat (14:20–21; 15:1).[29] This might then lead the "weak" to stumble in their undivided devotion to the Lord if they act against their conscience by eating unlawful meat. The danger is that their faithful orientation to Christ, the Lord, would be set adrift and even destroyed. Paul explains, "But those who have doubts are condemned if they eat, because they do not act from faith; for whatever does not proceed from faith is sin" (14:23). The person's eating "for the Lord" is undone in the process of eating for the approval of others.

Paul evaluates this situation in relation to Christ's self-restraining love. Because "Christ did not please himself" (15:3) neither should the empowered Roman Christians please their palates by demanding that meat be served during communal meals. Such a situation may result in a brother or sister "being injured by what you eat," and this would indicate that the meat-eaters "are no longer walking in love" (14:15a). To this possibility Paul exclaims, "Do not, by your eating, destroy that one for whom Christ died" (14:15b, author's translation). Destroying one for whom Christ died is antithetical to love since God's love works to save, reconcile, and glorify those who are weak, hostile, and susceptible to destruction (5:6–10; 14:15).

Paul's practical advice, then, is *not* for the Roman Christians to do what seems right in their own eyes but to walk in love and exercise self-restraint so that others may flourish—or at least not be destroyed. Those with the power to choose express their gratitude to God by restraining their own freedoms so that their eating practices support the flourishing and faith—rather than the destruction and infidelity—of others.[30] Paul expects Christians to recognize that the Kingdom of God is not focused on the enjoyment of food and drink. "By contrast, love, righteousness, peace and joy in the Holy Spirit *are* of ultimate value (14,15.17)."[31] Living according to these virtues helps God's people avoid destroying one for whom Christ died.

Although in the immediate context of Rom 14:15 the phrase "the one for whom Christ died" clearly refers to a brother or sister in Christ, the cosmic scope of God's salvation broadens its potential application. Since God intends to liberate the nonhuman creation from its slavery to destruction and since this liberation depends upon Jesus Christ's salvation of humanity,

29. Barclay, "Faith and Self-Detachment," 201.

30. Barclay argues, "This is not a compromise of the good news but precisely its necessary expression: only so can they act in love (14,15) which is the central characteristic and core product of the Christ-event (5,5.8; 8,39; 13,8–10). Like Christ, and because of Christ, their priority is to work for the good of their neighbour (15,1–3), such that their strength is expressed not in getting their own way, but in 'bearing the weaknesses of the powerless' (15,1; cf. Gal 6,2)" (ibid., 204).

31. Ibid., 199.

"the one for whom Christ died" can be said to encompass the whole of creation. Walking in love so as not to destroy "one for whom Christ died" means that we take thought—at the very least—for how procuring and eating food (as one of many human acts) might bring inordinate destruction to God's creation.[32] As we become increasingly aware of how our eating unnecessarily destroys not only human and nonhuman life but also soil, water, and air quality, we are encouraged by Rom 14–15 to exercise self-restraint in our eating choices because we are motivated by Christlike love. Our proper attentiveness to the world around us, our solidarity with the whole of creation, and our Christlike love enable us to express authentic gratitude for the gifts of life. In turn, these attitudes inspire and promote the kind of Christlike self-restraint that is required for the well-being and flourishing of others. In so living, we are not attempting to bring about God's new creation by our own efforts but to live in correspondence with that future reality by the Spirit's life-giving power that inhabits us now. We nevertheless continue to wait for the apocalypse of the children of God when God will complete our redemption and will finally liberate creation from its slavery to destruction (8:19, 21). But for now, we are motivated by gratitude and Christlike, self-restraining love so that even our feasting might be transformed in light of who God the Creator is and what Jesus the Christ has accomplished.

While Paul's concern here is to establish ecclesial health, chapters 14–15 also hint at ways in which people in the twenty-first century can support ecological health. Of course, Paul did not have our modern ecological problems in view as he wrote his instructions to the congregations in Rome. Therefore, we need to exercise discernment as we attend to the witness of creation (including its forms of suffering) so that we may understand how Christlike gratitude and self-restraining love can lead us to live now in congruence with God's future liberation. The contributions of natural and ecological sciences prove indispensible in such discernment as they reveal the ways in which human activity causes destruction throughout creation. Pursuing such discernment requires courage, patience, and solidarity as we come face to face with the suffering of creation. At the same time, however, we keep in view God's ultimate desire to liberate creation from its slavery to destruction. This God's-eye perspective provides the moral and spiritual guidance we need in order to follow Christ's ways of love and liberation.[33]

32. Perhaps the ethical principles drawn from Romans ultimately lead Christians toward vegetarianism. While vegetarianism still involves killing living things, plants as well as insects, it does not lead to the destruction of vertebrates—birds, fish, and mammals.

33. For a helpful study on how it often takes more than just knowledge to implement ecologically friendly practices, see Biviano, *Inspired Sustainability*.

Agriculture and Christlike Feasting

Attending to the suffering condition of the nonhuman creation exposes the ways in which our lack of gratitude and self-restraint has led us to inflict unnecessary and unhealthy amounts of destruction on species and eco-systems, even though these consequences are often unintentional. As an exercise in solidarity and attentiveness, then, let us consider one prominent way in which our agricultural efforts decrease the health of ecosystems and people: the use of toxic chemicals.

A central and persistent challenge in agriculture is overcoming the limiting and sometimes devastating effects of pests and weeds on crop yields. Insects eat crops. Weeds take up precious nutrients and space so that our crops are less productive and harvesting becomes more difficult. Thus, in order to eat the fruit of our delicate crops, we daily toil and sweat in our attempts to keep non-crop species at bay.

Since the middle of the twentieth century, people have attacked this problem by using pesticides and herbicides—chemicals that are toxic and deadly to the targeted intruders. A significant problem with this approach, however, is that the chemicals do not simply poison the invader. They also poison and kill the living things that make for healthy soils and the benefi-cial insects that prey upon such pests. We are left with dead soil that no lon-ger functions as the nearly miraculous place where bacteria "fix" nitrogen from the atmosphere into plant food and where insects, earthworms, and fungi transform waste and dead plants and animals into nutrient-rich soil. By applying toxic chemicals, we kill the soil biota since, as the prominent geologist Harvey Blatt notes, "Most pesticides destroy a broad range of liv-ing organisms, many of them either harmless or beneficial—like ladybugs, praying mantises, and earthworms—along with the undesirable pests."[34] The use of pesticides and other toxic chemicals effectively exterminates the living organisms that make new and nutrient-rich soil, undermining our whole food system.[35] In our attempts to feast easily and bountifully on the fruit of the earth, we have ignored the fact that "[f]ertile soil is alive" and

---

34. Blatt, *America's Environmental Report Card*, 110.

35. The long-term problem with killing the organisms in soil is that the soil is un-able to rebuild itself from the effects of erosion (effects that are multiplied through agriculture, especially ploughing). As Blatt has explained, "Six inches of soil are needed for crop production, a thickness that takes many hundreds or perhaps thousands of years to form, and human farming activities are causing it to erode an average of 10 to 100 times faster than this" (ibid., 106).

needs to flourish with a great variety of living things so that we might go on feasting for generations.[36]

But applying such chemicals not only kills pests, weeds, and soil biota but also damages human health as the poisons unleashed on pests and weeds infiltrate our water systems, remain on our food, and enter our bodies (and the bodies of other animals). Blatt captures the irony of such agricultural practices well:

> Given that the soil nourishes the plants that grow in it, and given that a great variety of living organisms in the soil contribute to a plant's health, it is little short of astonishing that farmers in the United States are so willing to spray poisons on their crops and into the soil. The United States consumes 35 percent of the world's pesticides. Cereal crops are sprayed an average of five or six times a season; potatoes thirteen times; apple trees eighteen times; and peaches are sprayed with forty-nine assorted pesticides and fungicides on a weekly basis from March until harvesting in July or August.[37]

Because farmers and farm workers apply and re-apply these chemicals and handle sprayed crops, their bodies are regularly exposed to the devastating, long-term health effects of these poisons. Consequently, they succumb to the chronic neurological, developmental, and reproductive problems brought on by these chemicals in greater proportion than the rest of the population.[38] Our agricultural system disables and sometimes destroys the people who work tirelessly (and often most vulnerably) in our fields so that we can feast.

Over the past two decades, scientists have attempted to reduce the need for pesticides and herbicides by using new technologies, such as genetic modification (GM), which introduces genetic material from another species into the crop species. Two different types of characteristics may be altered in the modified plant, depending on the crop and problems to be addressed. One type of modification makes a crop pest-resistant by transferring qualities that deter pests from one species to a pest-prone crop species. For example, genetic engineers introduce genetic material from the bacterium *Bacillus thuringiensis* (*Bt*), which produces a protein that is harmful to insects, into a crop plant (such as *Bt* corn) so that the plant itself now produces

36. Ibid., 109.
37. Ibid., 110.
38. Cimino et al., "Effects of Neonicotinoid," 156, 158, 160.

the insecticidal protein.[39] With this resistance, the farmer is able to use fewer insecticides (at least for a time) while maintaining high yields.

A second type of modification makes a crop herbicide tolerant by introducing genetic material from a species that is able to withstand specific herbicides into the crop species that would otherwise die when herbicide(s) are applied. For example, the herbicide glyphosate (patented as Roundup) kills weeds (as well as all bacteria and plants that are not tolerant) by interrupting their production of essential amino acids. In order to kill weeds but not harm crops, scientists have developed "Roundup Ready" crops so that weeds can be killed when glyphosate is sprayed on the fields. The crops themselves are protected from the deadly effects of Roundup because genetic material from the soil bacterium *Agrobacterium tumefaciens* has been incorporated into the crop species. This bacterium is able to continue producing essential amino acids even in the presence of the herbicide glyphosate.[40]

Nevertheless, because agricultural pests and weeds are living things with the ability to adapt to changing conditions, including poisons, even farmers of GM crops have had to rely on increasing amounts and varieties of herbicides to maintain high crop yields.[41] Thus, although GM crops often require less tractor power and fewer chemicals than do conventional crops—features that make them, at least in these respects, less environmentally damaging—they have not proven to be the technological savior they were heralded to be. In fact, researchers are becoming aware of the negative ecosystem and health effects of Roundup, the predominant herbicide used in agriculture, especially in growing soybeans and corn and in drying grain crops.[42]

39. For explanations see Monsanto, "Global Insect." For information about the development and safety of a wide variety of GM crops, see Center for Environmental Risk Assessment, http://www.cera-gmc.org/.

40. For a brief explanation of this process, see Center for Environmental Risk Assessment, "GM Crop Database."

41. In a study that examined GM agriculture from 1996 to 2013, increases in weed resistance to one of the most common herbicides, glyphosate, developed. Application of herbicides "put tremendous selection pressure on weeds and as a result contributed to the evolution of weed populations predominated by resistant individual weeds" (Brookes and Barfoot, "Environmental Impacts," 105). Consequently, farmers have had to apply more and different herbicides to their fields (ibid.). It should be noted, however, that farmers who planted conventional, non-GM strains of these crops also had to increase their applications of herbicides and still outpaced the applications of the GM crops (ibid., 105–6). See also Blatt, *America's Environmental*, 121–22.

42. "Drying" crops involves spraying non-herbicide-tolerant grain crops with herbicide toward the end of the growing season so that the plants die and the grains or seeds will dry sooner for harvest and processing (Kincaid, "Are GMOs Toxic?," 54).

Roundup, or glyphosate, kills not only targeted weeds and non-targeted microbes in the soil but also the bacteria that reside in the guts of the animals and humans that eat the crops. Thierry Vrain, a genetic engineer who began gardening extensively during retirement and started noticing the destructive effects of pesticides and herbicides on his soil's ecosystem, explains:

> A large number of published scientific studies—mostly done outside the United States—show that as little as 1 ppm [parts per million] of glyphosate will kill almost all bacteria—particularly beneficial bacteria—in the gut of animals; that endocrine disruption starts at 0.5 ppm; and that even just a few ppm can cause oxidative stress, chronic inflammation, DNA damage, and many other disruptions in mammalian organ cells and tissues.[43]

Vrain goes on to explain that in 2015 the World Health Organization conducted an investigation of glyphosate and concluded, "the scientific literature contains enough convincing evidence to classify glyphosate as a probable carcinogen."[44] Thus, although the foods produced by plants that have been genetically modified may not themselves be hazardous to human and ecological health (though the jury is still out), the herbicides used to produce them are indeed harmful to the community of living things in the soil, the farmers who handle the chemicals, and the consumers who eat them. We discover, then, that the foods on which we feast are slowly assaulting our bodies.

In our attempts to produce food easily, cheaply, and abundantly, we have ended up unintentionally "destroying those for whom Christ died" (Rom 14:15b, author's translation). Even for those who might not wish to extend the benefits of Christ's death to all of creation, such as bacteria and worms, we must recognize that our use of herbicides is destroying the health of *people* for whom Christ died. Although it is easier to turn a blind eye to this destructive and overwhelmingly complex situation, Christlike feasting requires us to express our love for one another through attentiveness and the kind of self-restraint that seeks to rectify the agricultural system so that vulnerable brothers and sisters, and indeed creation more broadly, are not "injured by what [we] eat" (14:15a).

43. Kincaid, "Are GMOs Toxic?," 54. Vrain also notes, "A German study suggests that glyphosate accumulates in all organs (liver, kidneys, intestines, heart, lungs, bones, and so on) of animals and people eating food products made from Roundup Ready crops" (ibid.). For the medical report of these findings, see Guyton et al., "Carcinogenicity." For an accessible overview of the World Health Organization's conclusions, see Cressey, "Widely Used Herbicide."

44. Kincaid, "Are GMOs Toxic?," 54.

A key way in which individuals and communities can work to remedy this situation and work to liberate creation from undue destruction is by supporting organic gardening and farming efforts. Growing food in our home or community gardens gives us the ability to withdraw from the deadly cycle of pesticide-intensive agriculture. Because organic, fresh foods are more expensive than processed and fast foods,[45] low and middle-income people find it difficult or even impossible to afford healthier options. On top of this, low and middle-income individuals and families often do not have the time and resources to grow and prepare fresh foods. As those who seek to follow Christ in alleviating destruction and supporting the flourishing of others, Christians have the opportunity to provide community support systems to ensure that all people—especially infants and children who are most affected by agricultural chemicals—are able to eat healthy food. One example of this effort is a community garden in Fairview, North Carolina, called The Lord's Acre, which "raise[d] three tons of vegetables on a mere quarter acre" through organic, intensive gardening methods and donated much of the produce to local food banks.[46]

Many people either do not have the opportunity to garden or do not like the work; and yet even they may be able to purchase and consume organically grown foods. Organic foods grown on local, small-scale, biodynamic, and polyculture farms (rather than large monoculture farms that depend on toxic chemicals or even large monoculture organic farms) best maintain the long-term vitality of the soil.[47] By supporting farmers directly through Community Supported Agriculture (CSA), we can encourage them to transition away from conventional, chemical-based agriculture to more sustainable and healthier approaches.[48] Admittedly, this transition involves highly complex factors. Many skeptics wonder whether we can

---

45. This is the case in large part because the U.S. government subsidizes the production of corn and soybean crops, which are processed into all kinds of ingredients used to make the apparent vast array of foods at the grocery store. Corn and soybean are also used to feed livestock for cheap (as well as more expensive) meat and dairy. Agricultural historian, R. Douglas Hurt, explains the complexities of agriculture subsidies in *American Agriculture*, especially chapters 8–9. Nutritionist Marion Nestle describes the relationship between agriculture and the foods we find in grocery stores in *Food Politics*. For an accessible explanation of corn agriculture, see Pollan, *Omnivore's Dilemma*, especially chapters 1–7.

46. Bahnson and Wirzba, *Making Peace*, 93. See the garden's inspiring website at The Lord's Acre, http://thelordsacre.org/.

47. For a picturesque depiction of one such farm (Polyface Farms, http://www.polyfacefarms.com/), see chapters 8–14 of Pollan, *Omnivore's Dilemma*.

48. To find a local CSA, see Local Harvest, "Community Supported Agriculture," at https://www.localharvest.org/csa/.

feed the growing global population with organic methods. But we might equally wonder whether chemical-based farming will be able to feed the world for the long haul. Because conventional farming undermines the long-term fertility of the soil even as it poisons our air, water, and bodies, it should at least occasion grave worries. Moreover, given that the production of meat is extraordinarily inefficient—the amount of grain necessary to produce a single pound of beef could feed a person for ten days[49]—a transition to more sustainable eating practices would lead us to eat less meat and thereby use the land's produce more efficiently. Such a change will demand self-restraint that is motivated by love for the well-being and flourishing of others, including future generations of people who must also till and reap fruit from the land.

In addition to these modifications, we can advocate for the well-being and flourishing of farmers and farm workers by supporting justice efforts.[50] We can elect and call on government officials to establish laws that limit the use of toxic chemicals in agriculture and establish clear safeguards for their proper use. In so doing, we exercise our power for the benefit and flourishing of those who are disempowered. In other words, "we, the empowered, carry the frailties of the disempowered and do not please ourselves" (Rom 15:1, author's translation).

We approach these tasks with Christlike love, giving thanks to God for the opportunity to stand in solidarity with creation in its suffering and ultimately in its liberation. In our attempt to follow the Christ who lived, loved, and died for the liberation of others and has shown us what it means to feast in ways that support the well-being of others, we direct our attention to the witness of creation (its dying soils, polluted waters and air, and diseased creatures) so that we might live into the liberation that God intends for all.

Bibliography

Bahnson, Fred, and Norman Wirzba. *Making Peace with the Land: God's Call to Reconcile with Creation.* Downers Grove: InterVarsity, 2012.

Barclay, John M. G. "Faith and Self-Detachment from Cultural Norms: A Study in Romans 14–15." *Zeitschrift für die neutestamentliche Wissenschaft* 104 (2013) 192–208.

49. Blatt, *America's Environmental*, 128.

50. Organizations that advocate for the rights and well-being of people and the environment are Farmworker Justice (https://www.farmworkerjustice.org/content/about-farmworker-justice-home), Alliance for Fair Food (http://www.allianceforfairfood.org), and Earthjustice (http://earthjustice.org).

Biviano, Erin Lothes. *Inspired Sustainability: Planting Seeds for Action.* Maryknoll, NY: Orbis, 2016.

Blatt, Harvey. *America's Environmental Report Card: Are We Making the Grade?* 2nd ed. Cambridge: MIT Press, 2011.

Blenkinsopp, Joseph. *Isaiah 1–39: A New Translation with Introduction and Commentary.* New York: Doubleday, 2000.

Brookes, Graham, and Peter Barfoot. "Environmental Impacts of Genetically Modified (GM) Crop Use 1996–2013: Impacts on Pesticide Use and Carbon Emissions." *GM Crops & Food* 6 (2015) 103–33.

Brueggemann, Walter. *Isaiah 1–39.* Louisville: Westminster John Knox, 1998.

Burroughs, Presian R. "Liberation in the Midst of Futility and Destruction: Romans 8:19–22 and the Christian Vocation of Nourishing Life." ThD diss., Duke University, 2014.

Center for Environmental Risk Assessment. "GM Crop Database: MON802 (MON-80200-7)," March 28, 2016. http://www.cera-gmc.org/GmCropDatabaseEvent/MON802.

Cimino, Andria M., et al. "Effects of Neonicotinoid Pesticide Exposure on Human Health: A Systematic Review." *Environmental Health Perspectives* 125 (February 2017) 155–62.

Cranfield, C. E. B. *A Critical and Exegetical Commentary on the Epistle to the Romans.* ICC 1. Edinburgh: T. & T. Clark, (1975) 1985.

Cressey, Daniel. "Widely Used Herbicide Linked to Cancer." *Nature: International Weekly Journal of Science,* March 24, 2015. https://www.scientificamerican.com/article/widely-used-herbicide-linked-to-cancer/.

Danker, Frederick W., Walter Bauer, and William Arndt. *A Greek-English Lexicon of the New Testament and Other Early Christian Literature.* 3rd ed. Chicago: University of Chicago Press, 2000.

Dunn, James D. G. *Romans 1–8.* WBC 38A. Dallas: Word, 1988.

Eastman, Susan. "Double Participation and the Responsible Self in Romans 5–8." In *Apocalyptic Paul: Cosmos and Anthropos in Romans 5–8,* edited by Beverly Roberts Gaventa, 93–110. Waco: Baylor University Press, 2013.

Fretheim, Terence E. *God and the World in the Old Testament: A Relational Theology of Creation.* Nashville: Abingdon, 2005.

Guyton, Kathryn Z., et al. "Carcinogenicity of Tetrachlorvinphos, Parathion, Malathion, Diazinon, and Glyphosate." *The Lancet* 16 (2015) 490–91.

Hannah Kincaid. "Are GMOs Toxic?: An Interview with Genetic Engineer Thierry Vrain." *Mother Earth News* 276 (June/July 2016) 51–55.

Hurt, R. Douglas. *American Agriculture: A Brief History.* West Lafayette, IN: Purdue University Press, 2002.

Jewett, Robert. *Romans: A Commentary.* Hermeneia: A Critical and Historical Commentary on the Bible. Minneapolis: Fortress, 2007.

Keck, Leander E. *Romans.* Abingdon New Testament Commentaries. Nashville: Abingdon, 2005.

Matera, Frank J. *Romans.* Paideia Commentaries on the New Testament. Grand Rapids: Baker, 2010.

Monsanto. "Global Insect Resistance Management." https://monsanto.com/products/product-stewardship/insect-resistance-management/.

Moo, Douglas J. *The Epistle to the Romans.* NICNT. Grand Rapids: Eerdmans, 1996.

Nestle, Marion. *Food Politics: How the Food Industry Influences Nutrition and Health.* Berkeley: University of California Press, 2002.

Pollan, Michael. *The Omnivore's Dilemma: A Natural History of Four Meals.* New York: Penguin, 2007.

Shogren, Gary Steven. "'Is the Kingdom of God about Eating and Drinking or Isn't It?' (Romans 14:17)." *Novum Testamentum* 42 (2000) 238–56.

Theokritoff, Elizabeth. *Living in God's Creation: Orthodox Perspectives on Ecology.* Crestwood, NY: St. Vladimir's Seminary Press, 2009.

The United Methodist Hymnal: Book of United Methodist Worship. Nashville: United Methodist Publishing, 1989.

Wenham, Gordon J. *Genesis 1–15.* WBC 1. Waco, TX: Word, 1987.

Wirzba, Norman. *From Nature to Creation: A Christian Vision for Understanding and Loving Our World.* The Church and Postmodern Culture. Grand Rapids: Baker, 2015.

Wolff, Christian. "Thanksgiving." *ABD*, 6:435–438.

12

The Pursuit of Peace and the Power of God[1]

MARY SCHMITT AND BISHOP SAMUEL ENOSA PENI

IN HIS LETTERS, PAUL uses Greco-Roman terms related to conflict[2] and also admonishes the recipients of his letters to pursue peace (e.g., Rom 12:18; 14:19; 2 Cor 13:11; 1 Thess 5:13). For many in North America, references to war and peace can feel far removed from our lived experience, and thus there is a tendency to spiritualize such concepts.[3] The Apostle Paul, however, lived and ministered in the first century CE in cities under the control of the Roman Empire. The military successes of Caesar Augustus had resulted in a period of unprecedented stability, such that this time is often referred to as the *Pax Romana* ("Peace of Rome," Seneca, *Clem* 1.4.1–2). Augustus was lauded as the bringer of peace to the empire, and the senate voted to build in his honor an altar of peace (*Ara Pacis*) located on the field of Mars, the god of war (*Res Gestae* 12).[4] Nevertheless, as argued by Klaus Wengst, Roman peace was the result of numerous violent battles throughout the empire and was sustained by the threat of violence.[5] For Paul, conflict

---

1. I (Mary) am honored to be able to write this for my teacher, mentor, and friend Dr. Susan Eastman. She first taught me to love the Apostle Paul. In addition, I am thankful for Bishop Samuel Enosa Peni, with the Diocese of Nzara for the Episcopal Church in South Sudan, for his willingness to co-write this article with me.

2. For a complete list of conflict terminology in Paul's letters, see catalogues in Gaventa, "Rhetoric of Violence," 63–69; Gaventa, "Neither Height nor Depth," 265–78. Lisa Bowens also considers this terminology in chapter 8 of the present volume.

3. This is a general comment based on the fact that there has not been a war fought within the continental borders of the United States in over a century; however, this does not deny the experiences of many who have been affected directly by violence in this country.

4. For a discussion of how Paul suggests that the Roman Christians relate to empire, see chapter 13 by Douglas Harink.

5. Wengst, *Pax Romana*, esp. 11–19.

and peace were not figurative terms but the concrete realities he and the members of his churches experienced.

Many Christians throughout the world continue to live in contexts where war and peace are part of daily life. Christians in South Sudan have experienced numerous violent conflicts. The two countries now referred to as Sudan and South Sudan fought two long civil wars. The first civil war went on for seventeen years (1955–72). This culminated with the 1972 Addis Ababa Agreement. The second war lasted for more than two decades (1983–2005), until the peace discussions of 2003–2004 created a six-year period of relative rest and autonomy for the southern territory. Following that period, the south voted in July 2011 to become the independent state of South Sudan. Even after achieving independence, internal political struggles in the newly constituted South Sudan have resulted in further skirmishes. The people of South Sudan thought that after overcoming the years of civil wars and chaos and after the hard-won independence through referendum, South Sudan would be tired of conflicts and wars; unfortunately, the new nation finds itself in further turmoil, destruction, and displacement. For Christians in South Sudan, Paul's words about conflict and peace are not figurative or spiritual but address Sudanese experiences.[6]

One Pauline text that addresses the intersection of conflict and peace is Rom 12:14–21. Paul begins by instructing Roman Christians to "bless the persecutors [of you]" (12:14).[7] Other instructions in this passage include "do not repay evil" (12:17), "do not take revenge" (12:19), and "do not be overcome by evil, but overcome evil with good" (12:21). Paul's instructions are challenging in contexts where real conflict exists, where Christians are experiencing persecution. In such settings, Paul's insistence that Christians bless and not take revenge is difficult, especially when revenge and repaying evil seem justified.[8]

The middle verse of this passage is 12:18,[9] which begins with two idiomatic phrases (*ei dunaton* and *to ex humōn*). Most English translators have settled on interpreting the verse basically this way: "If it is possible, so far as it depends on you, live peaceably with all" (NRSV). According to this translation, the pursuit of peace is qualified; peace is limited by the willingness

6. Charles Campbell also portrays a situation of real, deadly conflict in El Salvador and Archbishop Oscar Romero's courageous, unveiling response to it in chapter 3. Although not often attended by war, the American slave trade was full of deadly conflict, as Lisa Bowens illustrates in chapter 5.

7. Unless otherwise noted, all translations are by Schmitt.

8. Douglas Campbell, in chapter 14 of this volume, teases out the implications of Rom 12 and other Pauline texts for practices of restorative justice.

9. Wilson, *Love without Pretense*, 175–76.

of the other to engage in peacemaking. Alternatively, the same translation could be used to separate the pursuit of peace from the realization of peace. According to this interpretation, a person is responsible for pursuing peace as best she can, but the results are beyond her control. So, when conflict continues, a person is not responsible—she has done what she can.

Both of these are problematic ways of interpreting Rom 12:18. While the unusual phrasing of 12:18 frequently has been interpreted as Paul's concession that peace depends on two-party consent, closer inspection of Paul's concept of peace and the language in 12:18 reveals that Paul thinks peace is dependent on God's justifying power, which makes possible the pursuit of peace. What is not possible for humans alone in Romans becomes possible by the power of God. The shift of attention from human agents to the power of God has positive implications for countries like South Sudan, which are experiencing conflict. The efforts to pursue peace are not limited by the enemy's consent or dependent on individual striving but are guaranteed by the God of peace whose power is already at work to bring peace through the death of Christ and by the power of the Holy Spirit.

The Pursuit of Peace

Elsewhere in his letters Paul does not base the imperative for Christian pursuit of peace on the response of others. Paul uses the verb *eirēneuō* ("to pursue peace"), which occurs in Rom 12:18, in two other letters. In 1 Thess 5:13, he urges Thessalonian Christians to pursue peace with one another. Lest this claim be interpreted as the pursuit of peace only between Christians, Paul follows up this command with the instruction to "pursue good toward one another and toward all" (5:15). These imperatives occur in the same letter where Paul admits that there are those who falsely proclaim "peace and security," but cannot guarantee peace (5:3). The phrase "peace and security" was a popular slogan used to invoke the protection provided by the Roman Empire.[10] However, Paul insists that Rome cannot really guarantee peace. In the midst of Rome's failure to bring real lasting peace, Paul commands Christians to pursue peace and do good to all persons.

Paul also uses the verb *eirēneuō* ("to pursue peace") in 2 Cor 13:11, the end of one of Paul's most contentious letters. He repeatedly refers to his opponents in 2 Corinthians as those who have attacked him by calling him weak or inferior (e.g., 10:10; 11:5; 12:11). With no immediate reconciliation anticipated between himself and the "super-apostles," he instructs the Corinthians to pursue peace. He does not qualify this by making the Corinthian

10. Wengst, *Pax Romana*, 19–21.

pursuit of peace dependent on the response of the super-apostles. Paul simply instructs them to pursue peace, independent of how others respond.

Similarly, in the verses immediately surrounding Rom 12:18, Paul does not limit his instructions based on the responses of other parties. Twice Paul mentions other hostile parties: persecutors (12:14) and an enemy (12:20). Paul exhorts Roman Christians to bless those who persecute, to feed a hungry enemy, and to give a thirsty enemy something to drink. In addition, Paul exhorts the Romans to bless and not curse (12:14), never to repay evil (12:17), not to take revenge (12:19), and not to be overcome by evil (12:21). Paul does not limit these instructions to those who respond likewise. Furthermore, there is no indication that these activities will alter the actions of the persecutors or the enemy. Paul's commands do not depend upon how the other party responds. Similarly, Paul's imperatives in Rom 13 seem to be without regard for the action of the other party. Paul seems to give unqualified support to governing authorities.[11] In the immediately surrounding verses to 12:18, Paul offers only two limiting statements. First, the whole section is surrounded by the command to love (12:9; 13:8–10). All actions fall under the overarching insistence that Christians are to live in love. Second, while Paul instructs Christians not to take revenge, he does not limit God's power to enact righteous judgment. In fact, God's righteous judgment makes it possible for Christians not to take revenge. Paul instructs the Romans not to take revenge, but to leave vengeance to God.[12] Thus, the conditions for pursuing peace are made possible by God and not by the actions of other human beings.

11. Romans 13 should be read in light of the claims at the end of chapter 12—not to be overcome by evil, but to overcome evil with good. Legitimate governing authorities would be expected to overcome evil with good. This passage does not necessarily address governments that are not doing the good or are, in fact, supporting evil. Moreover, this passage must be read again in the context of expulsion of Jews by Claudius and their subsequent return under Nero (see Suetonius, *Claudius* 25). For more on this, see Donfried, *Romans Debate*. For a sustained treatment of Rom 13, see Douglas Harink's chapter in the present volume.

12. In Rom 12:18–19, the juxtaposition of the call for peace (12:18) and the image of the avenging God (12:19), though initially surprising, must be read in light of God's actions toward enemies throughout the epistle. According to Rom 5:8, we used to be God's enemies. At that time, God reconciled us through the death of the Son. Paul also refers to Israel as "enemies on account of [the gentiles]" (11:28). He claims that Israel has temporarily become an enemy of the gospel so that the gentile world will be reconciled. But Paul also anticipates Israel's restoration (11:15). "And thus, all Israel will be saved" (11:26). If the rest of Romans is any indication of how God treats enemies, peace in Rom 12:18–19 is not the hope that God will eventually destroy our enemies. Rather, the pursuit of peace is possible because we believe that God reconciles and saves enemies.

Given Paul's admonitions to Christians in other letters that they pursue peace no matter the context, one might suggest the emphasis in Rom 12:18 should be placed on trying one's best: if it is possible *as much as it depends on you*, pursue peace. This reading is based on the idea that the individual is admonished by Paul to do everything within her power that is possible to bring about peace. In Greek, the word *dunatos* has a wide semantic range. It can be translated as "able, capable, or powerful." It can also be translated as "possible."[13] However, closer examination of the phrase *ei dunaton* ("if possible")—the exact phrase that occurs in 12:18—reveals that this phrase is typically employed to denote an outlandish claim that is not really possible.

A brief survey of New Testament texts demonstrates that the phrase *ei dunaton* ("if possible") frequently denotes a hyperbole or something overstated that is not really possible. Paul uses the phrase *ei dunaton* ("if possible") in one other instance. He states that the Galatians, "if possible, would have dug out" their eyes and given them to Paul (Gal 4:15). Paul does not think that it is possible for the Galatians to do this nor is he suggesting that they should try it; it is a hyperbole. The other uses of *ei dunaton* ("if possible") in the New Testament can also be read as hyperbolic. In the gospels, Jesus prays, asking the Father if it is possible that this cup (= crucifixion) pass from him (Matt 26:39). It is, of course, not possible. The phrase *ei dunaton* ("if possible") also occurs in a warning against false Christs and false prophets, who would deceive, "if possible, the elect" (Mark 13:22; Matt 24:24). Origen notes that this is not to be read as a possibility that the elect could be deceived. He writes, "'If possible' is a hyperbole. For he did not suggest or indicate that even the elect are to be thrown into error."[14] As a final example, Jesus appears offended by the comments from the father of the epileptic boy in Mark 9: "If you are able (*ei ti dunēi*), help us" (9:22). Jesus replies, "'If you are able' (*to ei dunēi*)? All things are possible to the one who believes" (9:23). Jesus equates the father's use of the phrase "if possible" with unbelief. The phrase "if possible" is inappropriate in this instance; surely, Jesus can heal the boy. The phrase *ei dunaton* ("if possible") implies whatever is being described is not possible; Jesus rightly takes offense at the implication. These examples suggest that *ei dunaton* ("if possible") in the New Testament is typically hyperbolic, denoting something regarded as impossible.[15]

13. BDAG, 264; LSJ, 453.

14. Oden, *Mark*, 185.

15. In Acts 20:16, Paul is in a hurry to set sail so that if possible (*ei dunaton*) he may reach Jerusalem by Pentecost. Since no mention is made of Pentecost again in Acts, it is plausible to assume that this too is hyperbolic (cf. 1 Cor 16:8–9).

Moreover, a few examples from outside the New Testament demonstrate how widely recognized the hyperbolic use of *ei dunaton* ("if possible") is. In the *Letter of Aristeas*, the king appoints a librarian who is to collect and translate, "if possible, all the books in the inhabited world" (9). Collecting all the books in the world was not possible. Josephus uses the phrase *ei dunaton* ("if possible") to convey the Syrian General Bacchides' desire to end a siege and, "if possible, to return home without dishonor" (*Ant.* 13:31; cf. 4.130). From Josephus' perspective, the general under siege is already dishonored. Josephus also mentions that Bacchides returns home, and because he has been dishonored he disappears from power and never invades Israel again. Plato's *Charmides* is a debate about something that ultimately proves to be impossible to define—namely, temperance. But the discussion is introduced by a question that asks *if* it is *possible* to define temperance (*Charm.* 57).[16] These are a few examples that demonstrate that the use of *ei dunaton* ("if possible") as hyperbole occurs in a wide variety of texts.

Paul's use of the phrase in Gal 4:15, "gouging out their eyes," suggests that Paul was familiar with this hyperbolic usage of the phrase. As we return to Rom 12:18, then, this verse should be reexamined in light of the widespread use of the phrase *ei dunaton* ("if possible") to express hyperbole in Greek. But what is the hyperbole—the thing being overstated—in 12:18? Surely, it is not the command to pursue peace. Paul thinks the pursuit of peace is possible since he instructs both the Thessalonians and the Corinthians to pursue peace (1 Thess 5:13; 2 Cor 13:11). In most of the examples above, *ei dunaton* ("if possible") occurs immediately adjacent to the phrase being called into question (for example, "if possible, to *dig out your eyes*," Gal 4:15). If this same construction is assumed in Rom 12:18, the hyperbole involves the peace that depends on the Roman Christians: If possible (*ei dunaton*), *as much as it depends on you*, live peacefully. Paul does not think that it is, in fact, possible for peace to depend on the efforts of the Roman Christians. He does not lay the burden of peace on those following Christ. Neither does he lay that burden on those who oppose the followers of Christ. For, according to his imperatives to pursue peace in this and other letters, Paul thinks it implausible that peace depends on the enemy actually acting peacefully. Yet, again, careful examination of the widespread use of the phrase *ei dunaton* ("if possible") to denote hyperbole suggests that Paul does not expect Roman Christians to be able to establish peace either. So, who does Paul believe *is* responsible for peace?

16. See also Sextus Empiricus, *Phys.* 1.410–13; Polybius, *Hist* ix.vi; Plotinus v.3.1.

The Power of God

In Romans, *dunatos* and related words (*edunamoō, dunamis,* and *dunamai*) most frequently are associated with God. Power is one of God's eternal divine attributes (Rom 1:20). The resurrection of God's Son is a sign of power (1:4). The gospel is the power of God (1:16). The Holy Spirit is the conduit of power (15:13, 19). In Rom 9, Paul draws upon Israel's story, recalling that God's power was revealed to Pharaoh (9:17; Exod 9:16) and alluding to a text about God's wrath (Rom 9:22; Jer 50:25). This past power can be manifested again in the present time, because Paul insists that God also has power to graft the natural branches (= Israel) into the tree (11:23). *Dunatos* ("powerful, able") also denotes what God is able to do. God is able to fulfill the promises to Abraham (4:21), and God is able to establish the Roman Christians (16:25). Throughout Romans, God's power and ability are highlighted using the term *dunatos* and related words.

While God is the source of power in Romans, humans too can experience the power of God. According to Rom 4, Abraham was made strong or powerful (4:20). There is no agent explicitly stated. Often, when a passive verb occurs in Scripture without an explicitly stated agent, the implied agent of the verb is God.[17] So, in 4:20, the passive verb should be read as a divine passive: God made Abraham strong. In chapter 8, Paul contrasts those who are not able or strong (*ou dunamai*) with another group who live according to the Spirit (8:5–8). The former group lives according to the flesh and, as a result, is not able to please God (8:7–8). But those who live by the Spirit presumably are able to please God, and they experience in the Spirit life and peace (8:6). Those who live in the Spirit have power that is not accessible to those who live only according to the flesh. Finally, at the end of the letter to the Romans, Paul refers to "the strong" using the same word *dunatos* ("strong, able, powerful") and "the weak" with a negated version of this word (*adunatos,* 15:1). Interestingly, the label of "the strong" does not occur until the end of his discussion about welcoming the one whose faith is weak (14:1—15:6). Moreover, strength is immediately defined as acting how Christ acted (15:2–3).[18] Two things suggest that Paul thinks real strength comes from God. First, Paul introduces a thinly veiled analogy for God's role in strengthening Christians. In 14:4, Paul writes, "Who are you, the one who judges another's servant? To his own master, a servant stands or falls. And he will stand, for the Lord is able (*dunamai*) to make him stand" (14:4). The "Lord" could refer to the master of any servant. But here "Lord" clearly

---

17. Moule, *Idiom Book,* 25.

18. In chapter 11, Presian Burroughs considers this strength in relation to self-restrained eating on behalf of others' well-being.

is a reference to God, who bestows on God's servants divine power. Those who have power receive it from the Lord. Second, the strong are told to act like Christ (15:1–3). Power is associated with living the way Christ lived. Thus, "the strong" are not independently powerful but receive their strength as a gift from God and continue to be called "strong" only as long as they follow Christ's example.

Thus, in Rom 12:18, the use of the phrase *ei dunaton* ("if possible") draws attention to the contrast between human limitations and God's power. Throughout Romans, power is associated with God who makes others strong, like Abraham (4:20), God's servant (14:4), and even Paul and Roman Christians (15:1). The emphasis on God's power, then, makes clear that *ei dunaton* ("if possible") in 12:18 is marking the phrase "as far as it depends on you" as hyperbole. From Paul's perspective, the pursuit of peace cannot be dependent solely on *you*. Rather, the pursuit of peace is predicated on God's power.

Paul immediately follows up this claim in 12:18 with a quotation from Deuteronomy that highlights the centrality of God's power. He writes, "Beloved, do not yourselves take revenge, but leave room for wrath. For it has been written, 'Vengeance is mine; I will repay,' says the Lord" (12:19; Deut 32:35). Paul quotes Deut 32, the Song of Moses, three times in the letter to the Romans. He cites Deut 32:21 in Rom 10:19; Deut 32:35 in Rom 12:19; and Deut 32:43 in Rom 15:10. The number of citations from Deut 32, along with the fact that they are included in their original order, suggests that the citation of Deut 32:35 in Rom 12:19 is not random nor has Paul intended to use Deut 32:35 as a proof text. The original context is important. The central message of Deut 32 is a proclamation of God's power and God's authority to act in the ways God sees fit. God creates (32:6). God provides for Israel (32:7–14). But when Israel turns to other gods, the Lord rejects them (32:19–27). However, the Lord is also free to vindicate his people (32:36–43).[19] The reason that the Lord gives for not annihilating the people of Israel is the concern that God's enemies would say, "Our high hand [Greek, 'strong arm'], not the Lord, has done this" (32:27, LXX). The concern is to affirm that God's power, not human interactions, control history. The one known in Deuteronomy as "I am" has power to do what God's people do not have power to achieve. Moreover, the Lord vindicates Israel when their strength is gone (32:36). God's strength is contrasted with human weakness. Thus, in the text of Deut 32:35 cited in Rom 12:19, the emphasis should be placed on the first-person pronouns: "Vengeance is *mine*; *I* will repay." The first person pronouns in 12:19 contrast with the second person pronoun in 12:18: "as

---

19. Hays, *Echoes of Scripture*, 163–64.

much as it depends on *you*" (*humōn*). In 12:18–19, then, the possibility of pursuing peace is predicated on God's power and prerogative. Only God can take revenge; thus, humans are freed to pursue peace. The power for pursuing peace does not come from within but from the freedom created by acknowledging God's power.

Pursuing Peace by the Power of God

Peace in Romans is a marker of life in the Spirit (8:6). God is the source of peace. Paul refers five times to God as "the God of peace" (15:33; 16:20; 1 Cor 13:11; Phil 4:9; 1 Thess 5:23; see similar appellations in 1 Cor 7:15; 2 Thess 3:16 "the Lord of peace").[20] The peace intrinsic to God is then shared by the power of the Holy Spirit with those in the faith. In Rom 15:13, Paul prays that God will fill the Romans with all joy and peace by the power of the Holy Spirit. Paul makes clear that there is contrast between those who experience peace in the Spirit and those who do not. Those who live in the flesh do not experience peace, but those who live according to the Spirit have life and peace (8:6). Apart from the gift of God, humans do not know the way of peace (3:17). But those who have been justified have peace with God through Jesus Christ (5:1).[21] Paul also refers to the message of the gospel as the "gospel of peace" (10:15) and the Kingdom of God as a place characterized by "righteousness, peace, and joy" in the Holy Spirit (14:17). Thus, the source of peace is God, who through the Holy Spirit extends peace to believers.

The extension of God's peace to humans by the power of the Holy Spirit makes possible the pursuit of peace between humans. In Romans, the gift of "peace with God" (5:1) precedes and makes possible the human pursuit of peace (12:18; 14:19). Just as the master of the house makes his servants strong (14:1), the members of God's household are able by the power of the

---

20. Outside of Paul's letters, the phrase "God of peace" occurs only in Heb 13:20, making this a predominantly Pauline appellation. See Penna, "God of Peace," 279–302. Even Paul's standard greeting of "grace and peace to you from God our Father and the Lord Jesus" (Rom 1:7; cf. 1 Cor 1:3; 2 Cor 1:2; Gal 1:3; Phil 1:2; 1 Thess 1:1; Phil 3) reinforces the connection between God and peace.

21. A textual variant in 5:1 has led commentators to speculate on whether Paul considered peace to be the present experience of Christians (*echomen* [we have peace]) or whether he exhorts his hearers to strive for peace (*echōmen* [let us have peace]). The manuscript evidence is evenly divided. I am reading 5:1 as a testimony of the present experience of peace (*echomen* [we have peace]). However, perhaps the debate has created a false dichotomy between peace as gift and peacemaking as an activity to which Christians are called. In Romans, God secures peace, but Paul also calls believers to live out God's peace.

Holy Spirit to pursue peace and mutual edification (14:17–19). As argued by Corneliu Constantineanu, the structure of the book of Romans highlights the way in which reconciliation with God necessarily leads to the ministry of reconciliation with others.[22] In Rom 5–8, Paul first describes peace with God. Constantineanu refers to this as the vertical dimension of reconciliation.[23] Once the vertical relationship is reconciled, then the task of reconciliation is extended to horizontal relationships with others. In the last chapters of Romans (12–16), Paul exhorts Christians to pursue peace with each other (14:19) and with all persons (12:18). Reconciliation with God automatically results in the responsibility to pursue peace with others.[24]

That God's power makes peace possible is the best interpretation of Rom 12:18. Paul uses hyperbole to point out that peace is not dependent on human initiative. Rather, the citation from Deuteronomy underscores the real contrast between God's power and human insufficiency (12:19). Paul does not think it is possible for humans to pursue peace apart from the power of God. One other aspect of the text supports this reading. Peace is portrayed as a gift and thus as something about which one should not boast. Romans 12:3 introduces the topic of not thinking too highly of one's self because faith is received by grace. Similarly, in Rom 12:16, Paul returns to the same theme of not thinking too highly of one's self. This leads into Paul's claim that peace is made possible only because God makes it so. Thus, the pursuit of peace in Rom 12:18, which follows the caution to not be conceited, must also be understood as a gift from God. Christians pursue peace by the power and grace of God in Romans.

This insistence that peace is not dependent on either human party (the Christian or her enemy) but on the power of God could be misinterpreted to claim that humans do not have any responsibility to pursue peace actively. This potential misunderstanding is a legitimate concern. Both James and 2 Thessalonians could be read as correctives to similar wrong interpretations of Paul. In response to an emphasis on faith alone, James insists that faith without works is dead (Jas 2:17). Similarly, those in Thessalonica who are sitting around waiting for the Lord to return are encouraged not to be idle but to work (2 Thess 3:6–13). Clearly, Paul has been misinterpreted as an advocate for idleness. However, it would be a misreading of Romans to claim that emphasizing God's power decreases the importance of the human pursuit for peace. Rather, what Paul does is set things in their proper order.

22. Constantineanu, *Social Significance*, 21.

23. Ibid., 99–144.

24. Ibid., 145–84.

It is precisely because God is a reconciling God that Christians are called to pursue peace with each other (14:1—15:13), with governing authorities (13:1–7), and with all persons (12:14–21). If anything, the emphasis on God's power bringing about peace should urge Christians to pursue peace all the more. First, Christians are free to pursue peace because the outcome is dependent on God and not on their own actions. The ultimate judgments about justice and peace are left to the true Judge (see 14:10–12). Second, Christians joyfully pursue peace because God guarantees real peace. Christians know the end of the story. The God of peace is victorious. So Christians are actively encouraged to engage in bringing about God's final victory through the pursuit of peace and reconciliation. Emphasis on God's power to bring about peace incites Christians to pursue peace by the power of the Holy Spirit.

Pursuing Peace in South Sudan

In South Sudan, Christians have been at the forefront of pursuing peace. Reconciliation is never easy, but the God of peace calls us to this task, to participate with God in the restoration of broken relationships. Christian leaders in South Sudan seek to be agents of God's reconciliation and peace. They believe that God is opening doors for peace in order to overcome years of violent conflict and to bring about reconciliation between people groups that have long been divided. The following is one example of Christians pursuing God's call to act as agents of reconciliation in South Sudan.

The Episcopal Diocese of Yambio organized a religious peace conference in collaboration with local authorities from November 11–15 in 2004. I, Bishop Samuel Enosa Peni, was one of the leaders of this conference. The conference was held in response to intense tribal conflict between two opposing groups, the pastoralists and the farmers. The groups fought over land rights and the use of natural resources. There were many violent clashes between these two groups that left many people dead and much property destroyed. The church thought it wise to convene the peace conference in an attempt to mediate a peaceful resolution between the two groups. Over three hundred participants attended the conference.

The conference leaders approached the conference with a model for reconciliation that they had adapted from Roger Fisher and William Ury's book, *Getting to Yes: Negotiating Agreement Without Giving In*. Fisher and Ury suggest four basic steps for developing options in conflict solving. The four steps are: 1) establish the problem and current assumptions; 2) begin assessment of the issues at stake; 3) determine appropriate strategies for addressing the problems; and 4) implement specific steps for addressing the issues.[25] In particular, leaders of the Episcopal Church focused on the Christian responsibility to promote reconciliation and forgiveness as necessary elements in establishing peace between the fighting groups.

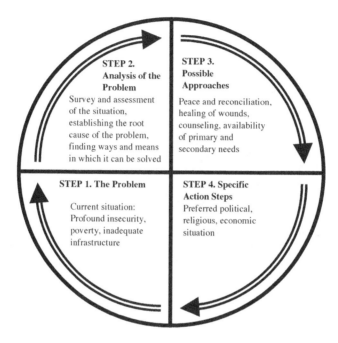

STEP 2.
Analysis of the Problem
Survey and assessment of the situation, establishing the root cause of the problem, finding ways and means in which it can be solved

STEP 3.
Possible Approaches
Peace and reconciliation, healing of wounds, counseling, availability of primary and secondary needs

STEP 1. The Problem
Current situation: Profound insecurity, poverty, inadequate infrastructure

STEP 4. Specific Action Steps
Preferred political, religious, economic situation

Figure 1: Steps toward gaining a desired situation[26]

This is how the conference proceeded:

Day One

Each of the ten counties that comprise Western Equatoria State sent representatives. Subsequently, these representatives were divided into special-interest groups: government officials, tribal chiefs, elders, women, church leaders, youth, farmers, and pastoralists. These subgroups were assigned the following questions to discuss: Why is there this conflict? How did it start? Who started it? What happened? Each group was to report back to the plenary session its findings regarding the anger and disappointments experienced by the participants and the people they represent. What was

25. Fisher and Ury, *Getting to Yes*, 68.
26. Ibid. Adapted from CMI Concord Group, Inc. 2008 to suit this situation.

not surprising was that each group blamed the other group(s). Most of the reports stated things like: "These people are bad. This is what they have done. They killed so and so. They stole our things. Our crops were destroyed by their animals. They need to change!" The facilitator and his crew took note of everything that was reported, posting all responses publicly on the walls where the conference was taking place.

Figure 2: Arrival of the governors of Western Equatoria State and the guest of honor for the official opening of the conference

Day Two

Each of the participants gathered in the same groups to discuss how the wounds that had been identified the previous day could be healed. The question that participants were asked to address was, "What could have been done by those who have wounded us to have prevented this conflict?" In other words, what could each of the two groups have done to maintain peace? Following the group discussions was the plenary session, in which the participants could compare their answers. In most cases, the answers were similar. They discovered that miscommunication or a lack of communication was responsible for much of the discord and enmity between the two groups. Each group demanded that the other group needed to act positively so all could live in peace.

Figure 3: The ECS Youth Choir saying "no" to conflicts
but "yes" to peaceful co-existence

Day Three

This was the day that the two groups brainstormed about how they could live together. They were asked to answer the question: How can we live as a Sudanese community and use our land and resources for the welfare of all Sudanese? A small group was formed, consisting of members from the two fighting groups, to come up with one cohesive, unified document with resolutions. This document was later presented to the whole group to amend and pass. This document was finally accepted by all the members participating in the peace conference.

Day Four

The peace conference culminated with a big, traditional celebration of reconciliation between the two conflicting groups. Previous offences between the groups were forgiven publicly, with each group member confessing to each other their mistakes and asking for forgiveness. Resolutions to establish cordial relations and improve communication between the two groups were signed and ways of solving any future problems were created. Because the church organized the peace conference, there was also a Christian reconciliation service. The service asked for God's forgiveness, absolution, and grace as we began seeking a new way of life together, renewing the old friendships that had fallen apart, and reestablishing former relationships as well. The Christian service of reconciliation is not included in most conflict resolution theories. However, it was absolutely essential to the success of the conference. The service enabled participants to move past the issues of the two groups and to see each other in light of God's forgiveness and grace.

Figure 4: The Reverend Samuel Enosa Peni leading the ecumenical liturgy

Christian churches in Sudan and South Sudan always have been at the forefront of the struggle to end violence and to achieve national peace. The conference in 2004 is only one example of the church's efforts to pursue peace in Sudan.[27] Overall, the conference was a fruitful conflict resolution and mediation process. The facilitators skillfully coordinated and interpreted the statements of the participants during the group discussions and plenary. Both parties admitted that they had contributed to the conflicts, and both sought reconciliation and new ways of interacting in the future. However, the county commissioners and traditional chiefs needed encouragement and support to disseminate the results of the peace conference. Unfortunately, the resolutions, the fruit of the negotiations, were not translated into the various tribal languages (vernaculars), and the traditional chiefs could not teach the resolutions to their people, beyond what they remembered. This was due to a lack of funding to pay for the needed translations. Therefore, the villagers were unable to receive the resolutions that had been designed and written specifically to help them avoid the recurrence of those problems that needed to be resolved. Thus, the conference was an important step toward pursuing peace, but there is still much work to be done.

27. For a list of other conferences, see Peni, "Role of the Church."

A Pauline Assessment of the Peace Process in South Sudan

How would Paul assess the 2004 religious peace conference between the pastoralists and the farmers in South Sudan? And what are implications of a Pauline understanding of peace for Christians in South Sudan today and any Christians who experience conflict around the world? Based on Rom 12:14–21, Paul most likely would be pleased that the church leaders were taking initiatives to pursue peace. Paul, in Rom 12, seems to lay the burden of pursing peace on Christians in Rome—telling them to bless even their persecutors. The Christian leaders in South Sudan saw themselves as active agents of God's reconciliation, and they led the way in pursuing peace not only among themselves but also with all people. Moreover, whereas most conflict resolution models stress the importance of each party admitting their responsibility, Paul places his hope for peace on divine reconciliation. The conference's final service of reconciliation mirrored this hope. Paul also would probably not be surprised by the way in which groups blamed each other, saying, "This is what they've done. . . . They need to change." Paul's appeal to Christians to pursue peace in 12:18 does not depend on either human party. Paul does not say to pursue peace once the other group starts acting justly. Instead, Paul expects Christians to pursue peace because of the nature of God, who is the God of peace and has the power to bring about peace. Finally, while the tendency might be to evaluate the 2004 peace conference on the basis of its immediate impact, Paul posits the prior act of God's reconciliation through Christ as the basis for success. The conference in 2004 followed the steps outlined in traditional conflict resolution models, yet it still did not bring about lasting peace. Thus, some people might question the conference's effectiveness. Yet Paul's vision of peace is based on God's overarching story of reconciliation. Despite individual episodes of conflict (or of peace), Paul insists that reconciliation is guaranteed not by a series of human successes but by God's victory through the cross of Christ.

By reflecting on the concrete realities of conflict and peace (as exemplified in South Sudan) in conversation with Rom 12:14–21, we find at least four principles for Christians today—whether in South Sudan or elsewhere—who seek peace in the midst of a violent world:

1. **Christians are called to be leaders in pursuing peace.** The Christian pursuit of peace is an imperative found in Scripture. It is also something Christians do because we are people being formed in the image of God, who is the God of peace.

2. **Christian peacemaking is not dependent upon the response of others.** Since peacemaking is at the core of Christian identity, we are not deterred when we encounter hostile forces. The refusal of enemies to engage in peacemaking is irrelevant to the Christian calling to be agents of God's reconciliation.

3. **Christian peacemakers have hope.** Christian peacemaking is founded on the premise that God already has reconciled the world through Christ. The victory is assured. This realization results in freedom and hope to continue to pursue peace even when the immediate results are limited. Individual failures and successes with regard to pursuing peace are viewed in light of the overall story of God's redemption.

4. **Christian peacemakers give credit to God.** Although Paul calls Christians to pursue peace with all, he also notes the absurdity of assuming the results are based on our efforts. Paul rightly places the responsibility for peace on God. From Paul's perspective, peace does not depend on us; peace depends on God. God is the guarantor of peace. Ultimately, peace is God's responsibility.

Bibliography

Constantineanu, Corneliu. *The Social Significance of Reconciliation in Paul's Theology: Narrative Readings in Romans*. LNTS 421. New York: T. & T. Clark, 2010.

Donfried, Karl P., ed. *The Romans Debate*. Rev. and exp. ed. Peabody: Hendrickson, 1991.

Fisher, Roger, and William Ury. *Getting to Yes: Negotiating Agreement Without Giving In*. Edited by Bruce Patton. 2nd ed. New York: Penguin, 1991.

Gaventa, Beverly Roberts. "Neither Height nor Depth: Discerning the Cosmology of Romans." *SJT* 64 (2011) 265–78.

———. "The Rhetoric of Violence and the God of Peace in Paul's Letter to the Romans." In *Paul, John, and Apocalyptic Eschatology: Studies in Honour of Martinus C. de Boer*, edited by Jan Kras et al., 63–69. NovTSup 149. Leiden: Brill, 2013.

Hays, Richard B. *Echoes of Scripture in the Letters of Paul*. New Haven: Yale University Press, 1989.

Moule, C. F. D. *An Idiom Book of New Testament Greek*. 2nd ed. Cambridge: Cambridge University Press, 1959.

Oden, Thomas C., ed. *Mark*. Ancient Christian Commentary on Scripture: New Testament 2. Downers Grove: InterVarsity, 2005.

Peni, Samuel Enosa. "The Role of the Church in Reconciliation and Peace Building in South Sudan." Lecture, Mission Theology in the Anglican Communion Project, March 2017.

Penna, Romano. "'The God of Peace' in the New Testament." In *Visions of Peace and Tales of War*, edited by Jan Liesen and Pancratius C. Beentjes, 279–302. Berlin: de Gruyter, 2010.

Wengst, Klaus. *Pax Romana and the Peace of Jesus Christ*. Philadelphia: Fortress, 1987.

Wilson, Walter. *Love without Pretense*. WUNT 2.46. Tübingen: Mohr Siebeck, 1991.

13

Messianic Anarchy: The Liberating Word of Romans 13:1–7[1]

Douglas Harink

R OMANS 13:1–7 HAS BEEN variously championed, questioned, contextu-
alized, despised, and rejected (sometimes as not authentically Pauline)
by Christians throughout the centuries. It has been embraced by both
Constantinians and Mennonites with, to say the least, divergent results. It
continues to be seen as a block, or stumbling-block, of text that bears little
relation to the rest of Paul's letter and is seemingly out of sync with what
Paul writes elsewhere in, for example, 1 Cor 2:6–8. But despite the multitudes of scholarly studies that have been written, whether in articles, mono-
graphs, or commentaries even in the last fifty years, I believe it is still worth
trying to see this text anew and ask whether it might still grip us—even as *a
liberating word*—in our time.[2] In this essay I track three themes intrinsic to
Romans in the first eleven chapters: "inheriting the world" (Rom 4 and 8);
"the justice of trust" (aka, "justification by faith"—Rom 3 and 4); and, more
briefly, "ruling in life" (Rom 5).[3] These themes are then applied to Israel in
Rom 9–11 and to the matter of "the ruling powers" in 13:1–7.

Much more could be done on the letter as a whole to firmly establish
the reading of Rom 13 I end up with. Most important would be to show how,
for Paul, the gospel of God is a comprehensive vision (or, rather, apocalypse)
of *the real*, of *life*, and of *justice* amidst the competing cosmic visions of the
pagan world that Paul sketches out in Rom 1:18–32 and the *nomos*-vision of

---

1. With this essay I express my deep gratitude for the work and friendship of Susan
Eastman. Her writings have been decisive for my work at critical junctures.

2. For a thorough recent discussion with extensive reference to the literature, see
Jewett, *Romans*, 780–803.

3. All scriptural quotations are from the NRSV, unless otherwise indicated.

Judaism (2:17—3:20).[4] The gospel apocalypse generates a new social body and "social imaginary" in the midst of these competing visions that testify to the reality, life, and justice of God in Jesus the Messiah and the Holy Spirit.[5] It creates a new movement of justice in the world that Paul takes to be world-historical in scope yet almost invisible according to the criteria normally used to discern movements of justice.

Inheriting the World

To a modern reader who pays attention, Paul's construal in Rom 4:13 of God's promise to Abraham seems bizarre: it is a promise that Abraham (with his "seed") should be "the heir of the world" (*to klēronomon kosmou*). One can hardly think of a more grandiose, indeed hubristic and dangerous promise being made to any human being. Imagine how such an idea might have been received by Rome in Paul's time, for which inheriting the world was its divine mandate.[6] Imagine any person, nation, or empire in Abraham's time or our own taking up such a promise—divinely given—and running with it. Unfortunately, with a quick glance through world history it is not too hard to imagine, from ancient Babylon and Rome to modern England, Spain, Russia, and the United States. Nevertheless, perhaps we could imagine—exceptionally—a perfectly wise and *just* ruler or "Founding Father" embodying, establishing, and fostering a perfectly just law among a people, as one who might rightly "inherit the world." We might even welcome such a one and work to advance his just cause throughout the earth.

Paul was not the first to think in terms of Abrahamic exceptionalism and world-historical destiny. The very idea is explicit throughout the stories of Abraham, Isaac, and Jacob in Genesis. It is declared to Abraham at the very moment of his calling: "I will make of you a great nation, and I will bless you, and make your name great, so that you will be a blessing.

4. By *nomos*-vision I mean the whole system of life of Judaism in which the Torah/Law (Grk.: *nomos*) is the comprehensive, even metaphysical, structuring reality. Of signal importance for filling out themes relevant to this essay are chapters 18 and 19 of Barclay, *Pauline Churches*.

5. The idea of "social imaginary" comes from Taylor, *Secular Age*, 171–76: A social imaginary is "the ways [people] imagine their social existence, how they fit together with others, how things go on between them and their fellows, the expectations which are normally met, and the deeper normative notions and images which underlie these expectations" (171). For connections between apocalyptic thought and our imaginings in relation to the vocation of preaching, see chapter 3 by Charles Campbell in the present volume.

6. As noted by Jewett, *Romans*, 325.

I will bless those who bless you, and the one who curses you I will curse; and in you all the nations of the earth shall be blessed" (Gen 12:2–3). It weaves its way through every major narrative block of the Old Testament. It is the meaning of Israel's election.[7] In Gen 15:18–21 Abraham's inheritance or "possession" is marked out in a limited way as the *land* between the boundaries of the Nile River to the southwest and the Euphrates River to the northeast. According to 1 Kgs 4:20–21, this inheritance was attained under Solomon's reign. Around two centuries before Paul one Jewish sage, Yeshua ben Sira, had greatly expanded the vision of Abraham's inheritance: it would be "from sea to sea, and from the [Euphrates] River to the ends of the earth" (Sir 44:21). Other Jewish writers before and in Paul's time shared that larger worldwide vision.[8] Precisely this world-historical Abrahamic exceptionalism becomes the focus of Paul's attention in Rom 4.

Who is the just man to whom a promise of world-inheritance might be given? To whom might it be justly entrusted? What is the character of his justice? From a Jewish perspective, Ben Sira had already answered this question: "Abraham was the great father of a multitude of nations, and no one has been found like him in glory. He kept the law of the Most High, and entered into a covenant with him; he certified the covenant in his flesh, and when he was tested he proved faithful" (Sir 44:19–20). Abraham, by this account, is the paradigmatic keeper of God's law, initiating (it seems) a covenant with God; he marks himself paradigmatically by circumcision, is paradigmatically tested, and proves to be faithful. He has thus proven himself worthy of the inheritance: "*Therefore* (*dia touto*) the Lord assured him with an oath that the nations would be blessed through his offspring; that he would make him as numerous as the dust of the earth, and exalt his offspring like the stars, and give them an inheritance from sea to sea and from the Euphrates to the ends of the earth" (44:21). For Ben Sira, Abraham achieved his rightful place in history and so too would his offspring if they walked in his footsteps.

---

7. "For the promise thus interpreted [that Abraham should inherit the world] was fundamental to Israel's self-consciousness as God's covenant people: it was the reason God had chosen them in the first place from among all the other nations of the earth, the justification for holding themselves distinct from the other nations, and the comforting hope that made their current national humiliation endurable" (Dunn, *Romans*, 233).

8. See ibid., 213, for further references to the literature.

The Justice of Trust

But Paul has a fundamentally different understanding of how Abraham is the just one, and why he receives the promise of inheriting the world. In Rom 4, Abraham is an "ungodly" one (*asebē*, 4:5), that is, a pagan, when God declares the promise to him. There is nothing glorious about him. By contrast, Sirach stresses the prior work of Abraham in attaining his "glory" through keeping the law, entering into a covenant with the "Most High," circumcising, and faithfully passing the test. For Paul no such "works" or "working" precede the promise of world inheritance. Rather, *God* declares the promise to the "not-working one" (*mē ergazomenō*, 4:5, author's translation), not to the Abraham who had himself attained a unique and universal glory through his piety, but to the *ungodly* Abraham. This Abraham *trusts* God's promise, and "to Abraham [that] trust was accounted [by God] as justice" (4:9, author's translation). To *this one whose uncircumcised trust is taken as justice*, God promises that he should be heir of the world. God counts him as the just patriarch of all peoples—not only of the circumcising people, but also of all those uncircumcised peoples, the "ungodly," who "walk the walk" (*tois stoichousin tois ichnesin*, 4:12, author's translation) of father Abraham's uncircumcised trust. They too are given a share in the Patriarch's world-historical destiny.

This is a revolution in the idea of the world-inheriting just patriarch. His justice and his inheritance are both "according to grace" (*kata charin*, 4:4,16); they are not established (as in Sirach and in most non-Jewish visions of the just ruler) by his glorious achievements in maintaining law, establishing treaties (with gods or God), proving himself in ordeals, or conquering the peoples of the earth. Abraham's justice and inheritance are established in and by "the God . . . who makes dead ones alive and calls things not-being into being" (4:17, author's translation). Abraham, in fact, has nothing to contribute: hearing God's promise of descendants and world-inheritance, he knew that his body, about a hundred years old, was already as much as dead (*nenekrōmenon*), and that Sarah's womb was indeed already dead (*nekrōsin*, 4:19). Nevertheless, the promise made by the resurrecting, creating God *energizes* (*enedynamōthē*) Abraham's trust, keeps his hope alive, and moves him not to attain glory for himself but to *give glory to God* (4:20). Paul does not say that the promise to Abraham was ultimately fulfilled in the birth of Isaac. Rather, Paul persistently draws our attention to the *inheritance-promising God* and to Abraham's *ongoing trust* in God's promise, which is a trust that *God counts as justice*—justice not only to Abraham, but also "to us who trust him who raised Jesus our Lord from the dead" (4:24, author's translation).

Justice and world-inheritance belong not only to Abraham but also to all those who trust as he did, with a trust that God reckons as justice.

Paul has just returned our attention to "Jesus our Lord." Not only was he raised from the dead; he "was handed over to death for our trespasses and was raised to render us just" (4:25, author's translation). Romans 4 is not an independent section on the justice of trust. The argument about justice of which chapter 4 is a part begins already in 1:16–18 and has its definitive center in 3:21–26: "But now, apart from law, the justice of God has been disclosed . . . the justice of God through the faithfulness of Jesus Messiah for all who trust" (3:21–22, author's translation). Justice *just is* what God does in and through *the faithful Jesus Messiah, whose redemptive death is the site, demonstration, and accomplishment of God's justice.* Those who share in the faithfulness of Jesus through trust are themselves made just. Reading backwards from 4:24–25, we realize that the justice reckoned to Abraham through his faithful trust is in fact none other than that justice of God enacted in the Messiah. By trusting in the resurrecting God *of* Jesus Messiah Abraham shares in the justice of God, *which is* Jesus Messiah.

Paul takes up the themes of death, resurrection, and inheritance again in Rom 8. The Holy Spirit is the power of life and justice by which God raises from the dead; not only the dead body of Jesus, but also our own Abraham-and-Sarah-like dead bodies (8:10–11). (Reading backwards again, we must also conclude then that this same Holy Spirit enlivened Abraham's and Sarah's as-good-as-dead bodies.) The life-giving, adopting power of the Spirit creates "sons of God" (*huioi theou*) and "children of God" (*tekna theou*) and *therefore* "heirs of God" (*klēronomoi theou*) and "co-heirs with Messiah" (*synklēronomoi Christou*, 8:14, 16, 17, author's translation). By the Spirit of life and adoption into Messiah, those who believe have been made sharers in the world-historical destiny promised to Abraham. As Paul had made clear already in Gal 3:15–18, being incorporated into the Messiah— the singular "seed" of Abraham—means being taken into Abraham's promised inheritance. Ultimately, *it is the Messiah who inherits the world*—and all those who, with Abraham, share *in the Messiah* through trust.

Inheriting the World, Reprise

World-inheritance for those in the Messiah! Isn't that also a very dangerous idea? "Christians" inheriting the world, claiming their right to it, marching imperially or "missionally" from one end of the earth to the other, declaring that the world belongs to them, establishing the rule of Christian "justice" in nations and empires wherever they can. This too has happened! We now call it European and American colonialism. The promise of world-inheritance whether to Abraham or to Christians seems like an inherently bad idea.

We might briefly add to this another potentially bad idea that Paul brings up in Rom 5: Christians "ruling." In 5:12–21 Paul writes of the entry of sin and death into the world upon the disobedience and injustice of Adam, spreading and establishing themselves as malignant ruling powers over all humankind (*ho thanatos ebasileusin*, "death reigned," 5:14, 17; *hē hamartia ebasileusin*, "sin reigned," 5:21).[9] Nevertheless, by contrast and superabundantly, through the obedience and justice of Jesus Messiah a new regime is established: it is the right and proper *ancient regime* that belonged to humankind in the first place: "dominion" over all living creatures (Gen 1:26–28). "Those who through superabundant grace receive the gift of justice will reign in life [*en zōē basileusousin*] through the one man Jesus Messiah" (Rom 5:17, author's translation). But here, as with inheriting, ruling is not achieved; *ruling is graciously given only through and in the Messiah*. Jesus Messiah, the singular heir, inherits the world and we in him; Jesus Messiah, by his singular life-act of justice and obedience, reigns in life and we in him.

So, not only inheriting the world but also ruling in life.[10] Without further gospel definition this may seem a mandate for disaster. In fact, however, Paul's gospel intrinsically, immediately, and decisively addresses this problem. The point is already obvious: the fact that world-inheriting and ruling in life are promised always and only *in Jesus Messiah* fundamentally qualifies, or rather constitutes, what world-inheriting and reigning in life are and what they look like for those to whom they have been promised. In Rom 8, no sooner has Paul written of the children of God sharing in the world-inheritance of the Messiah than he brings all hubristic ideas of what that might mean to a sudden stop. "Heirs of God and co-heirs (*synklēronomoi*) of Messiah, if indeed we co-suffer (*sympaschomen*) with him; *thus* may we be co-glorified (*syndoxasthōmen*) with him" (8:17, author's translation). *There is a single road to messianic world-inheriting and glory; it is the paschal road of the Messiah, the way of the cross.*[11] As Paul goes on to say, messianic co-suffering with Messiah also immediately

9. For a discussion of the way in which Paul draws on Gen 2–3 for his reflections about Adam and the implications of sin's entrance into the world for nonhuman creation, see Presian Burroughs's chapter 11.

10. We might also note the similar, indeed even more audacious, cosmic claim in 1 Cor 6:2–3, where Paul writes that "the saints will judge the world" and even "judge the angels."

11. In the same way, there is a single road to "ruling in life"; it is co-crucifixion in Messiah, as Paul makes clear in Rom 6. Michael Gorman, in chapter 1 of this volume, demonstrates that participation in Christ necessarily involves humiliation and suffering with Christ; such participation is what allows a minister to serve with integrity.

puts the "children of God" in fundamental solidarity with the groaning-in-travail of *all creation* (8:19–23) and again (as with Abraham) living not by sight, but in hope of the apocalyptic redemption of all things, bodies and creation alike, in the Messiah: "For who hopes for what is seen? But if we hope for what we do not see, we eagerly and patiently expect it" (8:24–25, author's translation). No powers in heaven or on earth can thwart this final victory and no "sword" can finally defeat the co-suffering paschal people (8:35–36) who will through suffering ("in all these things") become "more than conquerors through him who loved us" (8:37). The Messiah and his people receive the world-historical promise only in solidarity with those who are oppressed and with creation in bondage.

Justice for the People (of Israel)

God's promise of world-inheritance was made first and directly to *the people of Israel*, the flesh-descendants of Abraham: "to them belong the sonship [*huiothesia*] and the glory and the covenants and the gift of law and the worship [*latreia*] and the promises; to them also belong the patriarchs and from them the Messiah according to the flesh who is over all, God blessed into the ages" (Rom 9:4–5, author's translation). What would the vindication—the justice—of this world-historical promise look like for the Jewish people, especially in the time of Roman rule over Judea, when "Israel" is simply an occupied land and a conquered people subject to and often oppressed by the obviously glorious world-inheritor, Rome? Surely it would mean (according to someone like Ben Sira) that Israel seeks a glory like that of father Abraham, who kept the law of the Most High and kept covenant with him, certifying that covenant by circumcision and proving faithful when sorely tested. Perhaps it could also mean Israel striving to vindicate itself among the nations (as in the days of the Maccabees), attaining its rightful place in the world through zealous warfare.[12]

Perhaps. Or is it the case, now that Messiah has come "from them" and is himself the world-inheriting heir, that Israel's hope for vindication and justice as a people is gone? Will Israel *as a people* ever receive the inheritance promised to father Abraham by God? Or has that promise now been given instead to another people—perhaps the "church." Ultimately, Paul's answer to these questions is "never!" The Jewish people will not "be put to shame" among the nations (Rom 10:11, quoting Isa 28:16 LXX). But

---

12. Is it possible that Paul has something like this in mind when he writes in Rom 10:2–3 about Israel's "zeal" for God, a zeal by which Israel seeks to establish its own justice in the world rather than submitting to God's justice—in Messiah?

the road to their world-historical destiny (their justice) is no different from the one Paul discerned in Abraham—not the road of striving for glory that Ben Sira described, but the road of *trust*, which God *accounts as justice*. "I can testify," Paul writes, "that they [Israel] have a zeal for God, but it lacks understanding, for they have not truly grasped *the justice of God* [in the good news] and given themselves to it; instead they strive to bring about justice—that is, to attain their God-promised place in the world—through their own zealous efforts" (10:2–3; see also 9:31–32, author's paraphrasing). The Messiah does *not* cancel their hope of vindication, but justice will not come to Israel either through political compromise or a revolutionary uprising. Instead the Messiah himself establishes the mode of its arrival—trust. For Israel as an entire people there is *a single road to world-inheriting glory, to justice; it is walking the paschal road of the Messiah, the way of the cross: it is walking the walk of Abraham who trusted the resurrecting God* (10:6–13). That road of trust is a difficult and demanding road for any people or nation. But, Paul says, the word of this Messianic way to justice was *ever near* to Israel, "on their lips and in their heart" (10:8). In the moment of Messianic arrival, however, Israel did not hear it, for "God gave them a sluggish spirit, eyes that would not see and ears that would not hear" (11:8, quoting Deut 29:4; Isa 29:10). God did this strange thing to Israel for a specific purpose: because of it the word about the Messiah went out "to the ends of the world"; there it was "found by those who did not seek [it]"; it was "shown to those who did not ask for [it]" (Rom 10:18–20). In the meantime, Israel itself must wait and hope for its Messianic vindication (11:26–28). Israel, like Abraham and like those newly created believers from the gentile peoples, must trust the resurrecting and creating God—the one who in the first place created Israel by his promise (9:6–16). Such trust will be reckoned to Israel—God's chosen people—as justice.

Messianic Life

Among the pagan nations (those which were once "not-my-people," Rom 9:25, author's translation) there are those who hear and trust the good news of God's justice in the Messiah. Being thereby liberated from the powerful systems of idolatry and injustice, which had formed their life together throughout the ages (12:2; 1:18–32), they are now called into a new formation, a transformation of their mode of being in the world, a fundamental reframing and reforming of life. Among those who participate by trust in the justice of God in Messiah, God graciously generates a new social body and a new social imaginary.[13] In Messiah they present their bodies—together as one body (12:5)—as a "living sacrifice" (12:1) in the midst of an age of violence and injustice. In this new sociality and social imaginary they are given to "discern the will of God—that is, the good, the well-pleasing, the perfect" (12:2, author's translation)—in a fundamentally new way, not according to the enslaving and destructive cosmic principles governing the nations, nor according to the *nomos*-principle governing *ho Ioudaioi* ("the Judeans/Jews"), but according to the "mercies of God" announced and enacted as the good news. In this, they perform their "reasonable public service [*logikēn latreian*]" (12:1, author's translation) among the nations, for the sake of the nations.

The new form of public service (*latreia*) brought about by the gospel in the messianic community has a clearly defined (*logikos*) character, both in the internal life of the community and in its relationship to the wider world. "Living sacrifice" takes shape *within* the community according to the variety of *charismata* graciously given to form and bind together "the many" into the one social body of the Messiah (12:5).[14] That body is bound together in love and mutual honoring, in abhorring evil and clinging to the good. With Abraham, it rejoices in hope; with the Messiah, it is patient in suffering; with the Spirit, it perseveres in prayer (12:12; 4:18; 8:17, 26–27). It shares joys, sorrows, and finances. The high-minded rub shoulders with the lowly. It opens its life to strangers. In this form of life together it presents a living image of the Messiah—the justice of God. In *this way*, in *this time*, in *this place*, it receives and dwells in its messianic inheritance.

Messianic Anarchy

There is nevertheless a world—*the world*—that continues to operate otherwise. The messianic community encounters and engages—indeed, is embedded within and embodies—that world in many ways. It is not called out of the world but into a world in which, among much that is true, honorable, just, and worthy of praise (Phil 4:8), there is also sexual immorality, greed, theft, idolatry, injustice, and much more (1 Cor 5:9–10). Moved by malignant powers, it is sometimes a world that may curse, persecute, and

13. As noted before, the idea of "social imaginary" comes from Charles Taylor. We might also speak of a new *habitus*, as developed by John Barclay (borrowing from Pierre Bourdieu) in Barclay, *Paul and the Gift*, chapter 16.

14. Beverly Gaventa in chapter 4 and Emily Peck-McClain in chapter 10 of this volume further reflect on the metaphor of body and the Spirit's gifts, especially as these relate to gender identities and age-inclusiveness in church ministry, respectively.

do evil to the messianic community.[15] Avenging those curses with curses, persecutions with persecution, evils with evil—these are always the tempting options. But they are not messianic. No justice of God walks down that road. The relationship of the social body of the Messiah with those outside has a fundamentally different character—it is *messianic*. When the messianic community is persecuted or cursed, it blesses. When evil is done to it, it considers well how to respond with goodness, providing food and drink even to enemies. Whatever opposition or violence may be done against it, it determines to "live at peace with all" (Rom 12:14, 17–18, 20).[16] "Wrath" (*orgē*) and "vengeance" (*ekdikēsis*) are God's work; they are forbidden in the job description of the social body of the Messiah.

But what about the ruling powers (*exousiais hyperechousais*, 13:1)—the overlords, the commanders in chief, the princes, presidents and potentates, the kings and emperors? With "sword" (or whatever other "authorized" weapon) in hand, have they not also done their share—and possibly much more—of persecuting, evil, and vengeance? Even or especially to the Messiah (1 Cor 2:6–8); even or sometimes especially toward the messianic community? How shall those in Messiah respond to them?

Paul's word is *hypotassō*—translated variously as "submit," "be subject to," "be subordinate." Quite literally translated, Paul writes, "Let every soul be ordered under (*hypo-*) the higher (*hyper-*) authorities." Is this a recipe for the passive acceptance of whatever the ruling powers ask or require or demand? Or even more—and as it has been understood for centuries by Christian multitudes—is it a call for Christians to "obey" (*The Living Bible*) the rulers, to "be good citizens" (*The Message*), to be loyal to, pledge allegiance to, wave the flag of, sing anthems to, defend the cause of, march in the armies of, and destroy the enemies of the ruling authorities? This and much more has been absorbed into the meaning of *hypotassō*. It may be one of the most inflated words in Scripture. *Hypotassō* has warranted servile and grudging or loyal and willing Christian *obedience* to the ruling powers from Constantine to Hitler. It continues to do so.

However, if "submit" is too difficult a pill to swallow, then perhaps to "become" the ruling powers may be an option. Let those Christians who will not in good conscience submit seek for themselves the role and authority and power of ruling elites. Surely it is better if the ruling authorities are Christians. Let every soul be subject to *them*! If they conquer and colonize as the form of their Christian mission, all will be well. Justice and peace and

---

15. Lisa Bowens, in chapter 8, examines the ways in which Paul describes the Christian life as a life of resisting and combating such malignant forces.

16. Mary Schmitt and Bishop Samuel Enosa Peni consider this call to peace in chapter 12, as does Douglas Campbell in chapter 14.

life for all will prevail. Perhaps this is how the Messiah inherits the world. So also it has often been thought and continues to be.

That Paul means none of the above must be clear—or made clear. *Hypotassō* must be *emptied of all content but ordering*. Paul is saying, "There are the 'overs,' the *hypers*: acknowledge them as the 'overs'; take them as *given* in their being there—no more! And therefore messianics, you yourselves are the 'unders,' the *hypos*. But being the 'unders' is no disadvantage at all for messianics; it is in fact the mode of messianic being in the world. It was for Abraham, it was for the Messiah himself; it cannot be otherwise for those who 'walk the walk' of father Abraham's trust and who through trust have been taken up by God into the reality of the Messiah who gave himself for us." *Hypotassō* simply cannot mean "obey" in this context; Paul has another word for that (*hypakouō*), and it is owed to Messiah alone. It cannot mean "trust" or "allegiance"; Paul has another word for that (*pistis*, aka "faith"), and it is owed to Messiah alone. It cannot mean "offer your bodies in public service" (i.e., be good citizens); Paul has other words for that (*thusia zōsa* ["living sacrifice"], *logikē latreia* ["reasonable public service"], Rom 12:1), and these are owed to God, to the social body of the Messiah, and in self-giving service, hospitality, kindness, and blessing to strangers and enemies.

It is not as if the ruling powers are their own lords. They are there because God orders them to be there, to do the work that God allows them to do because the whole wide world is not yet offering "the obedience of trust/loyalty" (*hypakoē pisteōs*, 1:5; 16:26, author's translation) to the Messiah. But it is *an inglorious work*. The ruling powers, while serving God's purpose in some way, are nevertheless *moved by the powers of this age*. Their work is characterized throughout Rom 13:1–7 with words like "judgment," "terror," "fear," "sword," "avenger," and "wrath," and is infused throughout with the logic of reward and punishment.[17] According to the rest of Romans these words describe the workings of the power of sin. There is not a *hint* of the messianic in any of this. There is *no justice* here, no life, no grace and gift, no redemption or liberation, no reconciliation, no binding together as a self-sacrificing social body, no blessing, no peace, no glory, and finally *no promise to inherit the world*, despite the often ambitious and vaunted claims of the powers to rule over life and make the world their own. So when Paul says to let every messianic be ordered under the hyper-ruling powers, it can only mean that there is *nothing those powers are doing that is worthy of messianic participation*; in fact, the modus operandi of those powers is precisely that *from which messianics have been delivered through*

---

17. Douglas Campbell reflects on these aspects of punitive power in chapter 14 of this volume.

their participation in the Messiah. Hypotassō, in this context, is *a liberating word*. What do messianics owe the ruling authorities? Taxes. The simple acknowledgment of their being there ("submit"). The same kind of honor (*timē*)—but no more or greater than—that they owe their brothers and sisters in the messianic community (13:7; 12:9). And love, just insofar as the authorities too are their neighbors.

Messianics are called to a fundamentally different form of life (conformed to the image of God's Son, 8:29) and power of life (in the Holy Spirit, 8:10–11) than that which characterizes the *ruling authorities*. Those in the Messiah "inherit the world"—become agents within world history—by walking in trust as Abraham did and through co-suffering with Messiah in solidarity with all creation. They "rule in life" in Messiah, insofar as they share in his obedient life-act of self-offering on the cross. They participate in God's messianic justice in the world through trust, that is, through *holy anarchy*. They do not strive to serve, placate, oppose, rely on, or trust in the ruling powers. They do strive to communicate the power of messianic life in the world through love. Even love of enemies. Even when those enemies are the ruling powers. Paul says messianics fulfill the justice of law by one "word" (*logos*, 13:9): "Love your neighbor as yourself." In this they become the messianic justice of God in the world, and this is how that justice makes its way in the world. This one "word" is a word of fullness and abundance; it opens up to an infinite range of local, timely engagements, interventions, actions, practices, advocacies, polities, solidarities, and co-sufferings; it interrupts a world of "impiety and injustice" (1:18) with truth, reconciliation, grace, hospitality, and peace; that is, with the good news! There is no end to this "word."[18]

Messianic Time

Messianic anarchy operates "beneath" the ruling powers because it does not need them to pursue and fulfill its calling. It does not seek out and strive after the high places, but the low. It walks in the Abrahamic trust that God reckons as justice. But such messianic trust is not about sleep-walking through the time of trouble! It is not naïve about or unengaged with the state of the world or the neighborhood. It is not the lazy thought that "somehow good things will happen" or that "everything will be alright in the end." It is wide awake to the present moment, the *kairos*, a moment

18. For understanding messianic life as *peaceable anarchy* I am especially indebted to Eller, *Christian Anarchy*; and also to, *inter alia*, Ellul, *Anarchy and Christianity*; Osburn, *Anarchy and Apocalypse*.

full of dangers and possibilities (13:11). The dangers are real: there is always the temptation to numb oneself to the moment, to the demanding word, "Love your neighbor as yourself." That temptation to numbness was all around in Paul's time, as it is in ours: parties, entertainment, drunkenness, sexual immorality, pornography, fighting, and jealousy (13:13). These are the sins of the sleepwalkers, those who would shut themselves off from their neighbor by self-indulgence, diversions, exploitation, envy, and strife until the clock winds down. But for those who have "put on the Lord Jesus Messiah" the *kairos*, the hour, the day of salvation—in other words, the advent and claim of the neighbor—is "nearer now than when we first trusted" (13:11, author's translation); messianics, not being timed and lulled by the down-winding clock, are awake to the present time, to the gift that comes in the moment, to life in the Spirit, to doing the good, to struggling against the powers of darkness, and to inheriting the world.[19]

Conclusion

We live in an age—probably not really unlike others—in which our gaze is constantly being drawn to the ruling powers, not only the political ones but also all those who would grab our attention and call us to celebrate their glory and greatness. It is hard not to believe that *they* have inherited the world: it seems obvious. But the whole of the letter to the Romans draws our gaze elsewhere—to the justice of God in Messiah Jesus and the power of life in the Spirit. By the standard of what counts in our world this seems like next to nothing. Where are the visible signs of power and glory? But Paul's letter calls us to "hope for what is not seen" (8:24). It inserts itself, mostly unnoticed, into the world of the powers—in fact, into the center of worldly power in its worldly time—and proclaims (why not also to the powers?) an *other* word, an *other* form of ruling in life, and an *other* mode of world-historical influence. This good news neither affirms nor opposes nor hankers to become the *exousiai hyperechousai*, the "ruling powers." It carries on according to its own messianic mode of operation on the streets and in the neighborhoods, in marketplaces and offices, in public demonstrations and policy rooms, in homes and schools; *perhaps* (but there is no imperative here) even in the mayor's or governor's office. As it moves it proclaims that justice, peace, and life for all come from God alone, through God's grace in Jesus Messiah and the Holy Spirit, to those who trust.

19. An indispensable reading of Rom 13:8–14 is now Welborn, *Paul's Summons*.

Bibliography

Barclay, John. *Paul and the Gift*. Grand Rapids: Eerdmans, 2015.

——. *Pauline Churches and Diaspora Jews*. Grand Rapids: Eerdmans, 2016.

Dunn, James D. G. *Romans 1–8*. WBC 38A. Dallas: Word, 1988.

Eller, Vernard. *Christian Anarchy: Jesus' Primacy Over the Powers*. Grand Rapids: Eerdmans, 1987.

Ellul, Jacques. *Anarchy and Christianity*. Grand Rapids: Eerdmans, 1991.

Jewett, Robert. *Romans: A Commentary*. Hermeneia. Minneapolis: Fortress, 2007.

Osburn, Ronald E. *Anarchy and Apocalypse: Essays on Faith, Violence, and Theodicy*. Eugene, OR: Cascade, 2010.

Taylor, Charles. *A Secular Age*. Cambridge: Belknap Press of Harvard University Press, 2007.

Welborn, L. L. *Paul's Summons to Messianic Life: Political Theology and the Coming Awakening*. New York: Columbia University Press, 2015.

14

Paul the Peacemaker and the Ministry of Restorative Justice[1]

Douglas A. Campbell

Christians and Conflict

ONE OF THE MOST desperate needs of the world today is for peacemak-ing. Our globe is riven by conflict, and further conflict is generated by foolish and clumsy attempts at resolving clashes that have already taken place. Peacemaking is difficult, skilled work. And the church has been called since its inception to peacemaking. Surely, then, the world can look to the church for the leaders and tools it needs to resolve its cascades of bitter disputes.[2]

Of course it can't. The church is widely and rightly seen as an entity that is exceptionally proficient at *generating* conflict. It finds and creates conflicts where secular folk simply look on agog. "The name of God is blas-phemed among the pagans because of us."[3] Some Christian identities are even rooted in oppositional thinking, which is to say, in terms of fundamen-tal differences with others, not to mention, with other Christians. I worry that many Christians are only held in check, restrained from unleashing deadly violence on one another, by a secular state. (Note the ironic reversal here of Paul's viewpoint in 1 Cor 6:1–11.[4]) We must turn from our deadly

1. It is a privilege to contribute this essay in honor of my friend and colleague Susan Eastman, whose dedication to scholarship, to the gospel, and to the elucidation of Paul have been so significant during our time together at Duke Divinity School.

2. This essay draws heavily on chapter 13 in Campbell, *Pauline Dogmatics.* Per-mission from Eerdmans to reproduce much of this material is gratefully acknowledged.

3. Drawing here on Paul's rather caustic comment in Rom 2:24, which draws in turn on Isa 52:5 and Ezek 36:22. Translations are my own unless otherwise indicated.

4. We cannot make recourse to Christian adjudications of wrongdoing but must rely on secular institutions because they are so much more constructive and measured

misconceptions, from our deluded politics and priorities, and from our shameful divisions and relearn the patient skills of peacemaking.[5] And here we can follow Paul's costly practices of ecumenism and reconciliation, along with the restorative lead that some of his communities took under his guidance. Peace was one of his key emphases. Like grace, it opened and closed every letter and structured much else in his thinking.[6]

Paul's Diplomatic Career

If we approach Paul through a particular reformational lens, perhaps as an early Luther, and read him in terms of his fiery letter to the Galatians, we tend to build confrontation into the heart of his leadership. "Here I stand," he shouts to the rest of the leaders of the early church and to posterity.[7] Now, I agree that Paul stood firm on occasion. But this was in very particular circumstances. When the basis of his missionary work was under threat he defended it (and all Christians have to act like this on occasion). When certain issues are being attacked, we are called to stand firm—the practice of witness. But otherwise we are called to walk alongside those brothers and sisters who disagree with us. So perhaps we ought to think of Paul as a little less like Martin Luther and a little more like Martin Luther King Jr. King was not an aggressive person. He was fun-loving (and was initially uninterested in class and race relations until he received what was in effect a divine call). He was passionate, but he could compromise. Hence, he is remembered as both a courageous advocate of racial reconciliation *and* an ambassador of peaceful methods of protest.[8] Perhaps Paul was less of a Luther and more of an MLK. It is, at least, an interesting thought experiment to imagine and to see where it leads us.   → PURELY CONJECTURE

Galatians is frequently presented as a battle cry, and in certain respects it is. The basic truths of the gospel are not to be compromised. But when we press deeper into the events that led up to this letter's composition we find a strenuously diplomatic and reconciling effort on Paul's part, one that we see continuing well after this incendiary letter was sent. In

---

than our own approaches.

5. Schmitt and Peni also demonstrate that Paul insisted that God's people pursue peace; they provide a concrete example of pursuing peace in a war-torn situation in chapter 12 of this volume.

6. It characterized the resurrected mind—something that is quite significant. See esp. Phil 4:7; in counterpoint, more extensively, Rom 7:7–25.

7. A famous statement by Luther, and then of a famous, although dated, biography: Bainton, *Here I Stand*.

8. A useful biography of Martin Luther King, Jr. is Oates, *Let the Trumpet Sound*.

Galatians, Paul describes his relationship with several other key leaders in the early church who were based in Jerusalem—the brothers of Jesus and Jesus' original disciples led by James, Peter, and John (Gal 1:11—2:14). This group led the messianic Jewish wing of the early church, which was originally the dominant group. Paul recounts two visits to Jerusalem to meet with these leaders, one around three years after his call (1:18–20) and one as many as seventeen years later (2:1–10). He also briefly describes a confrontation with Peter in Syrian Antioch (2:11–14). But things will be clearer if we rearrange these events from their rhetorical order in Galatians into their probable historical order.[9]

Paul was converted some time in 34 CE (or perhaps very late in 33 CE). He visited Jerusalem as a Christian missionary for the first time late in 36 CE and stayed for about a fortnight (1:18–19). He met Peter and James at this time, as we have just noted (1:18–20). Then he worked independently of the Jerusalem leaders, mainly around the coastlands of the Aegean Sea, so quite some distance away, until a series of arguments broke out in Syrian Antioch. At this point he had to travel back to Syrian Antioch and deal with the debated issues late in 49 CE (2:11–14). However, everyone involved in the argument at Antioch realized that they had to travel back to Jerusalem for a major consultation to sort things out, since the origins of the conflict lay there, and this took place over the winter of 49–50 CE (2:1–10). In Galatians, Paul presents this meeting as ending well, with a shake of the hand by all the key players (2:9).

While present at this important Jerusalem conclave, Paul promised to gather a large sum of money from his churches and to send it to Jerusalem to assist their ministry among the poor—a gift or *charis* (2:10).[10] He was kept busy keeping this collection on track—especially at Corinth—through the rest of 50 CE and during the early part of 51 CE. His two letters written to Corinth in 51 CE open windows on various stages in this process.[11] Then, the crisis in Galatia broke out later in the same year. We learn from Galatians that hostile teachers were traveling through his communities in Galatia and trying to undermine his gospel there (1:6; 2:4; 5:7–10; 6:12). Paul seems to be uncertain in this letter of their exact relationship with the messianic leaders based in Jerusalem (2:2, 6), so another visit to the holy city looms in Paul's future to work this out. Had the Jerusalem agreement

---

9. The evidence underlying the following reconstruction is set out in Campbell, *Framing Paul*, esp. chapter 3.

10. More detailed support for this claim, made insightfully but too briefly by John Knox, can be found in Campbell, *Framing Paul*, chapter 3.

11. See esp. 1 Cor 16:1–4; 2 Cor 8, 9; and Rom 15:25–32.

collapsed? Or, were these hostile teachers traveling under a false flag, claiming the support of the apostles when they lacked it?

The rival teachers whom Paul addresses in Galatians weren't messing around. They arrived in Corinth, where Paul was working at the time. They proceeded to take him to court at the highest local level—before the Roman governor—who at the time was L. Annaeus Gallio. Their intention seems to have been to have Paul executed after the successful prosecution of a capital case. From their point of view, this would have put a stop to Paul's blasphemous activities quickly and emphatically. We learn about this nasty episode from Philippians, in particular, which was written while Paul was imprisoned awaiting this trial during the winter of 51–52 CE.[12]

In the spring of 52 CE, we implicitly learn from his extraordinary letter to the Romans that Paul won his case—as he expected to in Philippians. Now he plans to return again to Jerusalem with the money that he has collected, although he is not expecting an especially warm welcome.

> I urge you, brothers and sisters, by our Lord Jesus Christ and by the love of the Spirit, to join me in my struggle by praying to God for me. Pray that I may be kept safe from the unbelievers in Judea and that the contribution I take to Jerusalem may be favorably received by the Lord's people there, so that I may come to you with joy, by God's will, and in your company be refreshed. (Rom 15:30–32, NIV)

The pathos of this prayer is palpable. Paul has spent over two years collecting a massive sum of money, often at considerable personal cost, that he is now delivering, as promised, to the messianic Jewish community in Judea. But he asks for prayer because he might be killed on arrival. Moreover, he is not sure if his offering will now be accepted by the church.

Rather sadly, the book of Acts confirms that Paul's anxieties were well founded. Acts tells us how Paul ran into serious trouble in Judea (21:27—26:32), although he was not killed there. He was arrested by the Romans after a riotous disturbance in the temple (21:30–36) and subjected to a series of imprisonments and trials that immobilized him for years until—after a harrowing sea journey and a further incarceration—he was finally executed at Rome.[13]

---

12. Further details about this scenario can be found in Campbell, *Framing Paul*, chapter 3. The inscription attesting to Gallio's tenure is discussed succinctly in Murphy-O'Connor, *Paul*, esp. 15–24.

13. Paul's final journey begins in Acts 20:1. The book ends in 28:31 with Paul and his companions finally in Rome but under the shadow of execution (see esp. 20:25).

Now this is a dramatic tale. But I am not as interested here in the content of these events as much as the effort they involved. *Look at what Paul has done.* Think briefly about the lengths he has just gone to.

He has broken off his missionary work—to which he has been called by God—to make the long journey to Jerusalem twice, the second time at great personal risk, by way of Syrian Antioch. Think of walking hundreds of miles on foot through dangerous territory. He has then undertaken complex negotiations with the Jerusalem leadership concerning his disconcertingly radical missionary work, all while combating trenchant local opposition to his program. He has raised money, written letters, and crafted a joint declaration; he has challenged, interpreted, and cajoled. He has traveled, argued, and prayed. And he has done so even though it has become increasingly obvious that his involvement in these activities will lead to his death. (Hence, why I toy with the idea that he was a bit like Martin Luther King, Jr.)

This is an extraordinary level of commitment to ecumenicity. How many of us, faced with opposition from other Christians, would be willing to travel, fund-raise, write, and endure risk at this level, in order to preserve unity with figures who hate us so much that some of them are trying to have us executed? Paul's reconciling efforts within the early church put most of us to shame. However, at least in doing so they model the lengths to which Christian leaders should be prepared to go as they try to hold on to the visible unity of the church. This is the cost we should be prepared to pay to promote peace within the church. It is something of an understatement, then, when Paul exhorts his auditors to "labor to guard the unity of the Spirit through the bond of peace" (Eph 4:3). When we plug in Paul's own story, we know just how much force we need to give to the word "labor" here.

But the lessons we can learn from Paul about Christian peacemaking do not stop with his example of dedicated, patient, determined work of preserving church unity. We also find some highly practical advice in his writings about how to go about this. That is, we might accept that we desperately need peacemaking within our communities, as well as between them, and be committed to pursuing peace at great personal cost, but we might not know how to go about effecting it. Fortunately, we can detect a restorative practice unfolding through his letters to Corinth.

Restorative Justice at Corinth

In 1 Corinthians Paul lays out a series of sins that he wants the Corinthians to deal with, and there is quite a list![14] In 2 Cor 7, however, written some

---

14. See Campbell, *Paul*, chapter 7.

weeks later, he is able to praise the Corinthians for addressing something well—not everything but something. They have reacted with grief, repentance, and zeal to demonstrate that they are pure in a particular matter in which someone has committed a crime against someone else. Significantly, Paul's language here has a legal cast.[15]

> See what this godly sorrow has produced in you: what earnestness, what eagerness to clear yourselves, what indignation, what alarm, what longing, what concern, what readiness to see justice done. At every point you have proved yourselves to be innocent in this matter. So even though I wrote to you, it was neither on account of the one who did the wrong nor on account of the injured party, but rather that before God you could see for yourselves how devoted to us you are. By all this we are encouraged. (2 Cor 7:11–13, NIV)

The Corinthians seem to have acted communally against a person who has done something wrong. However, we also see in chapter 2 of the same letter that someone who has caused grief has now suffered enough from the grief inflicted on him by the majority. He is to be forgiven and encouraged, not overwhelmed.

> If anyone has caused grief, he has not so much grieved me as he has grieved all of you to some extent—not to put it too severely. The punishment inflicted on him by the majority is sufficient. Now instead, you ought to forgive and comfort him, so that he will not be overwhelmed by excessive sorrow. I urge you, therefore, to reaffirm your love for him. Another reason I wrote you was to see if you would stand the test and be obedient in everything. Anyone you forgive, I also forgive. And what I have forgiven—if there was anything to forgive—I have forgiven in the sight of Christ for your sake, in order that Satan might not outwit us. For we are not unaware of his schemes. (2:5–11, NIV)

It is most likely—we learn by reading between the lines—that the offender of 1 Cor 6 has been addressed by the community's court as Paul recommended in 6:1–11, hence by internal, not external, litigation. The offence itself was probably a theft. However, this "case" (Grk. *pragma*, which Paul uses in 2 Cor 7:11) has been fully resolved. So Paul is able to praise the Corinthians in 2 Cor 7 for their zeal and cooperation in this matter—something he cannot do for every item on his agenda. But Paul is also advocating forgiveness and support for the offender. He urges these actions in the letter

---

15. Campbell, *Framing Paul* discusses this important evidence in more detail.

in chapter 2, well before he describes the successful outcome of the case in chapter 7, arguing that to fail to extend forgiveness to an offender would be to fall prey to a satanic deception (2:11).

This all looks to me very like a traditional communal resolution of a dispute that tends to be known now as *restorative justice*. Modern western institutionalized justice, which is essentially retributive, has largely lost touch with the methods of conflict resolution that traditional societies practiced in ancient village and tribal settings—literally around campfires. But these methods are now being recovered as advocates recognize their superiority to modern procedures for addressing the harm caused by disputes and conflicts.[16]

Every approach to conflict resolution presupposes a narrative about the world. The narrative will supply an account of the nature of wrongdoing and of what to do about it.[17] And because of the ubiquity of conflict and its costliness, societies are deeply committed to the practices that their key narrative legitimizes. However, arguably the modern western narrative—in which we invest billions of dollars, endless years, and countless careers— has gone somewhat astray. The very different narrative often told in tribal contexts is arguably closer to the story of wrongdoing and its correction— rooted in revelation and resurrection—that emerges from Paul's theology.

The slightly divergent practices grouped together under the rubric of restorative justice—victim-offender conferences, talking circles, family group conferences, and so on—presuppose a fundamentally relational and covenantal story. These practices affirm the importance and dignity of every member of a community. When a dispute takes place or a conflict evolves, resolution in traditional terms is narrated as a process of communal healing and restoration within which all who have been harmed must participate. Everyone must have a voice. This process does not appeal to a third neutral actor—to some sort of state—to inflict pain on a key perpetrator; it does not assume that such an approach solves the problem. Framed by an unconditional commitment to all involved, restorative justice assumes the relationships that have been strained and torn must be mended or "restored" just as a tapestry, slashed by a knife, must have its threads patiently knotted and resewn. Furthermore, ancient communities knew that this work must ultimately take place face to face.[18]

16. This approach is described with typical charm by Jared Diamond in Diamond, *World Until Yesterday*, 79–170.

17. Two key contrasting narratives concerning conflict resolution widespread in the USA today are insightfully introduced by George Lakoff in Lakoff, *Moral Politics*.

18. The healing of conflict, which often involves the transcendence of shame, is introduced with particular wisdom and precision by Howard Zehr (the grandfather

Victims, in particular, must be allowed to speak their story in a secure space, thereby recovering their dignity and moving beyond their fear as they voice their anguish directly to those who have harmed them. This can be a deeply healing process. More than anything else, victims generally need those who have hurt them to experience directly from them—from their story and from all the emotions set in motion by it—the pain that they have had inflicted on them. And they need to see this deep emotional resonance taking place in those who have hurt them. Once this has happened people who have been victimized are generally satisfied and able to move forward.

But this process is generally transformational for people who have committed offences as well. As offenders experience the pain they have inflicted on others as a result of their actions, while they hear—in a face-to-face manner—the harrowing stories of the people whom they have hurt, they are placed in the ultimate learning situation. Often, crimes are thoughtless actions. There is little forethought and minimal appreciation of their consequences. But an appropriate restorative process brings the devastating consequences of an action home with full force. Only a psychopath can remain unaffected by the expressed anguish of a victim. Those who have committed an offence are generally deeply affected and transformed by this process. They learn to be ashamed of their criminal activities in an appropriate instance of shaming. And they invariably want to respond to their victims in ways that demonstrate their good faith in the future, making restitution.

In sum, restorative justice processes, which are in large measure a recovery of traditional communal practices, integrate smoothly with the basic truths of the Pauline gospel. They presuppose a relational, personal God, along with this God's powerful commitment to the healing and restoration of torn and damaged relationships. Hence, it is not surprising to see these practices at work in Paul's communities, especially in the troubled community in Corinth, where conflict was especially severe. Meanwhile,

---

of restorative justice in the USA) in Zehr, *Little Book*, and by Moore and MacDonald, *Transforming Conflict*. Also germane in this relation are some of Chris Marshall's important studies: Marshall, *Beyond Retribution*, and *Compassionate Justice*.

Shame is addressed by Nathanson, *Shame and Pride*, and ultimately by Tomkins in his seminal Tomkins, *Affect Imagery Consciousness*. Concise and accurate information can be found at www.tomkins.org, with a specific link provided to the connection between neuroscience and restorative justice. A jaunty but sadly inconsistent and somewhat unreliable introduction to Tomkins' thought and related issues is in Gladwell, *Blink*.

The church has much to learn from circle processes and especially from healing circles: see especially Pranis, Stuart, and Wedge, *Peacemaking Circles*; Kay Pranis's little primer, Pranis, *Little Book of Circle Processes*; and Rupert Ross's fascinating exposition, Ross, *Returning to the Teachings*.

Paul's relationship with Jerusalem also models the patient and faithful dedication to peacemaking that Christian leadership requires, whether within a conflict inside a local community or within conflicts that span churches and continents.

Dare we dream of modern churches in this sense, as incubators of conflict resolution rather than conflict propagation, and as nurseries of peacemaking? Dare we dream of church leaders who can work for reconciliation with as much dedication and courage as Paul? I hope so. But these realizations surrounding peace and peacemaking are so important it is worth spending a little more time exploring the ways in which they presuppose a number of other important Pauline virtues that Christians should be pursuing.[19]

Pauline Virtues for Peacemaking

Paul wrote a famous list of virtues in Gal 5:22–23a, referring to them, in biblical parlance, as "fruit."

> But the fruit of the Spirit is: love, joy, peace, patience, kindness, goodness, faithfulness, gentleness, and self-control.

We can see from this list that if love expresses itself in damaged situations as peacemaking, then love will also require *patience, kindness, faithfulness, gentleness*, and *self-control*. The first three subordinate virtues on this list

19. I am presupposing here the Pauline "virtue ethic" I articulate in Campbell, *Pauline Dogmatics*, esp. in Part 2. It is not a highly developed virtue ethic and is different in many respects from classical schemas. Susan and I share concerns when MacIntyre exerts too much influence on Pauline studies. A suitably Barthian use of MacIntyre is offered, however, by C. Kavin Rowe in his masterful Rowe, *One True Life*. See also, the excellent study, Miller, *Practice of the Body*. (In my view this book ought to receive rather more attention than it currently does.)

The connections between Barth and a virtue ethic are made constantly in more general terms within the work of Stanley Hauerwas: see especially Hauerwas, *Community of Character*, and *Peaceable Kingdom*. See also Hauerwas and Pinches, *Christians among the Virtues*. Hauerwas generously but perceptively criticizes Barth for lacking a full account of Christian formation in his *With the Grain of the Universe*.

An important figure bridging from Barth through virtue ethics and moving beyond MacIntyre's limitations—ultimately in conversation with social anthropology—is Michael Banner. The grounding in Barth is not overtly stated but is present in the important methodological chapter that begins Banner, *Ethics of Everyday Life*, 6–34.

The connections with Barth are important because of Barth's grasp of the revelatory epistemology that informs Paul's life and thought. See esp. J. Louis Martyn, "Epistemology at the Turn of the Ages," in *Theological Issues*, 89–110. For further discussion of this position in relation to an apocalyptic imagination, see chapter 3 by Charles Campbell in the present volume.

can be dealt with reasonably quickly. However, a more detailed articulation of the last two should result in some particularly illuminating insights from Paul for Christian discipleship.

Patience, Kindness, and Faithfulness

Determined believing in certain circumstances over time results in behavior we would call "faithful." And clearly Paul's reconciling efforts with both Jerusalem and Corinth were overtly faithful in this sense. His actions were deeply steadfast and enduring, to the point of arrest, imprisonment, and execution. Peacemaking is difficult work and needs this sort of perseverance. It also needs leaders who are kind and who possess supernatural degrees of patience!

It goes without saying that peacemakers need to be kind, while I often insist that Christians should simply be kind in general. Paul wrote entirely correctly that love is kind, and I am tempted to add that it covers a multitude of sins. Kindness denotes a gentle attempt to enter into the situations of others, even when they might seem initially to be forbidding or just plain wrong. Judgment is set to one side (as best as it can be), and people are given the space to be what they need to be. In fact, when we let people tell their own stories we often go on to learn that we have misunderstood things in the first place. So kindness can save us from the tyranny of some of our own assumptions.

Peacemakers also need to be patient. I recently attended an intensive training for leaders in restorative circle practices led by the renowned circle keeper Kay Pranis.[20] She began the training as she usually does—by placing a bag containing a pile of driftwood in the middle of the group next to a small table and instructing us to proceed as a circle (i.e., one by one, in sequence). We could take one or more pieces of wood out of the bag—as many as we wanted—and arrange them on or around the table. Or we could put them back in the bag, whether one, several, or all of them. This had to continue until the entire group "passed" in a circle indicating its acceptance of whatever arrangement of wood had eventuated. Nothing was to be said at any point.

I knew the driftwood exercise was coming and had fortified myself internally with the suitably chilled attitude, but even with this foreknowledge it turned out to be difficult to sit in silence—with occasional sculptural moments in the middle—for the sixty-five minutes that it took our group to eventually settle on something. (We eventually tipped over the table and

20. It took place at the National Humanities Center, March 31–April 2, 2017.

then created the word "LOVE" on the floor, with a mirror image of the word next to it so that both sides of the circle could benefit.) I was well aware that people around me were huffing and puffing, especially when I and a few others still insisted late in the piece on getting up and rearranging things. Even more testing was experiencing a beautiful arrangement of small drift-wood sculptures that had taken several rounds to create being swept to the floor by someone to begin again!

I knew that we were supposed to be learning something, although I didn't know exactly what it was. First impressions suggested that the exercise was silly, and it certainly drove everybody nuts. But this was just the point. As Kay explained after we had concluded, leading a circle involves "sitting with the discomfort," especially when it involves any resolutions of harm or conflict. A circle-keeper has to keep still and silent and to accept that she has no control over the outcome of the process. The process will end when everyone in the circle is ready for it to end and not before. It does not end when we might be ready for it to end. Hence, circle-keepers can only keep circles effectively, especially circles addressing challenging issues, if they live fully into this posture of patience.

Kay went on to observe that our group had shown unusual restraint because no one had put all the wood in the bag with a fairly strong signal that the stupid exercise should just stop. (We had all thought about doing this.) Usually someone does this—and on one occasion, a person took the bag and locked it in their truck outside in the carpark! But when this happens, *someone else invariably goes and gets the bag and gets some wood out and keeps going*. In other words, no one person can ever take control over the process and say when it has to end. The entire group controls the process, and it ends when everyone is ready for it to end. This is the only way in which communities can move forward with every person, important or unimportant, hurt or hurting, having been included and felt heard and valued. This is how conflicts are resolved and harm is addressed effectively. Harm is only addressed when everyone who has been affected has been included and has spoken. Until this has happened, anyone leading the process and maintaining the fragile quality of the space within which the conflict is being addressed must "sit with the discomfort."

But a way of naming this attitude—of sitting with the discomfort until everyone has reached a point of resolution and the entire circle has settled— would be to say that the circle-keeper needs *patience*. Proper, deep conflict resolution and peacemaking require patience at a level our modern culture can barely imagine.

In a *New York Times* op-ed Timothy Egan cited a study undertaken by Microsoft in Canada that had discovered that the average attention span of a person in 2015—"the amount of concentrated time [spent] on a task without being distracted"—had dropped from the twelve seconds recorded in 2000 to eight. Apparently, this is a shorter attention span than a goldfish.[21]

Many of us experience the same phenomenon in traffic. I seethe with frustration if someone is too slow moving off on a green light and I am forced to wait for another change of lights—maybe a minute or two of my time—and I not infrequently see drivers around me reacting even more impatiently than I do. Things have changed for me since I have started treating traffic and traffic stops as small exercises in patience training. I am pleased to say that I have made some progress and can now happily endure a light change or two. But we will need to be more patient than this if we want to sit with the discomfort of conflict resolution as we make peace within fractured communities. The Truth and Reconciliation Commission (TRC) that brought so much healing to post-apartheid South Africa met in multiple ways *for five years*.[22] (The TRC was by no means a perfect restorative justice process, but it has been constructive and significant, especially when some of the alternatives are considered.[23])

In short, as Paul said rightly, love is patient (1 Cor 13:4); and we can now add the coda that peacemaking is the place where patience is needed in an especially large measure. It requires training in a way that our modern culture constantly militates against. "Driftwood not cellphones" might have to be our motto moving forward, at least when it comes to certain group activities. The exercise of loving patience, in turn, depends upon self-control.

Self-Control

Our prevailing cultural narrative of peacemaking tends to involve force. Problems are solved, we are told, by the application of an amount of pain on perpetrators that is equal to the amount that they have perpetrated on others. This feels equal, equivalent, and balanced. We might even name it "just." The word we often use to describe this broader theory of conflict resolution

21. Egan, "Eight-Second Attention Span."

22. See esp. Tutu, *No Future*, and Storey, "Different Kind of Justice." Note, the latter essay was written while the TRC was in the midst of its work, which ran from 1995–2000. Storey was on the committee charged with selecting the TRC commissioners. He notes, "Selecting the truth commissioners was . . . a challenge. They had to be people of proven integrity and capable of impartiality, with a track record of commitment to human rights and the inner strength to cope with the emotional strain *of the job*. A balance of race, gender, region and vocational or professional background was also crucial" (2, emphasis added).

23. See Gibson, "On Legitimacy Theory," and Jones, "Truth and Consequences."

is punishment. The underlying Latin *punire* means "to inflict a penalty on" or "to cause pain for some offense." However, although it contains important insights, this narrative of conflict resolution, despite its cultural dominance, is not fundamentally informed by the Pauline gospel.

God's way of dealing with the problem of a disordered and fractured world was to enter into it and to bear its pain, terminating it, and then to reconstitute a reality that is now accessible to those still struggling within the old dispensation. And on the way, anyone who was implicated in the wrongdoing of the old order—which includes everyone—was forgiven. The new reality now draws us into deeper relational wholeness, restoring us, and teaching us about the consequences of wrongdoing.[24] This is God's solution to wrongdoing, including conflict, *and force is nowhere in sight*, except as a possible means of effecting termination, although even there it is unnecessary.[25]

As appropriately tutored Christians we must consequently resist the introduction of force into conflict and dispute resolution. Force will more than likely take a bad situation and make it worse. As the old adage goes, "Two wrongs don't make a right." The infliction of an amount of pain on people equal (supposedly) to the pain they have inflicted is a deeply pagan account of problem solving and a thoroughly nasty one to boot. It is, at the end of the day, problem solving understood as revenge.[26]

We should recall that Paul himself was originally a violent man. Few would have felt as justified as he did in inflicting pain on the bodies of the messianic Jews he apprehended before he was called so dramatically to the apostolate. His use of force was righteous and, presumably, thoroughly supported by statements in the Scriptures. But he was, of course, utterly mistaken. It is highly significant that Paul did not prosecute his Christian mission violently. He clearly renounced this, even as he endured it from others. His martyrdom, following in the footsteps of Jesus and echoed by so many other Christian leaders, places a final accent on the disclosure that violence is something evil on which the Christian community must turn its back.

---

24. A more detailed account can be found in Campbell, *Pauline Dogmatics*, chapters 5 and 6.

25. The gratuity of the crucifixion of Jesus—of the infliction of pain on Him resulting in death—speaks primarily of our deep hostility to God and of the evil of the powers who oppose Him. They apply force and pain, and kill: see 1 Cor 2:8. All Jesus had to do was die; he didn't have to be tortured to death.

26. These dynamics are articulated brilliantly by Alan J. Torrance's essay Torrance, "Theological Grounds."

But if force is not the way to solve a problem—recalling instead the healing offered by processes like restorative justice—we still need to give some account of force.

By this I mean only to suggest that occasionally it might be right to do something coercive to someone else's body. When my children Emile and Grace were small, although still large enough to get into trouble, I would restrain them at times. I would stop them from—to put matters generically—jumping into a river or into a fire or from running in front of a car. This involved force, and this was the right thing to do; force here was good. But note carefully how it is not a fundamentally constructive act even in these circumstances. I was not solving anything or creating anything. I was simply acting preventively. I was stopping a further slide into evil.

I suggest then that we follow Paul's lead and renounce force as a constructive thing—that is, renounce it as "violence"—and apply it only rarely and preventively, as we are informed by the virtue *of self-control*. This virtue prevents the unleashing of force as violence and revenge, even when our emotions and culture are screaming for it. It holds force within its necessary but limited preventative role. Can our communities model an exercise of force that is only ever self-controlled? And, when even preventative force fails, as it sometimes must, can we turn our other cheek and, if necessary, accept the fate of a martyr, exposing the evil of violence more fully? This would be like Paul—and, rather more importantly, it would be like Jesus.[27]

One final virtue now needs to be noted here. It is a critical part of peacemaking, although it extends well beyond this particular practice into every aspect of Christian life. We ought to pursue gentleness.

27. I fear, of course, that we are some distance away from this. In the wake of the relatively recent horror that took place in the Emanuel African Methodist Episcopal Church in Charleston, South Carolina, where nine African-American worshippers were massacred by a young, gun-toting racist, the Huffington Post published Graulau,"Pastors And Faithful Pick Up Gun Training." Bianca Graulau reports in this article how Pastor Geof Peabody recommends a much more aggressive policy of gun-training and gun-ownership in the wake of the Charleston tragedy. He has already trained over four hundred pastors, he says. The ministers "first learn about safety. Then, they move over to the shooting range to get hands on practice." One of his students commented in the same article: "We need protection. People that go through classes and get licenses and stuff to carry a gun. I fell [*sic*] like we need this in our lives. We need it in church and in our businesses."

But force dependent on the practiced use of a gun is unlikely to be merely preventative. It is much more likely to be fatal to the aggressor, if it isn't fatal to the gun owner. And prevention based on the rationally perceived threat of deadly force is not the same thing as force applied in a directly preventative way. (Preventative force in relation to Charleston could presumably involve restraining people from obtaining access to the tools of deadly force, in this case guns—something that multiplies their capacity to do harm to others.)

Gentleness

Self-controlled force, as opposed to violence, is acting in a way that is *gentle*. Peacemaking requires constant, enduring, gentle actions. Kindness is in many respects simply gentleness. And I can think of few better ways of learning to be gentle than by working with plants or with animals. Most plants and animals can't fight back. But we learn from the way we treat them that gentleness elicits flourishing, along with obedience when that is relevant, while harsh and bullying ways elicit damage and recalcitrance.

When pondering these things I often think of my grandfather. He was a great influence on my life and was a famously encouraging, kind, and gentle person. He was a farmer and was particularly skilled with sheepdogs and horses. Sometimes other farmers would send him talented dogs that had been rendered useless through bullying and poor training, and he would patiently regain their trust, rebuild their confidence, and teach them again to do their highly skilled jobs. He would never beat them, this usually being the root of their problems. He did the same with horses.

For much of my early adulthood he rode a horse imaginatively named Red, who had been traumatized and was profoundly nervous. On one occasion, as a young horse, a canvas horse cover had detached from his hind legs and swung around to cover his head. He had gone through two wire fence-lines, getting tangled in them, before he could be caught and calmed. But Red was a magnificent chestnut who would do anything my grandfather asked him, whether it was cutting stock or dressage. I watched Red touch his arm gently in the stables from behind one day and my grandfather turned to me and said, "Look, that's the way a horse tells you that he loves you."

But I think of my grandfather here not just because he modeled these virtues to me but because of the way he acquired them. My grandfather learned to be gentle. He was a wonderful grandfather and a terrible father. Prior to being a farmer he had worked doing deliveries and then had volunteered to serve in the New Zealand division during the war. In those days he was a man's man who played rugby and boxed and frequently got into bar fights and brawls. Only close friends saved him eventually from his demons, which were worked out with a conspicuous lack of self-control in relation to alcohol. Then animals taught him to be kind and gentle, because that was really what he wanted to be.

If we want to learn how to be gentle, there might be few better ways of doing this than by picking up a nervous dog from the pound. We will have the opportunity to learn to be gentle, as well as self-controlled, patient, and kind. If we can't develop these patterns of behavior with a dog, we should think twice before we take charge of other human beings, especially small ones. Dogs are much more compliant and forgiving partners, with far fewer demands than people, as my grandfather often used to say.

But gentleness should characterize more than our direct actions on the bodies of other things and people. It should characterize speech—a particularly important area of human behavior for peacemaking, not to mention, for relating in general.

Gentle Speech

The eleventh step of humility in the *Benedictine Rule* begins, "When [a monk] does speak, he should do so gently and without mockery, humbly and seriously, in a few well-chosen words."[28]

One of the most curious things about Paul's more generic ethical instructions to his communities is how much time he spends on speech ethics. He is concerned about other sins as well—behaviors like theft and drunkenness. But the only ethical preoccupation comparable in extent to his concern with speech is his anxiety about aberrant sexual activity. Paul spends a great deal of time exhorting his converts to speak in the right way, not merely truthfully, but constructively and lovingly. And I imagine that this instruction was highly countercultural.

The lower echelons in hierarchical cultures tend to develop "strategies of resistance," as James Scott calls them.[29] It is usually too dangerous for poor and low status people—especially servants and slaves—to confront a hierarchy directly, and it requires considerable organization, talent, and courage to do so. But it is always possible to do things that cause a bit of trouble or at least get back at one's superiors to some degree—things like loitering, pilfering, and sabotaging. Particular language games are a key weapon in this resistance. The lower ranks use double entendre and tone to mock their superiors to their face and, then, also parody them behind their backs. As Scott's seminal Ethiopian proverb puts it, "When the great lord passes the wise peasant bows deeply and silently farts." In any hierarchical society like the ancient Greco-Roman empire, language is caught up tightly with this generalized pattern of resistance. It is used to express resentments, hatred, and scorn.[30] This makes Paul's frequent admonitions about appropriate Christian language all the more remarkable.

---

28. See Benedict, *Rule of St. Benedict.*

29. See his classic study Scott, *Domination.*

30. I am not excusing higher status figures from challenge here. They probably faced particular challenges in relation to the intense competitiveness of ancient society, especially its partisanship. This tends to provoke unethical speech as well.

He insists that Christians—the vast majority doubtless converted from the lower orders and hence well-used to these special language games—speak out of the interpersonal reality that they now overtly indwell, which is the divine communion. They are to speak in love, with gentleness, to build up and to correct one another and not to mock, deride, or attack. And this all makes perfect sense, however challenging it might prove in practice. Relationships are profoundly affected by how we speak within them. To a large degree they exist through our language practices, so how we speak is very important. But speaking rightly is very difficult. Paul's point is not so much, then, as many modern Christians seem to suppose, whether godly folk should cuss or not. He doesn't approve of this (Eph 4:29; 5:4), but it is not his main concern. His principal priority is the constructiveness of Christian speech. Are the relationships within the body being nurtured and enhanced by our speaking, or are they eroded and damaged?

A quick glance at the plethora of Christian blogs on the internet will reveal that many Christians are woefully out of touch with Paul's mediation of divine relationality and their dynamics here (and I count myself among them at times). How much writing, preaching, and teaching conveys the spirit of the world and the flesh rather than the Spirit of God? Is our internet presence a gentle one? Moreover, we see here very clearly that the how is as important as the what. We can be right in substance and utterly wrong in style, which is in fact to be wrong in substance. Marshall McLuhan's famous adage, "the medium is the message," springs to mind. This dictum applies *exactly* to how Christians speak.

I suspect then that Paul would simply ask a lot of us to step up here, to repent of our linguistic partisanship and aggression, and to practice speech that is self-controlled and gentle—speech that by its very manner conveys the gentle and loving relationality with which we are involved. Our communities should offer the world the gift of a community that speaks gently both to its members and to outsiders, a community that knows how to speak both rightly and kindly. Only communities who have learned speech like this can make peace after conflicts have escalated emotions and vicious and aggressive language has compounded harm with harm, whether these conflicts take place in the office, at the local café, after a church meeting, across international borders, or over the kitchen table. Where violent speech deepens a dispute, gentle speech can begin to defuse it. Such speaking flows from peace and fosters peace—something that Paul summons all those learning from him to embrace and to pursue.

In sum—and contrary to how he is often portrayed—Paul was a dedicated peacemaker. He pursued peace doggedly and courageously with other church leaders in his day and encouraged it when his communities fractured as a result of incidents like theft and adultery. Behind his specific recommendations, we can detect a more traditional approach to conflict and dispute resolution that differs markedly from the retributive and punitive story that so dominates modern U.S. society. Paul sought to knit together the human threads that had been unstitched and torn. Leaders involved in this sort of work today will probably need to be inordinately virtuous. Peacemaking and restoration requires love. But it also needs patience, kindness, faithfulness, gentleness, and self-control. Susan Eastman has called our attention like few others to the importance of imitation in Paul's life and teaching. Paul calls us to imitate him, even as he himself imitated the one who had called him so dramatically on the road to Damascus. Those imitating Paul, we can now add, will hopefully figure forth specifically with the virtues of peacemaking, virtues so badly needed in the dislocated world that we are called, like Paul, to engage patiently, kindly, gently, faithfully, with self-control, and in love.

Bibliography

Bainton, Roland H. *Here I Stand: A Life of Martin Luther.* London: Meridian, (1955) 1995.

Banner, Michael. *The Ethics of Everyday Life: Moral Theology, Social Anthropology, and the Imagination of the Human.* Oxford: Oxford University Press, 2014.

Benedict of Nursia. *The Rule of St. Benedict: A Contemporary Paraphrase.* Edited by J. Wilson-Hartgrove. Brewster, MA: Paraclete, 2012.

Campbell, Douglas A. *Framing Paul: An Epistolary Biography.* Grand Rapids: Eerdmans, 2014.

———. *Paul: An Apostle's Journey.* Grand Rapids: Eerdmans, 2017.

———. *Pauline Dogmatics in Outline: From Revelation to Race.* Grand Rapids: Eerdmans, 2018.

Diamond, Jared. *The World Until Yesterday: What Can We Learn from Traditional Societies?* New York: Penguin, 2012.

Egan, Timothy. "The Eight-Second Attention Span." *New York Times,* January 22, 2016. https://www.nytimes.com/2016/01/22/opinion/the-eight-second-attention-span.html?_r=0.

Gibson, James L. "On Legitimacy Theory and the Effectiveness of Truth Commissions." *Law and Contemporary Problems* 72 (2009) 123–41. https://scholarship.law.duke.edu/cgi/viewcontent.cgi?referer=https://www.google.com/&httpsredir=1&article=1522&context=lcp.

Gladwell, Malcom. *Blink: The Power of Thinking Without Thinking.* New York: Little, Brown, 2005.

Graulau, Bianca. "Pastors and Faithful Pick Up Gun Training: 'We Need It in Church.'" *Huffington Post, June, 23, 2015. http://www.huffingtonpost.com/2015/06/23/gun-training-church_n_7647788.html.

Hauerwas, Stanley. *A Community of Character: Toward a Constructive Christian Social Ethic.* Notre Dame: University of Notre Dame Press, 1981.

———. *The Peaceable Kingdom: A Primer in Christian Ethics.* Notre Dame: University of Notre Dame Press, 1983.

———. *With the Grain of the Universe: The Church's Witness and Natural Theology: Being the Gifford Lectures Delivered at the University of St Andrews in 2001.* Grand Rapids: Brazos, 2001.

Hauerwas, Stanley, and Charles Pinches. *Christians among the Virtues: Theological Conversations with Ancient and Modern Ethics.* Notre Dame: University of Notre Dame Press, 1997.

Jones, L. Gregory. "Truth and Consequences in South Africa." *Christianity Today* 43 (1999) 59–63. http://www.christianitytoday.com/ct/1999/april5/9t4059.html.

Lakoff, George. *Moral Politics: How Liberals and Conservatives Think.* 2nd ed. Chicago: University of Chicago Press, 2002.

Marshall, Christopher. *Beyond Retribution: A New Testament Vision for Justice, Crime, and Punishment.* Grand Rapids: Eerdmans, 2001.

———. *Compassionate Justice: An Interdisciplinary Dialogue with Two Gospel Parables on Law, Crime and Restorative Justice.* Eugene, OR: Cascade, 2012.

Martyn, J. Louis. *Theological Issues in the Letters of Paul.* Edinburgh: T. & T. Clark, 1997.

Miller, Colin. *The Practice of the Body of Christ: Human Agency in Pauline Theology after MacIntyre.* Princeton Theological Monograph Series 200. Eugene, OR: Pickwick, 2014.

Moore, David, and J. McDonald. *Transforming Conflict in Workplaces and Other Communities.* Sydney: Transformative Justice Australia, 2000.

Murphy-O'Connor, Jerome. *Paul: A Critical Life.* Oxford: Oxford University Press, 1996.

Nathanson, Donald L. *Shame and Pride: Affect, Sex, and the Birth of the Self.* New York: W. W. Norton, 1992.

Oates, Stephen B. *Let the Trumpet Sound: A Life of Martin Luther King.* New York: Harper & Row, 1982.

Pranis, Kay. *The Little Book of Circle Processes: A New/Old Approach to Peacemaking.* Intercourse, PA: Good, 2005.

Pranis, Kay, Barry Stuart, and Mark Wedge. *Peacemaking Circles: From Crime to Community.* St. Paul, MN: Living Justice, 2003.

Ross, Rupert. *Returning to the Teachings: Exploring Aboriginal Justice.* Revised ed. Toronto: Penguin, (1996) 2006.

Rowe, C. Kavin. *One True Life: The Stoics and Early Christians as Rival Traditions.* New Haven: Yale University Press, 2016.

Scott, James C. *Domination and the Arts of Resistance: Hidden Transcripts.* New Haven: Yale University Press, 1990.

Storey, Peter. "A Different Kind of Justice: Truth and Reconciliation in South Africa." *The Christian Century* 114 (1997) 788–91. *Expanded Academic ASAP.* go.galegroup.com/ps/i.do?p=EAIM&sw=w&u=duke_perkins&v=2.1&id=GALE%7CA198448 84&it=r&asid=77367b262a91c5d19954bec4ba712df8.

Tomkins, Silvan S. *Affect Imagery Consciousness.* The Complete Edition. Philadelphia: Springer, 2008.

Torrance, Alan J. "The Theological Grounds for Advocating Forgiveness and Reconciliation in the Sociopolitical Realm." In *The Politics of Past Evil: Religion,*

Reconciliation, and the Dilemmas of Transitional Justice, edited by Daniel Philpot, 45–85. Notre Dame: University of Notre Dame Press, 2006.

Tutu, Desmond Mpilo. *No Future Without Forgiveness.* New York: Doubleday, 1999.

Zehr, Howard. *The Little Book of Restorative Justice.* Intercourse, PA: Good, 2002.

15

Toward an Evangelical Art of Dying[1]

Philip G. Ziegler

> *What is to be feared is not death or hardship*
> *itself, but the fear of hardship or death.*
>
> —Epictetus, *Discourses* II.1.13

> *O death, where is thy victory?*
> *O death, where is thy sting?*
>
> —1 Corinthians 15:55

THE EPISTLE TO THE Hebrews is, by all accounts, a rhetorically and theologically sophisticated tract written to display and vindicate the saving work of Christ. The letter as a whole reads as an extended gloss upon the primitive kerygma reported by Paul that "Christ died for our sins" (1 Cor 15:3).[2] It is fundamentally concerned with the character of Christ's saving work and the nature of Christ's person as the worker of his work. Soteriologically, both the letter's profound interpretation of Christ's death in terms of the Day of Atonement and its exposition of the Savior's identity by appeal to the priestly order of Melchizedek are highly innovative. Christologically, the argument is as equally devoted to the defense of

---

1. I am delighted to present this essay in honor of Susan Eastman, a fellow laborer in the vineyard. I am privileged to have learned much from her scholarship and benefitted greatly from her generous encouragement over many years.

2. All scriptural quotations are from the NRSV, unless otherwise indicated.

Christ's genuine humanity as it is to the declaration of his heavenly origin and incomparable divine reality.[3] It has been suggested that the author of Hebrews "ranks with Paul and the Fourth Evangelist as one of the three great theologians of the New Testament."[4] Here we encounter an apostolic witness to the reality and consequences of "Christ's odd triumph" whose relevance, Stephen Long has recently remarked, is "found precisely in its irrelevance, its willingness to stand in tension with some of our contemporary sensibilities."[5]

Death is a theme integral to Hebrews' core concern with Christ's saving triumph and one on which its witness cuts across our contemporary sensibilities. In this brief essay I want to reflect upon the difference that Christ's own death makes for Christian thinking about our own confrontation with the end of life. The enigmatic witness of Heb 2:14–15 will serve to provoke and (dis)orient us in this, as it represents an important watchword for our understanding of salvation as the fruit of Christ's own victory over death.[6] After some reflection on that text itself in part one, I turn briefly in part two to consider the medieval tradition of the *ars moriendi*—the "art of dying"—and the understanding of death and salvation at work therein. I suggest that this tradition can be understood as a kind of spiritual catalogue of some of the manifold ways in which the *fear* of death assaults and threatens to corrode and degrade both faith and life. In the final part of the essay I offer a brief evangelical supplement to traditional *ars bene moriendi*, or instructions on the art of dying well, particularly inspired by the witness of Hebrews and Paul's gospel.[7]

To Be Delivered from Death's Fearful Captivity

Speaking of Jesus Christ, Heb 2:14–15 reads:

> Since, therefore, the children share flesh and blood, he himself likewise shared the same things, so that through death he might destroy the one who has the power of death, that is, the devil,

3. On the specifically Christological witness of Hebrews see Webster, "One Who Is Son," 69–94.

4. Kindars, *Theology of the Letter*, 1.

5. Long, *Hebrews*, 1. Long himself is particularly interested to draw out the letter's "untimely metaphysics" (6) in this regard.

6. As noted very recently again by MacLeod, "Work of Christ," 262–63.

7. Throughout, I simultaneously ascribe to the adjective "evangelical" with its plain sense meaning, "of the gospel," and its traditional European meaning of "Protestant."

and free those who all their lives were held in slavery by the fear
of death.

Even at first blush it is clear that something curious is afoot as regards the
meaning of "death" in this passage.[8] Death is here an instrument of the
Savior's proper work, something by means of which salvation is worked
out: indeed, immediately before this we read that the very purpose of the
incarnation is this saving work as the Son is "made lower than the angels
for a time . . . *so that* by the grace of God he might taste death for every
one" (Heb 2:9). But at the same time, death is also an instrument of the
devil's proper work, something by whose power women and men are held
in fearful captivity (see 1 Cor 5:5; 10:10). In the first case, Christ takes death
upon himself for the sake of others; in the second, the devil threatens and
inflicts death upon those very same ones for whom Christ comes to save.
Human life itself—"flesh and blood"—stands in the midst of this deadly
contest over who controls death and is fundamentally at stake in it. In this
frame of reference, death is anything but natural for it has been weaponized,
as it were, within the disorder of the fallen cosmos.[9] The Latin Vulgate gives
fitting expression to this in verse 14 where it speaks of the devil's "empire of
death" (*mortis imperium*).

Later in the letter, the author points to the effective power of Christ's
priesthood—which is to say his office as Savior—as a function of the
"power of an indestructible life" that is uniquely his (7:16). As Howard
Marshall remarks, the author envisages that in Christ "the devil came up
against a life over which he simply had no power."[10] The contest of divine
life and demonic death is, finally, no real contest at all. But this divine life
triumphs precisely by giving itself over into death. When Hebrews speaks

8. On the general New Testament semantics see Bultmann, "Death in the New
Testament," 85–107. Curiously, Lindars' thorough study of the *Theology of the Letter to
the Hebrews* includes no reference to or discussion of Heb 2:15.

9. As Jean Hering aptly observes in his commentary on these verses, "The modern reader must not let himself be seduced by a naturalistic philosophy which regards
death as no more than a law of nature. The New Testament does not deny these laws;
it presupposes them; but it views them from a theological angle and does not regard
them as conforming in every case to the original intention of the Creator. 'The laws
of nature are not natural,' said the elder Blumhardt" (Hering, *Epistle to the Hebrews*,
20). On this question of the place of death between nature and sin, see Sonderegger,
"Finitude and Death," 385–99. Sonderegger notes that sorting the question represents a
particularly "delicate task" for Christian theology (385). For further discussion of death
as an unwelcome intruder, see chapters 6 and 11 by Ann Jervis and Presian Burroughs,
respectively, in the present volume.

10. Marshall, "Soteriology in Hebrews," 259; cf. Acts 2:24: "But God raised him up,
having loosed the pangs of death, because it was not possible for him to be held by it."

of Christ as our "captain" and "forerunner" (2:10; 6:20) it refers, not least, to this saving transit through death itself. For the death Christ dies is not a hero's death; it is the Savior's death. And so he dies, as Gerhard Forde has stressed, not "instead of us" but "*ahead of us,*" drawing sin's captives into and through his own death as to break their allegiance to death's empire and to win them anew for freedom within God's reign.[11] Here we are not spectators. We are subjected to divine action, and our reality is itself implicated in its movements.

The patristic theologian John Chrysostom took an uncommon interest in these particular verses. He was particularly struck by the surprising role played by death in the outworking of salvation to which I have drawn attention just now. Of this he wrote,

> Here [Paul] points out the wonder that, by that through which the devil prevailed, [the devil] was himself overcome. By the very thing that was [the devil's] strong weapon against the world—death—Christ struck him. In this Christ exhibits the greatness of the conqueror's power. Do you see what great goodness death has wrought?[12]

Yet, Chrysostom's comments on verse 15 indicated that he found the idea of people being "subject to lifelong bondage to the fear of death" more puzzling: he wonders aloud and indecisively whether the phrase might mean that death exercised a power that had not yet been done away with, or whether we ought to understand that fear of death drains the pleasure from present living, or perhaps finally that "he who fears death is a slave and submits to all things rather than die."[13] Each reading is suggestive, but the matter is left undecided.

John Calvin—who appreciated Chrysostom in many things—also catches sight of these motifs and draws out their importance in his commentary on these same verses.[14] The coming low of the Son in the flesh unto death is, he says, an act of "infinite love" whose benefits are very tersely named in these verses. He observes that "there is in this brevity of words a singularly striking and powerful representation, and that is, that he has so delivered us from the tyranny of the devil, that we are rendered safe, and that he has so redeemed us from death, that it is no longer to be dreaded." Though the devil "had the power to reign to ruin," from the "abolition of his

---

11. See Forde, *Where God*, 28.

12. Chrysostom, *Hebrews*, 46–47. The material in brackets is provided by the volume editors.

13. Ibid., 47.

14. On Calvin's relationship to Chrysostom, see Lane, *John Calvin*.

tyranny by Christ's death" comes the "great consolation . . . that we have to do with an enemy who cannot prevail against us."[15] However, by contrast with Chrysostom's seeming comfort with the ambiguity of the meaning of verse 15, Calvin takes a particular and intense interest in resolving the matter firmly. As he explains:

> This passage expresses in a striking manner how miserable is the life of those who fear death, as they must feel it to be dreadful, because they look on it apart from Christ; for then nothing but a curse appears in it: for whence is death but from God's wrath against sin? Hence is that bondage throughout life, even perpetual anxiety, by which unhappy souls are tormented; for through a consciousness of sin the judgment of God is ever presented to the view.[16]

It is notable that it is not death as such but rather the vision of death as divine judgment upon sin—death fundamentally repurposed and denatured by sin—that terrifies. It is equally notable that Calvin emphasizes how the power of death as the future and final horizon of life reaches back into life itself to torment, alarm, oppress, and so to enslave: death's power is exercised by its coming "back from the future," as it were, always already governing the present in this way. The present symptom and poisonous fruit of the powerful presence of that future death is *fear*.

Calvin concludes his commentary on this passage with the firm declaration: "*from this fear Christ has delivered us.*" The oppressive fear of death of which the author of Hebrews speaks is simply not a Christian possibility; or, said positively, freedom from the enervating fear of death is the very essence of Christian life. Calvin even treats this as a kind of visible evidence of faith, punctuating his discussion of these verses with the stark claim: "If any one cannot pacify his mind by disregarding death, let him know that he has made as yet but very little proficiency in the faith of Christ."[17] A bracing claim.

I would like to dwell a little longer upon the importance of this matter of the *fear* of death and the life of faith. Many since Calvin have been less willing to speak so firmly of faith's power to completely dispel the fear of death, however. Dale C. Allison opens his recent personal reflection on human mortality and Christian hope with a chapter simply entitled "Death and Fear." A series of poignant anecdotes and honest discussion of his own confrontation with the fear of dying is punctuated by a quotation from Paul

15. Ibid., 71–72.
16. Ibid., 72.
17. Ibid.

Ramsey's essay "Death's Pedagogy," where the ethicist characterizes death as "an irreparable loss, an unquenchable grief, the threat of all threats, a dread that is more than all fears aggregated together, an approaching 'evil' . . . the background of every background."[18] Ramsey distills something essential to our understanding of the witness of Hebrews at issue here: for the living, death is as present as *fear*, and this fear is an imperious power that effectively shapes the lives we live here and now. For it is "an *approaching evil*," known—and feared—as such. To this we usefully also add a programmatic statement of William Stringfellow's—undoubtedly one of our most acute theological writers on the subject of death in recent decades—who describes the imperious presence of death in this way:

> Death is the contemporaneous power abrasively addressing every person in one's own existence with the word that one is not only eventually and finally, but even now and already, estranged, separated, alienated, lost in relationships with everybody and everything else, and—what is in a way much worse—one's very own self. Death means a total loss of identity. Death, in *this* sense—death embodying this awful threat—is the death which is at work not only on the day of the undertaker, but today.[19]

The impersonal chemical images of "dissolution" and "abrasion" are powerful and apt; so too, paradoxically, is the dramatic personal representation of death addressing us every day with a threatening—even annihilating—"word" that has the power to shake us profoundly and perhaps even to shatter our faith. Death's future advent is already a corrosive power "today," bearing down upon us "even now and already."

In the next section we turn to consider the medieval tradition of the *ars moriendi*. We would do well to understand it as an attempt to dramatize and illuminate the struggle against fear for those confronting death. This tradition manifestly displays death's power to assault and overcome a person by way of fear, but it also reveals the power of Christ's own death and of Christian teachings that may brace one against such fear. Standard manuals from this tradition equip ministers as they journey with the dying through fear toward death.

---

18. Ramsey, "Death's Pedagogy," 501, cited in Allison, *Night Comes*, 10.

19. Stringfellow, *Instead of Death*, 22.

The *Ars bene moriendi*—Fear's Temptations,
Faith's Encouragements

By the fifteenth century, Western Christianity had come to possess a variegated tradition of practical Christian counsel for the dying, of which the short block-book entitled *Ars bene moriendi* ("The Art of Dying Well") was a quite popular and widely circulated example.[20] This particular book was an anonymously authored tract compiled, at least in part, from earlier works on the theme by the Dominican theologian, Jean Gerson (d. 1429). The text chiefly consists of five pairs of "temptations" and "encouragements," each being graphically illustrated by an accompanying woodcut image of the death bed of "*Moriens*"—literally, "the dying one"—surrounded by contentious devils and angels. While demonic voices tempt the dying man in turn with doubt, despair, impatience, pride, and greed, angelic ripostes respectively encourage him to the virtues of faith, hope, patience, humility, and voluntary poverty. There is much in this short work of both note and interest. For present purposes my concern is only to suggest that we might read this work as a kind of expansive catalogue of the shape of our fear before death as well as a particular vision of how faith might resist and overcome such fear. We should see the five temptations as species of the fear death enjoins and the encouragements as species of answering faith. In this way, I venture, we may take it as a kind of practical commentary on Heb 2:14–15.

The text literally begins with fear: while death of the body is a terrifying thing, all the more "terrifying and detestable" is the prospect of the "eternal death" of the soul.[21] The devil's temptations always have fear as their singular grim aim, but "those near death face more serious temptations than they have ever had before."[22] Doubt, the first temptation, attacks the foundation of Christian life by attacking faith itself. With death pressing in, the dying are beset by the fear that faith is "a big mistake," ventured without proper

---

20. There is a beautiful facsimile reproduction of the original Latin text and woodcut illustrations, *The Ars Moriendi*, which is readily had in reprint or online. In what follows I make use of the English translation of the text of this shorter edition provided at §76, "Art of Dying Well," 525–36, and all quotations of the text are drawn from here. For an accessible contemporary account of the wider Western tradition of these *ars moriendi*, see Verhey, *Christian Art of Dying*, especially the extensive discussion on 79–171, which also includes reproductions of the woodcuts from the famous shorter edition.

21. The reference to Aristotle is to the *Ethics*, 3.6: "Now death is the most terrible of all things; for it is the end, and nothing is thought to be any longer either good or bad for the dead."

22. Shinners, *Medieval*, 525–26.

warrant, and is powerless to stave off inevitable death.[23] Despair comes next. Here the dying are made to fear that they are irredeemably "sunk in sin," that their sins are manifold, unconfessed, and unforgiven, and that they can only be counted among the goats at the final judgment (Matt 25).[24] The third temptation to impatience leads the dying to resent their suffering and to fear that—"unbearable" and "utterly useless" as suffering is—it will finally overtax the charity of others and so alienate them.[25] The fourth temptation is to pride. Here the devil reverses the angle of attack, tempting the dying now with their "spiritual self-satisfaction" and "presumption" of salvation in the face of death.[26] In fighting off the fear of death, they are now lured to forget the "fear of the Lord," as it were. The fifth and final temptation is to greed or avarice. Here the dying are tempted to fear the loss of their worldly possessions, but also more widely the dissolution of their achievements and the forfeiture of their relationships with friends and family: the devil "especially vexes" people with the fear that death will devour all that they have achieved, acquired, and made of themselves in this world.[27]

All five temptations—doubt, despair, impatience, pride, and avarice—can thus be understood to have the anxious fear of death at their root. The singular substance of the fear of those who are dying is the conviction that death should prove to be sovereign, or at least that its sovereignty is incontestable *in their case*, whether because of their lack of piety, the failure of their faith, or because of the failure of that on which faith has wagered. In any case, fear of death is the engine and organ of the soul's demonic subjugation long in advance of the actual end. Its work is ever to isolate and to drive the soul back upon itself, to turn it in upon itself in anxious spinning scrutiny. Sin and death clasp hands once more as the soul, subjected by the fear of death, once again curves in upon itself. It is striking how in this text the fearful temptations of the devil conspire to aggravate the self-regard and self-concern of the dying: the figure of God is rendered remote, almost undiscussed, something abstract and indistinct. God is at best a cold, indifferent, and threatening justice. So, too, the wider world and other people appear in the discourse of the temptations only as elements in the calculus of one's own threatened identity. And while the drama of the "Art of Dying Well" itself is concentrated upon a single death-bed scene, we can extend

23. Ibid., 527.
24. Ibid., 528–29.
25. Ibid., 530.
26. Ibid., 531–32.
27. Ibid., 533.

and extrapolate the dynamics of that single scene to illuminate the entirety of a life threatened and pressurized by the fear of death.

But what of the angelic "encouragements" in the manual offered to the dying in the hope that they might resist the fear of death refracted in the temptations? To what extent do they reflect the gospel of Christ's "destruction of him who has the power of death" and his deliverance of "all those who through fear of death were subject to lifelong bondage" (Heb 2:14–15)? The encouragements appear as collections of citations from biblical and traditional authorities. The unfolding of the first encouragement is typical of them all: tempted by doubt, the dying are instructed that they "should think first how necessary faith is since without it no one can be saved" and then "how useful it is since it makes all things possible." They should, therefore, trust that "with the merit of God's blessing, [they] will receive faith" with which to "resist the Devil" who is "a liar."[28] To this end, the dying are encouraged "to recite the Creed" in order to stir them to "constancy of faith" so they may "bravely and firmly believe."[29] The strategy is at once to insist upon the importance of the virtue of faith in the face of temptation and also to call to mind the promises of God in relation to the gift of faith. This pattern—instructing the dying about the importance of exercising their salvation with virtue (whether faith, hope, patience, humility, or poverty), summoning them to cleave to and practice the respective virtue all the more in the face of temptation, and then reminding them of God's promise to provide and assist in this effort—recurs in each of the five encouragements. At points, one might worry that the angels seem simply to counsel the dying to redouble their own struggle for virtue, vigorously "pointing out" once again to the dying "those things that are necessary for salvation." Even still, the dying also rely on and are buoyed by the gracious promises of the church and received in its sacraments.[30]

At other points the encouragements do reach more decisively toward the unconditional reality of Christ's saving work. For example, in the conclusion, prayer displaces striving when the dying are invited to beseech God—as well as Mary and the saints—that through God's "inexpressible mercy and the power of his passion," the Lord "may deign to receive him."[31] In the end, the author attests, the dying can only take Christ's prayer as their own, saying, "into thy hands I commend my spirit" (Luke 23:46).[32]

---

28. Ibid., 527–28.

29. Ibid.

30. Ibid., 526.

31. Ibid., 534.

32. Ibid.

The introduction of the manual also includes an appeal that "whoever is so disposed, let him commit himself totally to Christ's passion, constantly holding it in mind and meditating on it. For through this, all the Devil's temptations, especially those against faith, are overcome."[33] However, what is striking about this last passage is its ambiguity: is it Christ's passion *as such* by which the devil's temptations are overcome, or is it by the believer's "holding in mind and meditating" upon that passion?

The evangelical consolation of the angelic encouragement lies most plainly in the opening and closing moments of the text when it is most "eccentric," that is, when it draws the attention of the dying away from concern for the self, its losses and gains, and toward a firm recollection of the reality of divine grace that breaks in from outside. In these moments grace holds the dying self firmly, and the divine promise of the God whose identity is specified by the person and work of Christ upholds them. Indeed, I take this to be the force of the specific encouragement to "recite the Creed in a loud voice" and to "repeat it many times."[34] Why rehearse the Apostles' Creed? Not so that, mantra-like, it might exclude other realities from consciousness, but rather so that the world described by the creed, with its center of gravity in the second article, can be received and owned as the reality of final consequence, especially by the dying. For the world of the creed concerns us. Indeed it graciously presses upon us precisely what is "*for us and for our salvation*." To recite the creed is to be reminded in the midst of death that by grace we have been made to dwell in *this* house, and so need not occupy the house fashioned by the conspiracy of our own anxiety, uncertainty, and terror before death. In short, to recite the creed is to rehearse the gospel truth from Hebrews once again: Christ came to break the annihilating power of death and so to liberate us from the profound tyranny of fear that death extends into life itself.

"Who by the Grace of God Tasted Death for Everyone"

It is fair to say that we live in a culture that is simultaneously death soaked and death denying. Both our fascination with and denial of death give contradictory expression to a singular, deep-seated fear of death. "Death is a provocation" to our modern way of living, John Grey writes, "because it marks a boundary beyond which the will cannot go," the terminus of all our striving, projecting, and self-making.[35] Such a provocation is an oppres-

33. Ibid., 526.
34. Ibid., 528.
35. Grey, *Immortalization Commission*, 205.

sive terror to us moderns. But not just to moderns. Wherever humanity confronts denatured death under the power of sin, it knows all too well the "lifelong oppression" by the fear of death, which is the point made by Hebrews. Indeed, the power of death to insert itself in the midst of life by way of fear has been a particular point of emphasis in our understanding of Heb 2:14–15 and our reflections upon the "Art of Dying Well." Sergei Bulgakov once observed that "the horror of death can appear only in the land of the living."[36] And so it does. The horror itself is the present and powerful presence of death in the midst of life.

Perhaps if we are to do justice to the witness of Heb 2:14–15 we must say something more concerning the meaning of Christ's overcoming of the one who "has the power of death" precisely as the One who "tasted death for everyone" (2:9). Christ's overcoming has denatured death once more. Christians confront their own death as one "doubly denatured," as it were: once as something weaponized by sin, but then as something suffered and undertaken by Christ himself, that saving death which is itself "the death of death." In Christ—on the other side of that odd triumph—those who are dying face death now shorn of its empire. Calvin's strident suggestion that Christians may—nay, must—live "disregarding death" gives voice to this uncanny freedom.

I would suggest that, from a Protestant perspective, one way to conceive of the limitation of the traditional instruction in the art of dying well is to note its sustained concentration upon the subjectivity and mental and spiritual actions of the Christian facing death. This comports with the medieval construal of faith primarily as practical assent to teaching (*assensus*) and knowledge (*notitia*), rather than trust (*fiducia*). For, the cooperating subject plays a crucial role in the realization of faith and so the achievement of salvation; indeed, the text of the *Ars bene moriendi* explicitly stresses that both sin and faith require the exercise of free will.[37] As we have seen, both temptation and encouragement are addressed to and concern this cooperating subject, seeking to (re-)establish the dying person's orientation, movements, and aims. Much—perhaps everything—hangs upon the person's decisions, since while divine grace aids and abets, it does not dictate or determine. On such a view, when the temptations and the fear of death confront Christians, they can be *encouraged* but they cannot, finally, be *assured*.

For such assurance, according to a Protestant perspective, the evangelical truth that salvation is given by grace alone (*sola gratia*) through Christ

36. Bulgakov, *Philosophy of Economy*, 192, cited in Cunningham, "Is There Life," 123.

37. Shinners, *Medieval*, 527.

alone (*solus Christus*) is crucial. The construal of faith as trust (*fiducia*) in a deliverance that befalls us from beyond ourselves stands as a corresponding truth. This reframes the entire matter: for now what it means to "die well" is not a matter of the movement of the cooperating self from *vice* (doubt, despair, impatience, pride, and greed) to *virtue* (faith, hope, patience, humility, and poverty). Rather, it is a movement of the dying person out of the whole vice-virtue scheme, with its focus on the abilities and actions of the cooperating self. Instead, the self, according to the Protestant Reformers, exists in the sphere called *Christian freedom*. One of the marks of this freedom is a decided disinterest in certain features of one's own inner life and status. What is more interesting and far more important than the movements of my soul—even in the face of death—is the reality, surety, and graciousness of Christ's saving movements toward and for me. The eccentricity of Christian attention here is total: even as the Christian "tastes death," the fact is that Christ, who "by the grace of God tasted death for every one," is faith's sole concern and ground of hope (2:9). While, as we saw, elements of this aspect of faith were not entirely absent from the traditional teaching about the art of dying well, a fully evangelical account must augment and amplify this aspect. Indeed, it must make it the central and controlling feature of its thinking about Christian life in relation to the fear of death.

And so, on such an evangelical recasting we would expect to hear that the temptation to doubt is outbid by Paul's proclamation that "while we were yet sinners, Christ died for us" the "*ungodly*" (Rom 5:6–8). The temptation to despair is sapped by the fact that faith is never anything other than a "hope against hope" (Rom 4:18). The temptation to impatience is overreached by the fact that "the patience of the Lord is salvation" (2 Pet 3:15). Human pride is rendered uninteresting by faith's boast in the cross alone (Gal 6:14), and human avarice is bypassed by faith's joy in "counting everything as loss for the sake of Christ" (Phil 3:8). The art of dying well becomes here the art of self-forgetfulness in the face of the wonder of the gospel of God. Those who are already dead to sin, whose allegiances to the passing age and its death-empowered-regent have already been broken by Christ's triumph, need not fear the end of life. Neither need they suffer death's oppressive anticipatory burden in life. This is because, as Ray Anderson has argued,

> The core of this Christian perspective on life and death is faith. It is faith in the God who has overcome death and who lives through Jesus Christ that enables Christians to surrender their time and history to God and to receive it back again from Him as the gift of life through death.[38]

38. Anderson, *Theology, Death and Dying*, 126.

For these reasons, a self-consciously evangelical recasting of the traditional "Art of Dying Well" should take the form of a patient theological reflection on the strange freedom of those whose lives are firmly set and held within the saving movement of Christ against, through, and beyond death as attested in Heb 2:14–15. It should invite faith to contemplate this movement, and like Chrysostom—with renewed astonishment at the self-giving of the Lord—it would ask of itself and others, "Do you see what great goodness death has wrought?"[39] In all this, it should look to own the liberating power of trust in the One who "tasted death for everyone," the One whose work of "perfect love casts out fear" (1 John 4:8), including the enervating fear of death. Finally, it would do well to take as its governing epigraph the joyous exclamation with which Paul punctuates his own telling of the apocalyptic gospel of God: "O death, where is thy victory? O death, where is thy sting?" (1 Cor 15:55). The final service of the Protestant minister to those who are dying is thus simply to call the promise of all of this to mind with clarity, love, and humility. For the fact that Christ himself died well *for us* is the assured hope and encouragement for the soul.

Bibliography

Allison, Dale C. *Night Comes: Death, Imagination, and the Last Things.* Grand Rapids: Eerdmans, 2016.

Anderson, Ray S. *Theology, Death and Dying.* Oxford: Basil Blackwell, 1986.

The Ars Moriendi. Edition princeps circa 1450. Edited by W. H. Rylands. London: Wyman & Sons, 1881.

"The Art of Dying Well (c. 1430–35)." In *Medieval Popular Religion, 1000–1500,* edited by J. Shinners, 525–36. Peterborough, ON: Broadview, 1997.

Bulgakov, Sergei. *Philosophy of Economy: The World as Household.* Translated by C. Evtuhov. New Haven: Yale University Press, 2000.

Bultmann, Rudolf. "Death in the New Testament." In *Life and Death: Bible Key Words from Gerhard Kittel's Theologisches Wortebuch Zum Neuen Testament,* by Rudolf Bultmann, 85–107. Translated by P. H. Ballard et al. London: A & C Black, 1965.

Calvin, John. *Hebrews.* Translated by J. King. Calvin's Commentaries 44. Edinburgh: Calvin Translation Society, 1853.

Chrysostom. *Hebrews.* Edited by E. M. Heen and P. D. W. Krey. Ancient Christian Commentary on Scripture. Downers Grove: InterVarsity, 2005.

Cunningham, Connor. "Is There Life Before Death?" In *The Role of Death in Life: A Multidisciplinary Examination of the Relationship between Life and Death,* edited by J. Behr and C. Cunningham, 120–53. Eugene, OR: Cascade, 2015.

Forde, Gerhard. *Where God Meets Man.* Minneapolis: Augsburg, 1972.

Grey, John. *The Immortalization Commission: The Strange Quest to Cheat Death.* London: Penguin, 2011.

---

39. Chrysostom, *Hebrews,* 47.

Hering, Jean. *The Epistle to the Hebrews*. Translated by A. W. Heathcote and P. J. Allcock. London: Epworth, 1970.

Kindars, Barnaba. *The Theology of the Letter to the Hebrews*. Cambridge: Cambridge University Press, 1991.

Lane, Anthony N. S. *John Calvin: Student of the Church Fathers*. Edinburgh: T. & T. Clark, 1999.

Long, D. Stephen. *Hebrews*. Louisville: Westminster John Knox, 2011.

MacLeod, Donald. "The Work of Christ Accomplished." In *Christian Dogmatics: Reformed Theology for the Catholic Church*, edited by Michael Allen and Scott Swain, 262–63. Grand Rapids: Baker, 2016.

Marshall, I. Howard. "Soteriology in Hebrews." In *The Epistle to the Hebrews and Christian Theology*, edited by R. Bauckham et al., 253–77. Grand Rapids: Eerdmans, 2009.

Ramsey, Paul. "Death's Pedagogy." *Commonweal* 20 (1974) 497–502.

Shinners, J., ed. *Medieval Popular Religion, 1000–1500*. Peterborough, ON: Broadview, 1997.

Sonderegger, Katherine. "Finitude and Death." In *The T&T Clark Companion to Sin*, edited by Keith L. Johnson and David Lauber, 385–99. London: Bloomsbury T. & T. Clark, 2016.

Stringfellow, William. *Instead of Death*. New and expanded ed. Eugene, OR: Wipf & Stock, 2004.

Verhey, Allen. *The Christian Art of Dying: Learning from Jesus*. Grand Rapids: Eerdmans, 2011.

Webster, John. "One Who Is Son: Theological Reflections on the Exordium to the Epistle to the Hebrews." In *The Epistle to the Hebrews and Christian Theology*, edited by Richard Bauckham et al., 69–94. Grand Rapids: Eerdmans, 2009.

Made in the USA
Coppell, TX
13 April 2024

31273660R00156